"*The Lives of Reilly* is an astonishing account of an amazing man on an epic journey of super-heroic proportions. Just reading about this honourable man will make you a better person."

Pat Nevin
Broadcaster, pundit and ex-professional footballer

"Inspiring."

Keith Jackson
Chief Sportswriter, *The Daily Record*

"I've known wee Mavis for several years and he never fails to impress me with his dedication, commitment and drive."

Kevin McGowne
Ex-professional footballer

THE LIVES OF REILLY

MARK 'MAVIS' REILLY

WITH DAVID MCCARTHY AND DICKSON TELFER

The Lives of Reilly

Published by Nameless Town (2023)

namelesstownbooks.com

ISBN: 978-1-914400-04-9

Edited and typeset by Dickson Telfer
Proofed by Gillian Gardner

Front (main) and back cover photographs courtesy of the MDS Foundation.
Front cover left lens photographs (from onlooker's perspective) courtesy of
The Daily Record and the MDS Foundation.
Front cover right lens photographs (from onlooker's perspective) by
Monica Reilly and Michelle Dalziel
Author photographs by Monica Reilly, *The Daily Record* and Dickson Telfer

Photographs on page 133 courtesy of *The Daily Record*. Photographs on page
134 by Michelle Dalziel (top) and Mark Reilly (bottom). Photographs on
page 135 by Mark Reilly. Photographs on page 136 by Monica Reilly.
Photographs on page 137 courtesy of *The Daily Record*. Photographs on page
138 courtesy of Kilmarnock F.C. (top) and *The Daily Record* (bottom).
Photographs on page 247 by Monica Reilly. Photographs on page 248
courtesy of *The Daily Record* (top) and by Mark Moffat (bottom).
Photographs on pages 249 and 250 courtesy of the MDS Foundation.
Photographs on page 251 by John Harris (top) and Sean Rice (bottom).
Photographs on page 252 by Sean Rice (top) and Mark Moffat (bottom).
Photographs on pages 253 and 254 courtesy of *The Daily Record*.
Photograph on page 345 courtesy of the MDS Foundation.
Photograph on page 346 by Monica Reilly.

Jacket concept by Dickson Telfer
Design and layout by stonedart

Printed and bound by Martins the Printers, Berwick-upon-Tweed

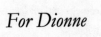

For Dionne

WHAT IS THIS BOOK ABOUT?

*T*he *Lives of Reilly* chronicles the various lives of Mark 'Mavis' Reilly, ex-professional footballer, athlete, long-distance runner, Ironman finisher, police officer and fundraiser. However, this isn't a book exclusively about him; it's also about his daughter, Dionne, who suffers from Rett Syndrome, a currently incurable condition meaning she requires 24/7 care.

If you're a fan of any of the clubs Mavis played for during his football career, or are just a football fan in general, you'll no doubt be keen to hear the football stories, of which there are several (and many we'll hope you'll get a laugh at). Likewise, if you're an ultra-event enthusiast, long-distance runner or fundraiser, you'll be interested in Mavis's participation in the Marathon des Sables in 2021 and the various events he completed in the lead up to that monumental challenge.

As a publisher, deciding chapter order was not a straightforward process. *The Lives of Reilly* covers a lot of ground and taps into three quite different aspects of Mavis's life. The link, however, is that all three are underpinned by positivity, determination and hope.

Thousands of young lads want to be professional footballers, but only a tiny percentage fulfil their dream. Such a dream cannot be achieved without fierce determination, discipline and dedication to the cause.

Likewise, competing in the Marathon des Sables in extreme temperatures is not something just any runner can turn their hand to. Endurance, resilience and great physical and emotional strength are fundamental to be able to get through even the first day. As you'll discover, the Sahara offered Mavis the ultimate opportunity to prove the power of his positive mindset and never-say-die attitude.

In 2011, just under three years after Dionne was born, she was diagnosed with Rett Syndrome. Following her diagnosis, Mavis could've kept his head down and wallowed in self-pity, but that would only serve to fly in the face of the attributes and character traits he'd honed over many years as a professional footballer. Such a response wasn't in his DNA, so once the initial shock had worn off, he took a step back and began to see opportunity in the challenges; opportunity to 1) make Dionne's life the best he possibly could, and 2) get involved in fundraising for Reverse Rett in the hope a cure could one day be found.

Without Dionne, this book would not exist, nor would the Marathon des Sables have been run by Mavis to raise funds for Reverse Rett. His football days framed his ability to respond to the needs of his disabled daughter in a positive light, in turn fuelling the fire to take on the Marathon des Sables in the name of charity. It was tempting to open the book with a funny football story, but in the end we decided to kick things off with the chapters about the incredible little girl who changed Mavis's life forever. It's a mix we hope you'll appreciate and enjoy.

A quick note about memoir: sections of this book are based on events that occurred only a few years prior to publication, whereas others span back as far as the 1970s. Specifically for the latter, it is not possible to accurately recall the specifics of who said what and the exact words used, but all the important facts and events in *The Lives of Reilly* are as relayed. Additionally, occasional colour has been added to some scenes for pace and entertainment purposes and no pseudonyms have been used. Every effort has been made to ensure accuracy, but if any misrepresentation is present, this is entirely unintentional and likely due to memories being clouded by the passing of time.

Nameless Town
February 2023

FOREWORD

by Ally McCoist

I have been very fortunate to meet some extraordinary people in my life. Mark Reilly – or Mavis as he is known by absolutely everybody – is one of them, although he is so unassuming that he would never in a million years describe himself in such a manner.

I first came across Mavis when playing against him in Rangers-Kilmarnock matches and I thought he was a good, solid player, comfortable on the ball and able to sense any danger. I didn't really appreciate his value to that Killie team until I played with him, though, and that's the gospel truth.

There are players within teams who, when you look at the team sheet and you see certain names on it, you're happy. Mavis was one of those players. Your team was always better with him in it than without him. He was invaluable to us. The work he would do was incredible. He was absolutely tireless and selfless and had an unbelievable work ethic, and I came from Ibrox, where a lot of boys had those attributes in abundance, so I know it when I see it.

He was never in the limelight and didn't want to be. Didn't need to be. But none of us ever underestimated his value to the team. Every single day in training, he was a nine out of ten because he wanted to be the best he could be every time he pulled on his boots. Afterwards, he'd head to the gym and look after himself to such a degree that he might just have been the fittest footballer I've ever known. He was meticulous and a great lad as well. He might not have been as loud as some were in the dressing room, but Mavis had a wicked, dry sense of humour and loved the banter and the patter. He would sit next to me in the dressing room and just revel in the camaraderie.

The Lives of Reilly includes the story of how he and I ended up in the Rogano one night with a Hollywood legend, someone I was lucky enough to work alongside, and with whom I became good friends. At the next training session, Mavis was holding court in the dressing room, loving every minute of it. Then on the Friday, he sidled up to me and said, 'Who are we meeting this week, Coisty? Jack Nicholson?'

After his football career finished, he was never going to be a lad who sat on the couch every night eating crisps. His challenges for charity became well-known in Scotland, but even I raised an eyebrow when I heard he was taking on the Marathon des Sables in 2021. The level of physical fitness needed to take on a challenge like that is extraordinary, but a lot of people don't understand the mental strength you need to have to carry it out.

I remember talking to Eddie Izzard one night after the comedian had done some ridiculous marathon challenge; something like a marathon a day for a month. Eddie told me that there was absolutely no doubt that the mental strain was far, far greater than the physical.

That, I'm sure, was the same for Mavis, but if it came down to sheer iron will and refusal to accept defeat, it was going to take something extraordinary to stand in his way of completing the Marathon des Sables. Those are the same qualities he exuded every day in a football career that spanned 20 years at the top level. You don't do that unless you are physically *and* mentally strong. I was lucky enough to play with some fantastic footballers and Mavis was one of the strongest, mentally, that I ever came across.

We've all had family issues, real tough times that we've needed to get through and he is no exception. It must have been incredibly difficult for him when his darling daughter Dionne was diagnosed with Rett Syndrome, but it's entirely in keeping with the Mavis Reilly I know that he would channel every ounce of his being into making her life the best it can be.

He feels blessed to have Dionne, and Mavis talks about how he doesn't know how much she can take in or understand the challenges that he undertakes on her behalf. Well, I'll tell you right now – on some level she knows. I have no doubt about that. You see the way she looks at him, and the love that comes pouring out of her. She knows, all right.

I know Mavis thought the world of Tam Burns, who I was also honoured to know and love as a friend. He explains in this book how Tam helped shape him into the person he has become. Well, the best thing I can say is that Tam would be proud of the way Mavis has conducted himself, in and out of football, all throughout his life.

It's an honour and a privilege to write the foreword for *The Lives of Reilly*, a book that's as poignant and inspiring as it is entertaining and motivational. Enjoy the journey.

Ally McCoist
February 2023

CHAPTERS

PROLOGUE

On Sunday, October 3rd, 2021, 672 competitors stood on the start line for what was to become the hottest Marathon des Sables since records began. Six days later, only 354 made it to the finish line, a dropout of around 47 percent. During day two of the race, one of my tentmates suffered a cardiac arrest, but thankfully he survived. Proof, if it was ever needed, that the Marathon des Sables is the toughest, most punishing footrace in the world.

What follows is an edited and embellished version of one of the many blog posts I wrote after returning from the Sahara in mid-October 2021. The day in question, the fourth – which will be covered in more detail later in the book – was the toughest, most excruciating and most physically and mentally challenging day of my life . . . so far.

It was the usual night in camp for me: a few hours' sleep and the continuing stomach issues. The little sleep I managed was disturbed by the sound of two of my tentmates, John and Terry, vomiting. They were both looking strong the previous day, so this was desperately unfortunate for them.

At sunrise, John told me he wasn't continuing. Although understandable, given his night of vomiting, it was a hammer blow and everyone in the tent was gutted for him. We'd all put in 19 months of training with ultra-marathon fanatic, Rory Coleman, so losing someone off the back of a sickness bug wasn't in the masterplan. Terry, despite looking far from well, decided to soldier on.

So, weak and sleep-deprived, Terry and I, our other remaining tentmate, Sean, and Jack from the tent next to us, made our way to the start line, which was the usual 30 feet long by 15 feet high red and white inflatable arch. As per the previous days of the race, we were greeted by the bizarre sight of Race Director and Marathon des Sables founder, Patrick Bauer, dancing on the roof of his Land Rover, head to toe in khakis. Microphone in hand, he blared out details about the competitors in French, dutifully translated by his less animated translator. I could feel the usual mix of apprehension and excitement in the air and did my utmost to ignite the athlete in me, ignoring as best as possible the sickness bug and the absence of John.

AC/DC's 'Highway to Hell' blared through the PA, a song chosen, allegedly, to remind us that we were running to hell via the most treacherous route possible; a track to test our resolve and remind us that the race is more about resilience and endurance than it is running.

Once the starting klaxon had sounded and we were on our way, navigating the stony, sandy and ever hostile terrain, it was clear Terry was struggling, his gait awkward and breathing laboured. The stomach bug had got the better of him and, once we got to checkpoint one at 12.7km, he reluctantly withdrew.

With Sean already out of sight, Jack and I rested for about half an hour, absorbing the reality of our ever-diminishing pack and mentally preparing ourselves for the next leg, a 9.6km stretch to checkpoint two. Three and a bit kilometres[*] in, the temperature was a gruelling 55 degrees Celsius[†] and sweat was pouring down my face. Having spotted a bush, Jack agreed that a ten-minute rest was a good idea. I say bush, but it was more like a cluster of twigs. Anything to provide even the slightest bit of reprieve from the relentless sun was welcome though. However, as we soon discovered, half a dozen others had had the same idea. From an aerial view perspective, it must have looked crazy; eight knackered runners clumped together around a poor excuse for a bush, as if it was a power source responsible for providing energy and preserving life.

Grateful for the rest, Jack and I set off into the furnace once again, checkpoint two as our sole focus. It was around 4km away, but it felt like it took an eternity to get there. Once we arrived, sand covering our salty, sweaty bodies, I realised just how much I was suffering from the sickness and diarrhoea bug that had swept through the camp, eliminating John and Terry in its wake. I was even finding walking taxing, but – bizarrely – I was grateful for the blisters on my feet, purely because

---

[*] About 2 miles
[†] 131 Fahrenheit

they detracted from the intense nausea I was experiencing.

In an attempt to lower my core temperature, I lay on the ground and placed a couple of water-soaked cloths on my head and neck. Jack's tentmate, Chris, turned up shortly after, looking like someone who could only be described as ill: no colour, unsteady on his feet and dead behind the eyes. It made me wonder if I looked as bad, but fortunately there are no mirrors in the desert, so I couldn't check.

With short, erratic breaths, Chris lay down next to me and announced to anyone who was listening that the bug had done him in to the extent that he couldn't even eat and he was therefore pulling out of the race. Judging by the look on his face, there was no doubt he was making the right call. In that very moment, I'd be lying if I said I wasn't a little envious, but I told myself that I was over the worst of the bug and that giving up wasn't an option. Because it wasn't.

Chris was ex-special forces, so he'd probably be taking his withdrawal quite hard. Words were unlikely to offer much, so we just lay there together for a bit, breathing and resetting ourselves. He was heading home, but I was heading back out there. I had to keep going.

Feeling marginally better from the rest at checkpoint two, Jack and I resumed the race and were soon joined by Ian, a South African guy I'd met during the previous leg. However, less than two kilometres* in, I started vomiting. Maybe I wasn't over the worst of the bug after all. Coughing and retching, I told Jack and Ian to go on without me. We were all on our own journey and I didn't want to hold them back.

---

* 1.2 miles

I had another 60-odd kilometres* to go, and genuinely wondered if I'd be likely to make it. Given that I could barely think straight or see properly, running seemed out of the question, but somehow my subconscious took over, drawing energy from somewhere, fueling the mechanics of putting one foot in front of the other.

Feeling so ill, and being away from Jack and Ian made it a lonely and dark period for me, but I did what I could to keep moving forward one step at a time. I lifted my head, determined to endure the cards I'd been dealt, and noticed a lake in the distance. Yes! I couldn't wait to steep in it, to enjoy its coolness on my sandy, salty, gritty skin, to drink in abundance, rehydrating before tackling the remainder of the leg.

But then I remembered the map.

And the fact that I was in the Sahara.

It was a mirage.

The grin fell from my face, but secretly I was pleased. It meant I hadn't entirely lost my marbles . . . I kept going, delighted to see the sun setting, taking its suffocating heat with it. The only downside was I'd be in darkness in a matter of minutes.

When I got to checkpoint three, I immediately went to the medical tent, made the doctor aware that I'd been sick, and asked her for something for my nausea. I lay down, drank some water and she gave me a couple of tablets. She then asked me what I'd been eating. I told her I'd had some nuts and showed her a roll of fruit pastilles with two sweets missing.

Unimpressed, she told me to get some rest and said she'd be back later to check on me and make the call as to whether or not it was safe for me to continue.

* 37-odd miles

I lay there battling demons, convincing myself there was no shame in withdrawing, especially since guys tougher than me, like Chris, had already pulled out. But the difference was, I had a purpose: Dionne.

I got a bit emotional thinking of all the donations people had given me for Reverse Rett. I also thought about the promise I'd made to my wife, Monica, that I'd be sensible when it came to my health . . . It was a promise I had no intention of keeping.

I waited until the doctor was out of sight, got myself together and merged my way back into the race, knowing fine well that my greatest strength – my determination to succeed – had the potential to also be my biggest downfall.

I was running on empty but, deep inside, I had the undying belief that there was another 25 percent somewhere – an extra-special reserve that was only accessible in times of great need. Times like these.

If I stayed strong mentally, my body would follow. That was the party line I was going with and nothing was going to convince me otherwise. I also formulated a simple plan: keep drinking; take my salt tablets; try to eat; get some sleep; find company.

I let a couple of guys, whose names I soon discovered were Simon and James, catch up with me. Ten minutes or so later, we were joined by another guy called Andrew. They were a great bunch of guys and Andrew and I decided we'd stick together to help each other through the remainder of the leg. Simon had a few extra packets of Shot Bloks[*] and kindly gave me one. Okay, it was no gourmet meal, but it was all the food I needed and I was immensely grateful.

---

[*] Gel-based energy capsules

Once we reached checkpoint four, Andrew and I decided to take an hour's kip before plunging ourselves into the 62km stretch to checkpoint five.

As we covered the distance, one blister-ridden step at a time, it occurred to me that I'd chalked off all three parts of my plan. The difference sleep, food and company had made was heartening, albeit not surprising. I made it through the leg without any more mirages and without too much more vomit.

When we got to checkpoint five, we decided to sleep for two hours. The next leg involved climbing a jebel* as the sun came up, so we knew our resilience would once again be challenged and our spirits would need to be as strong as they possibly could be.

Thankfully, we made it up the mountain before the sun fully flexed its muscles. After that, knackered and bedraggled, but somehow still motivated, we plodded our way through a series of sand dunes before heading for the last checkpoint.

When we arrived, we were greeted by the sight of a doctor pouring water over the head of a fellow competitor.

'Would *you* like a shower?' she asked with a smile.

'Definitely,' I replied, laughing.

I quickly took off my backpack and stood where the now soaking wet other competitor had been. Without any preamble or hesitation, the doctor proceeded to pour four 1.5 litre bottles of water over me, washing away the sand that had irritated my skin and eyes for hour after hour. For the first time in my life, I was delighted to be drenched in my clothes, laughing as if every millilitre of water contained a cracking joke.

---

* The name for a hill or mountain in an Arab country

The doctor laughed along as she continued to douse me. Andrew then started laughing too. It became like a scene from a weird film, but it was the most invigorated I'd felt in ages.

The last six kilometres* genuinely felt like they were never going to end. It was as if I was destined to spend the rest of my life running in the Sahara. But then that glorious moment came: the sight of the finish line. Not a mirage. This was the moment that would draw a line under the fourth day of the 2021 Marathon des Sables. It was a brutal, unforgiving day. But I got through it.

Like cars running on fumes, Andrew and I crossed the finish line more than 26 hours after setting out. We managed to muster enough energy to congratulate each other before heading off to our respective tents.

As I hobbled towards mine, I thought about Dionne. The muscles in my legs were sore and tight, and my feet were agony, but I could walk. Dionne can't.

I wondered if I'd have withdrawn under normal circumstances, like if I'd entered the Marathon des Sables exclusively for a personal challenge. I wondered too if that doctor would have recommended I pull out for health reasons, albeit perfectly justifiable ones. Dionne may not be able to walk, but I was pretty damn certain she gave me that reserve, that back-up 25 percent. I was proud I pushed through, and equally as proud that she was my driving force.

When I reached my tent, I was greeted by the usual sight of Sean resting up. It was weird that there were only two of us left and it did cross my mind that Sean might've thought that he could've been sleeping there alone that night.

But I made it. I was still in the race. Just.

_____

* 3.7 miles

DIONNE

B ehind every fact and statistic about Rett Syndrome is a real life afflicted by the condition. One of those lives is the centre of my universe: my third child, Dionne, born September 9th, 2008, the day my life was set to change forever.

When Dionne was around 11 months' old, my ex-wife Michelle and I began to notice that something wasn't quite right. By this stage, babies can usually crawl, with some making their first attempts to walk – but Dionne was showing no signs of either, nor was she showing any attempt to form words. Our concern was exacerbated by the onset of severe reflux, which saw her vomiting up to a dozen times a day.

Hearts heavy with concern, we did all we could to make sure she was as comfortable as possible, the washing machine whirling constantly as we scratched our heads, wondering what was happening to our beloved daughter.

As a family, we would often go out for dinner, but as Dionne's vomiting showed no signs of appeasing, we had to put a halt to visiting restaurants. A kid being sick in a place where food is being served was no fun for anyone, least of all Dionne.

Naturally, we made many appointments at our GP's surgery as well as paying regular visits to the Sick Kids' Hospital, which was at Yorkhill in Glasgow at the time. With no changes in Dionne, this went on for the best part of a year, until – eventually – in the summer of 2010, a doctor at the Sick Kids' Hospital diagnosed her as having Global Development Delay. Frustratingly though, all this meant was, *There's something not quite right here, but we don't know what, exactly.* Michelle and I just wanted answers for our little girl, but it appeared Dionne had the experts stumped. Collectively, we'd hit a dead end – and it hurt.

Then, not long after Dionne's second birthday, she showed minor signs of improvement, managing a bit of what we called couch cruising. This involved using the couch to pull herself up for a few moments, gripping the fabric to give herself the stability she needed to take a few independent steps. It was always short-lived, a few seconds at best, but it was heart-warming to see her achieve some degree of progress. Around the same time, she also developed a bum-shuffling system that allowed her to move from A to B, which we took as evidence of the development of problem-solving skills. Michelle and I encouraged her with enthusiasm and praise, but – as we would soon discover – it was all temporary. Before long, she was confined to a buggy and, subsequently, a wheelchair.

Although the couch cruising and bum-shuffling was short-lived, we had hoped the reflux issue would improve, but that wasn't to be the case either. The reality was it became worse, heightening our unease, making us feel helpless as parents.

Towards the end of 2010, Dionne was referred to an Early Learning school in Hamilton, which specialised in kids with disabilities. Over the following eight months, Dionne showed no improvement, leading Michelle and me to slip into a period of just getting on with it, almost as if we were accepting the stalemate. Although we never vocalised it to each other, it felt like we'd conceded that our daughter was unlikely to ever be able to walk or talk. That didn't mean we'd given up trying to find out what was wrong though; we were still at it daily, but no useful information was coming our way.

Then a two-week summer holiday to Florida in 2011 changed everything.

Three days before we were due to come home, the heavens opened and the rain pelted down, fast and hard in long, thick needles, drumming aggressively on each and every surface and drenching anyone who dared step outside. We had planned to visit the theme parks for the umpteenth time, but the downpour put paid to that, holding us captive in our villa, or indoors at least.

Dionne had been struggling with her reflux. In fact, it was as bad as it had ever been. She could barely keep anything down, the acid in her stomach plotting against her any time she attempted to live as normal a life as possible. Now, people who know me well will verify that I'm a pretty levelled guy and not someone who gets upset easily, but on this occasion I was at the end of my tether. Things had plateaued in Scotland – we weren't getting any answers and Dionne was continuing to suffer – so I decided to investigate what America might be able to offer. After all, I was in a country where I hadn't explored the options, so it made sense to make the most of that opportunity.

I opened my laptop and searched online for nearby neurologists. My search was vague and unfocussed, so I was pleasantly surprised to learn that there was one only a 20-minute drive away. I punched the phone number from the website into my phone and spoke to the receptionist. Within an hour, the three of us were sitting in the neurologist's office.

27

Probably in his mid-50s, he was a plain looking man with a professional demeanour and impeccable posture. He was dressed casually and wore an expression that could only be described as neutral, a practitioner seasoned in not letting emotions cloud his judgement, advice or interventions. I imagined his expression would be the same when ordering a coffee as it would be when providing a life-saving treatment or delivering devastating news. It might seem like an odd thing to say, but I felt a kinship with him. Not to say my expression would be identical if faced with similar day-to-day situations, but I admired his demeanour because I felt it mirrored my own. Based on this, I knew that whatever news he might deliver to us, it'd be accurate, evidence-based and completely void of emotion. This was something we'd never experienced in Scotland, and it's what we needed.

With our consent, he used his hands to touch and move Dionne's limbs while she sat on my lap. He then moved her to his lap as he carried out some more tests, his expression – as fully expected – giving nothing away.

Once the physical assessment was complete, he returned Dionne to my lap and sat back in his chair and asked us some questions about Dionne's day-to-day life, her mobility, how often she was sick, how she communicated with us, and so on.

'I've got to be honest with you,' he said, resting his hands on his desk. 'I think what your daughter has isn't curable . . . I don't know exactly what it is, but if you're looking for a diagnosis, I can get you one within three weeks.'

He had delivered the news as if we were ordering a rare part for a vintage car. It's the kind of approach that I imagine would turn people off, but what he'd said and how he'd chosen to deliver it was music to my ears.

'And if I'm honest,' he continued, leaning forward slightly, 'I'm flabbergasted that you haven't been able to get a diagnosis in the UK.'

If Michelle and I hadn't been in shock, we might have laughed, because while he'd announced he was flabbergasted, his expression and tone couldn't have been more neutral. It was like someone admitting something was funny, only without even a flicker of a smile.

Three years we'd waited back home to get . . . well, nothing really, unless you consider the vague diagnosis of Global Development Delay as useful, which I didn't. Yet here we were in America, being told by a neurologist that we could have a diagnosis for Dionne in less than a month.

We sat in silence for a bit, letting everything sink in. On the outside, I maintained the image of the levelheaded, optimistic person I knew myself to be, but inside I was devastated. The hope I'd clung onto that there'd be a cure had been crushed by a single sentence, trampled and annihilated, like plastic beer tumblers after a gig. To be clear, I wasn't deluded; I never expected a doctor to prescribe a miracle pill that would allow Dionne to live an entirely normal life after a couple of weeks, but I had hoped there'd be evidence somewhere in the world that the right combination of medication, diet, treatment and support would make things considerably better for her.

On the plus side though, I knew this feeling of devastation wouldn't last. I'm not the kind of person who lets things fester. The sting would soon subside and my focus would shift to what we *could* do, rather than wasting energy feeling sorry for ourselves. That'd be no good to anyone, especially Dionne.

Another obvious positive was that a diagnosis would give us a baseline; something to work from; clarity as to what we were dealing with. But we were going home in three days, so how was this going to work?

Thankfully, it was all fairly straightforward. We went back the following morning and the neurologist took 17 blood samples from Dionne, some of which were sent away to the other side of the country for analysis, hence the three-week turnaround.

However, since we were in Florida for a holiday, we only had basic travel insurance, which wouldn't be a problem if the U.S. had the equivalent of the NHS – but with that not being the case, we knew it was likely that the diagnosis would be expensive.

Although his face never showed it, the neurologist must have been cognisant that he was dealing with a couple craving the need to know what was wrong with their child. Much to our amazement and gratitude – and on the condition that we paid cash or by credit card – he charged us only half the fee, a total of around £800. This expunged that unfair conception that all Americans are only ever about the dollar.

There was no hesitation. I trusted this neurologist to provide us with the information we so desperately wanted. Needed. Even if the diagnosis was grim, we'd know what we were dealing with and could move forward from there.

About a fortnight later, the results arrived via email. I was at work at the time, but Michelle had read it and contacted me at work to tell me the news. As I made my way from office to car, phone clutched tightly in my hand, I took a deep breath and asked her what the diagnosis was. It was then, for the first time in my life, that I heard the words 'Rett Syndrome'.

NO CURE . . . YET

The neurologist's email was a dagger to our hearts. Despite him telling us that he thought what Dionne had wasn't curable, there was still a small part of me that believed he might be wrong. Unfortunately, though, it was me who was wrong. In his email, the neurologist advised we research Rett Syndrome online, which we duly did, and soon discovered there was no known cure – or certainly not at that time. It's weird how something as perfunctory and everyday as an email was capable of blowing all our hopes and dreams out of the water.

As we continued to read and research, it quickly became apparent that Rett Syndrome was going to rob Dionne of the quality of life any parent would hope their child would have. I remember thinking that she'd never have a boyfriend and that the only people who would love her would be her family. In that moment, I felt great sadness. Most fathers dread the moment their daughter brings home their first boyfriend, but I was gutted that it was now a moment that wouldn't feature Dionne's future or mine.

The Mavis Reilly 'flat-liner' aura I'm told I project, i.e. I'm never too high and never too low, you always find me the same way – which I happen to think is a good thing – was under threat in these moments. The wind was well and truly knocked out of my sails. Heartbroken for my little girl and the life she was destined to lead, I had moments over a period of about a week where I locked myself way and cried my eyes out.

Then – and some people might consider this to be exceptionally quick – I started to get my head round it. I told myself, *C'mon, Mavis, you've always been strong when it comes to processing things. You can't change what it is, so what are you going to do about it? Go on feeling sorry for yourself, or start getting on with making things as good as possible for Dionne?* Looking back, I might have been on autopilot, it's hard to tell, but I think I did pretty well in coming to terms with it.

Naturally, we visited our GP to inform her that we'd paid an American neurologist to provide Dionne with her diagnosis. Interestingly, when we revealed that Dionne had Rett Syndrome, our GP had never heard of it and had to look it up on her computer. Some people might have been annoyed at this, but I took it as proof as to how rare a condition Rett Syndrome was. And to be fair, whilst some people might expect a GP to know about every single condition, disease, ailment and disability, I don't think it's realistic. I'd also much prefer a doctor is honest and transparent about what they do and don't know, rather than purporting to know everything just because they're wearing a white coat.

For Michelle and me, the priority was learning about the complications and nuances of the condition, so we could be as prepared as possible. We soon learned that seizures could occur frequently and that scoliosis, a progressive curvature of the spine, may feature as Dionne became older.

Whilst difficult to take in, it was important to develop our knowledge and awareness of the condition. If we hadn't gone through this process and Dionne was to have a seizure one day, we wouldn't be prepared to respond in the correct manner.

In order for the NHS to help as best they could, all the documentation had to be sent over from the USA. Although, if truth be told, there's not a great deal the NHS can do, as Dionne is not on any medication for Rett Syndrome, simply because no medication or cure exists. Well, not yet anyway.

Fortunately, Dionne hasn't suffered many seizures and only one resulted in hospitalisation, although we're not sure Rett Syndrome was 100 percent responsible for it as she'd had a bug a few days beforehand, so her immune system was likely to be weaker than usual. On another occasion, she had what's referred to as a silent seizure, which happened when she was at school. She'd lapsed into a 15-minute period of silence, which is not a common occurrence for Dionne, but she had been experiencing poor sleep at that time, so it could have been nothing more than tiredness catching up with her.

If I'm honest, the seizures are a regular concern, as there's never any indication as to when one might come on. That said, in contrast to other Rett Syndrome sufferers, Dionne's seizures have been infrequent and mainly mild, so we have to look at the positives.

A significant turning point in terms of Dionne's quality of life occurred in 2011, when she underwent fundoplication surgery to deal with her reflux. The procedure involved wrapping the upper curve of her stomach around her oesophagus, which sounds horrible, but is proven to prevent acid reflux and regular vomiting. Much to everyone's delight, the surgery was a success and Dionne was left with a much better quality of life.

Despite this silver lining, sleep patterns became a bit of a problem. Dionne would sleep for periods far beyond the recommended seven to eight hours, but this was then followed by the opposite extreme, meaning she'd be awake and lively most of the night.

Another aspect of the condition is the early onset of puberty, meaning Dionne began menstruating at only eight years old. This is down to a symptom of Rett Syndrome being the acceleration of development, which also contributed to the curvature in her spine becoming progressively worse, as was intimated shortly after her diagnosis. In time, it began to fuse, putting pressure on her internal organs, which led to major surgery being recommended.

The surgery took place at the Sick Kids' Hospital in Edinburgh one month after Dionne's 11th birthday. Unfortunately, it's not possible for the spine to be realigned entirely, but the outcome was still a positive one for Dionne, despite having to stay in hospital for a full week. I was delighted it was all worth it, because as any parent who's been in a similar situation will verify, it's heavy going watching over your child lying in a hospital bed with tubes down their throat to the soundtrack of machines whirring, buzzing and beeping. But like the trooper she is, Dionne embraced the procedure with a smile and recovered brilliantly.

As I'm sure you can appreciate, Dionne has had a lot to endure in her life, certainly far more than the average person. If you were to meet her, you might expect to see someone suffering, wrestling with a condition that's having a detrimental effect on their quality of life. But that's not what you'd get. Instead, you'd be greeted with a smiley face, an infectious giggle and a desire to make friends. Anyone who meets Dionne leaves elated, not deflated. Unless she's tired or hungry, Dionne is a happy young lady who spreads that happiness effortlessly.

Although she can't talk, she can make noises and uses body language and facial expressions to communicate. With food being her big love, she's great at using her eyes to let us know what she wants. If I hold up a yoghurt and a bar of chocolate, I'll know within a second which one she wants . . . usually the chocolate!

Similarly, if she's feeling under the weather, she communicates this through expressions, sounds and body language. It may not be as instant and obvious as a kid saying, 'I've got a sore tummy', but it never takes us long to become aware of what's going on. Interestingly, sufferers of Rett Syndrome have a high pain threshold, which might explain how accommodating Dionne has been over the years with the various interventions and procedures she's been exposed to.

It's difficult to know how much Dionne is aware of, but she definitely recognises people she's met before. She loves going out and people-watching from her wheelchair. Whether we're in a park, a shopping centre or just moseying down the street, it's clear she's drinking everything in, fascinated by people, their movements and their behaviours.

You may have noticed in the Prologue that I mentioned my wife Monica and that earlier in the book I referred to Michelle as my ex-wife. My marriage to Michelle fell apart in 2015 for reasons it's not necessary to cover in this book, but I feel it's important to highlight that our separation had nothing to do with Dionne. The reason I say this is that it may be easy to assume that a child with 24/7 care needs would contribute to a marriage becoming strained. I'm sure there are couples out there who have split as a result of disagreeing on what's best for their disabled or impaired son or daughter, whether that be medication, treatment, education, or the extent of integration with able bodied, impairment-free children, to name just a few. This was not the case with Michelle and me. After we split up and later divorced, Dionne, who was six at the time, showed no signs of being affected. Of course, it was difficult to truly know what she was thinking, but there was no outward display of emotions, either negative or positive. It's highly likely she wouldn't have understood what was going on, but she did show awareness of new, different surroundings. There were now two houses and two bedrooms! My guess – and hope – is that she saw it as something exciting. It's not like her mum or I loved her any less, far from it. It just meant we weren't all under the same roof.

Back in 2012, when Dionne was nearly five, we hit a bit of a stumbling block. The ideal school for her to begin her education was the Craigalbert Centre in Cumbernauld, but Cumbernauld is in North Lanarkshire and that time we lived in South Lanarkshire, a different catchment area altogether. The Craigalbert has a fantastic reputation for teaching kids with complex needs to a high standard, so, understandably, Michelle and I were keen that Dionne be considered. We wanted her to get the best start possible, so we were willing to do whatever it took. Thankfully, after some extensive to-ing and fro-ing between councils, the powers that be showed sensitivity towards our dilemma and agreed that Dionne could attend the Craigalbert. We were delighted and, as we later found out, the Craigalbert lived up to its reputation, providing a level of care to Dionne that could only be described as exemplary.

Inevitably, though, the years rolled on and, in 2019, the time came for Dionne to go to secondary school. During this period, Michelle and I had separated, but we were both equally concerned about this step up, as was Monica, especially given the excellent standards Dionne had experienced at the Craigalbert. Thankfully, though, we had nothing to worry about. South Lanarkshire Council had been reviewing things on an annual basis and, once the time came, Dionne began her secondary education at Sanderson High in East Kilbride, where, despite being one of the least mobile pupils, she was welcomed warmly and treated well.

The coronavirus pandemic meant things ended up being a bit disjointed, but Dionne was happy, so that was the main thing. Her teachers told us that she was fascinated by the other kids, often fixating on them, watching them do all the things she couldn't. It was great to learn that she wasn't passive or feeling isolated and instead was curious and engaged, absorbing everything that was going on around her.

THE CHAIN CAROUSEL

As a couple, Monica and I do the best we can to give Dionne as full a life as possible. Monica has to be given credit, though, for helping me enhance the way I spend time with my daughter. In the past, I may have been a little too protective, but Monica has helped me overcome that, drawing out an approach that's more fun and exhilarating for Dionne – and for me!

One time that sticks in my head was Christmas 2016. The three of us took a trip to George Square in the centre of Glasgow, where, as is always the case at that time of year, there was an ice rink and a funfair, all illuminated by lights of multiple colours, twinkling and flashing to the soundtrack of whoops, playful screams and jingly, happy, Christmas music. Dionne was mesmerised by two rides in particular, the Big Wheel and the Chain Carousel.

In case you're not sure what the Chain Carousel is, it's the one where there's a large centre piece, kind of mushroom-shaped, with loads of swings hanging from it, as in swings you would see in a play park, only with metal sides and a security bar. Some have only single seats, but this one was kitted out entirely with double seats. When the ride starts, the mushroom-shaped bit rotates and the seats move round in a circle, but when it picks up speed and begins to dance, as if it's dropping a shoulder and standing tall again, the chairs end up diagonal, whizzing through the air, catching the breath of the riders, most grinning in delight, but with the occasional one looking like they've regretted their decision to strap in.

When the chairs were spinning at maximum speed and the centre piece was grooving and gyrating as if it had entered a dance competition, Dionne laughed her head off, exhilarated by the experience as if she was on the ride herself, the flashing lights reflecting in her eyes, illuminating her joy.

'Why don't you take her on it?' Monica said, out of the blue.

'No way!' I replied, instantly. 'Look at the speed it goes at!' The safety-conscious Mavis had kicked in, the sensible parent who would protect his disabled daughter by only allowing her to watch fun things from afar. Even typing this makes me realise how ridiculous that sounds.

'Go on,' Monica urged. 'You can't keep her wrapped in cotton wool forever, you know. Let her experience life.'

The look on Monica's face told me she was right. And I knew she was. I had to let go. If I wanted Dionne to lead as normal a life as possible, I couldn't continue treating things like a funfair ride as some sort of perilous life-threatening monster. After all, all that was required to ride the Chain Carousel was a bum and the ability to sit. Dionne possessed this ability as much as I did, so I bit the bullet and we went on.

Once the chairs picked up speed, Dionne screeched and screamed, but these were screeches and screams of pure joy. I would've loved to have shared that joy with her, but I'll be honest, I was terrified, gripping onto the chains for dear life! Maybe my earlier reservations were more self-preservation than fatherly concern! Scottish

Cup Final? No problem. Marathon des Sables? No reason why not. Chain Carousel at Christmas time? Hmm, Monica can go on next time.

Later on, we rode the Big Wheel and, as I expected, Dionne absolutely loved it. These are simple things that other children perhaps take for granted – my guess is that most kids similar in age to Dionne would have ridden a whole host of funfair rides several times before – but these were completely new experiences for my little girl. Up there on the Big Wheel, seeing her grinning ear to ear and shrieking with delight, was a turning point for me. I vowed that from that point on that there would be no more cotton wool.

I was in awe of my daughter. Prior to taking Monica's advice and biting the bullet, I suppose I thought Dionne might be scared of these rides, maybe see them as dangerous or threatening. What if she'd become terrified once she was strapped into her seat and the ride was in motion? That point of no return would be the beginning of five minutes of torture, a torture I'd have been responsible for. But what's the point in thinking like that? Negativity only breeds negativity and it was clear from Dionne's reaction to her surroundings before we went on the Chain Carousel that these were things she wasn't in the least bit scared of.

As an athlete, I know all about stepping outside my comfort zone to reach goals and live a meaningful, fulfilling life. That day in George Square, Dionne stepped outside her comfort zone with a great big smile on her face, but more importantly, I stepped outside mine by untying the apron strings and letting go. The result was the sharing of unforgettable experiences with my daughter and wife, experiences that taught me that personal development can occur as much on a football field or battling through illness to run in unbearable heat as it can on a day out at Christmas with the family.

Off the back of Dionne enjoying the funfair rides so much, I took her to a place called Calvert Trust in Northumbria, which specialises in outdoor adventures for disabled kids. One of the things on offer is zip wiring, something I never thought for a moment Dionne would be able to experience. These guys are experts though, so they had a special seat with a back brace that ensured Dionne's spine was protected. Having put all my unnecessary concerns to bed, I was then strapped onto the back of her, so we could experience the adrenaline rush of zip wiring as a father-daughter combo. Monica found a suitable position to take a video from and shot us flying through the air on the zip wire, Dionne hee-hawing with glee. Any time I watch that video, it warms my heart. Her euphoria is so uplifting, it's impossible to have any other reaction.

I have to thank Monica for encouraging me to get out there more with Dionne to share these experiences. I think it's all too easy to end up being over-protective when disability is a factor. It's hard not to assume that vulnerability is increased and the chances of things going wrong or becoming more complex are likely. But that's not the way we've chosen to live. To be clear, I am by no means saying that parents with a disabled child (or disabled children) should throw caution to the wind and instantly sign up for the next available bungee jump. I appreciate the word 'disability' encompasses a lot and, of course, that there are wide spectrums within disabilities. But that said, I never thought I'd see Dionne on a Chain Carousel, in a canoe or on a zip wire. Sometimes it's about reading the room, listening to experts and loved ones and thinking about what's possible, rather than assuming most things aren't. Monica used to work as a head teacher in a school for children with disabilities, so she brought that experience to the table and helped me eradicate my unwarranted fears.

As is evident in the Marathon des Sables chapters, mindset is massive. It may sound like a cliché these days, but never underestimate the power of your mind. Everyone is capable of rewiring their brain to change the way they perceive things. I'm not saying you can convince yourself to survive a sky dive without a parachute or play professional rugby at the age of 67, but you can certainly push your boundaries, whether physical or mental, whether in relation to attitudes and beliefs towards yourself or to others. You have the capability to open the doors you thought were bolted tight forever. A shift in mindset and treating your brain like a muscle that can be developed – like any other muscle in your body – can help push away the negativity, exterminate the unnecessary catastrophising and make things rewarding and fruitful, both for yourself and your nearest and dearest.

Having read quite a bit about Dionne now, it's likely you'll have developed some sort of emotional response. One that we get all too often is that of sympathy. People tell us that it must be really hard, that they feel sorry for us having a daughter who needs 24/7 care, that it's a shame she has to live with such a complex condition. The one that I dislike most though is, 'How do you cope?'

I don't mean for this to be harsh or insensitive, and I know 100 percent of people who offer their sympathy or ask that question do so with the best of intentions, but here's the thing: I wouldn't change Dionne for the world. This might come as a surprise, based on what you've read about her reflux, her inability to walk, talk or carry out basic day-to-day activities. It might also seem an unusual thing for me to say given that my Marathon des Sables venture was to raise awareness and funds for Reverse Rett. But I shall explain.

Dionne is happy.

How many people do you know – who have no diagnosed disability or impairment – who are either unhappy or not particularly happy? How many people do you see walking down the street, on trains and buses, or even on TV, whose faces are glum and whose body language suggests doom and gloom? If you were to meet Dionne, you'd get a warm welcome and a big, hearty smile. She would have no pre-conceived opinions or attitudes based on what you look like, the colour of your skin, your gender identity, age, sexuality or political persuasion. She would just accept you for who you choose to be and would do so with warmth.

Sure, it's sobering knowing that Dionne will need round the clock care for the rest of her life. I've accepted it'll be challenging, especially as I grow older, but I am deeply fortunate to have Dionne in my life. She has made me see things differently and appreciate the things I took for granted before she was born. Every morning when I wake up, I'm profoundly grateful that I can swing my legs round, place my feet on the carpet and stand up. This is something I wouldn't even have thought of being grateful for before Dionne was in the world, but I now experience this all-encompassing gratitude every single morning. I can walk, talk and go about my daily business without even thinking about it. Dionne not being able to do these things places emphasis on how appreciative I am to have them as default.

Another major thing Dionne has brought to my life is my lack of fear of death. A lot of people don't like to think of their mortality, but if someone said to me tomorrow, 'That's it, Mavis, your time's up', my attitude would be, 'Oh, well, I've had a brilliant life. I've been a professional footballer, won the Scottish Cup Final, had a great job with the police, met some fascinating people and visited loads of interesting places, including Austria, Croatia, Finland, New York, San Francisco and South Korea'.

What have I got to moan about? Nothing, that's what. Absolutely nothing.

I look at Dionne and, despite her being able to do so little, she's exceptionally happy. What an inspiration! She has no ego, no obsession with material things, and never judges or gossips. It would be great if more people could adopt her values. She's taught me so much about myself, and the human condition.

Motivational speakers, gurus and life coaches often talk about the need to live in the moment, to appreciate the present, rather than focusing on the past or the future. The contemporary world is so frantic and unpredictable, and it seems like it's full of people chasing their tails, regularly announcing they're immensely busy, like it's some sort of accolade or badge of honour, as if an unmanageable, over-populated diary is a sign of success. So many people miss the moment because they're either planning their future moves or they're stuck in the past, ruminating over bad decisions as if perfection is the only option.

But none of this applies to Dionne.

Dionne appreciates the simple things in life like no other person I've met. When the weather is decent, she loves nothing more than being outside surrounded by nature with the air in her face. When we go to the park in the spring, her contentment is transparent. She's in the moment, focusing entirely on what she's experiencing there and then, unconcerned about what might happen next or what has come before. Her response to something as simple as a trip to the park is to smile and laugh. Sitting there in her wheelchair, having endured everything she's had to endure, if my daughter is smiley and happy, what right do I have to be miserable? What right does *anyone* have?

If you think about spiritual leaders or monks living in a monastery, they all live in the moment and have peaceful auras that exude calm and serenity. This is because they have all their basic needs met and are not concerned with material things. Dionne is the same. She knows her basic needs are met and that her necessary care will continue to be provided across two homes by her loving family, so she's happy. A happy soul with a kind heart who lives in the here and now. That's not something, in my book anyway, that warrants the question 'How do you cope?'

Make no mistake, if it wasn't for Dionne having Rett Syndrome, I wouldn't have developed the vision, motivation and enthusiasm that led me to run the Marathon des Sables. Not that I was a negative person before she was born, but Dionne has guided me into a life where I always take a negative and do what I can to turn it into a positive. Running the Marathon des Sables wasn't exclusively about a guy running a crazy race to cure his daughter, it was about raising awareness and funds to make things better for Dionne and people like her. She has made things better for me, so I want to make things better for her. To do this, I used one thing I have that she doesn't and two things she's helped me develop over the years: my ability to walk, my positive mindset, and my mental strength.

I don't think there will be a cure for Rett Syndrome in Dionne's lifetime, but I'd be delighted to be wrong. Whether a cure is found or not, it feels like Dionne was meant to have it, if for no other reason than to show the world that genuine happiness is possible regardless of the cards you've been dealt.

Monica and I have two dogs, a Giant Schnauzer called Milo and a South African Mastiff called Manny. If you're knowledgeable when it comes to dog breeds, you'll know that these are big, imposing dogs, both about 25 inches tall, with Milo coming in at 40kg and Manny a whopping 60kg. If you're nervous around dogs, or have had an unfortunate experience with one in the past, you'd likely be intimidated by Manny, if for no other reason than his tank-like physical presence and slobbery chops. But, as is the case with any dog who's well cared for, he's gentle, affectionate, dedicated and shows lots of love to his family. The same goes for Milo.

Like a lot of dogs, when someone comes to the door, Manny and Milo become excitable, keen to find out who's coming into their home, what they want and why they want it. I assume this comes from them seeing it as their job to protect the estate, playing the part of a bouncer or quality controller. Of course, it could also be straightforward excitement, the anticipation of having someone new to interact with, someone who might want to play their favourite game or pet them in a way that hits the spot.

What's interesting, though, is that when Dionne arrives, they're nowhere near as excitable and never jump up. They're still pleased to see her and give her a warm welcome, but they're much more careful around her. I'm not sure if the wheelchair has an influence, but they show awareness of Dionne's condition and adjust the way they engage accordingly. You could call it a sixth sense, but they definitely tune in to what's going on and know that a different set of behaviours is necessary.

When she was about eight or nine, Dionne could pick things up with her hands and there was even a period where she could feed herself. Sadly, though, she gradually lost the use of her fingers, a common symptom of Rett Syndrome. Her fingers are now clenched inwards, hooked at the middle knuckles, meaning her ability to grip is minimal to non-existent.

Due to this, the way Dionne shows affection to the dogs is different to what they receive from everyone else; she manages to ruffle their ears a bit and run the back of her hand against their fur. Manny has floppy ears, so Dionne can sometimes get them between her fingers and tug at them. A neutral onlooker might show concern for Manny as sometimes it looks uncomfortable, especially if his ears are being tugged quite hard. What's fascinating, though, is he just sits there and takes it. If Dionne has one hand on his ear, Manny will lick the other, returning the affection. This makes Dionne giggle, providing Manny with immediate feedback that she likes what he's doing. All these communication loops fly back and forth without a single word being uttered.

Very often, when Dionne is sitting on the sofa, Manny jumps up and lick her cheeks, tail wagging vigorously, whip-like. Whether this behaviour is a sign of submission, tenderness or a method of picking up messages, it sends Dionne into hysterics. From her reaction, Manny gets the positive reinforcement he desires, meaning he can continue doing what he's doing and carry out the same behaviour in the future.

When he's not licking her face or having his ears tugged, Manny can often be seen lying at Dionne's feet, protecting his queen like a head lion, assured in his role to safeguard his pride. There's a true kinship there, not just between Dionne and Manny, but Milo too, the only difference being that Manny's behaviours and mannerisms (or Manny-erisms) are overt, while Milo shows affection in a more implicit, aloof way. When I take a step back and think about it, it's awe-inspiring: three members of my family, all communicating non-verbally, all respecting each other in their own individual ways, all living in the present moment, and all showing unbridled, unconditional love.

REVERSE RETT

B ack when Dionne was first diagnosed with Rett Syndrome, it took a while for the shock to wear off. Once it did, though, I thought it would be a good idea to find out if there were any Rett Syndrome charities out there.

I figured it would be good to hear from other parents, to learn from their experiences of caring for a child with Rett Syndrome, but I was also interested in helping out in terms of fundraising and raising awareness. As I had no knowledge of Rett Syndrome until Dionne was diagnosed, I was sure there were plenty other people out there with no knowledge of it either – and that was something I was passionate about changing. At that point, I never thought for a second that my initial research and enquiries would lead to me – several years later – running 251km* over the Sahara.

I soon came across Rett UK, a charity that does fantastic work, placing their focus on supporting families and parents. However, I wanted to look at the bigger picture, to find a charity that focusses on treatment and cure. And that's when I came across Reverse Rett.

I did some further research and found a study carried out in 2007 in which Rett Syndrome was reversed in laboratory mice. The researchers concluded their paper by stating that Rett Syndrome could be the first ever

---

* 156 miles

curable neurological condition. I found this to be extremely encouraging and remember feeling slightly light-headed when I read those words.

Nevertheless, I'm not naïve, so whilst something sparked inside me that day, I didn't become deluded, convinced that all I'd have to do was a bit of fundraising and Dionne would be cured in a couple of years. The chances of a cure being available in Dionne's lifetime are slim, but slim still means it's possible. I felt it was important not to be selfish though – this wasn't exclusively about Dionne. Sure, my motivation and enthusiasm to make changes and influence progress clearly came from having a daughter with Rett Syndrome, but I told myself that even if my contribution could lead to a cure being available for future generations, it was worth doing.

Reverse Rett doesn't have government funding, nor does it receive any lottery money, meaning all their work is driven by donation and sponsorship. Part of their work involves funding clinical trials. For instance, if a child is having difficulty swallowing, Reverse Rett will fund trials to help find medication to treat or manage that symptom. So, whilst finding a cure is their goal, they also invest in helping alleviate problems and complications associated with the condition.

Another thing I did as part of my initial research was to find out which percentage of a donation goes directly into funds for research and how much goes towards administration costs. I did this for Reverse Rett but then picked another ten charities to compare it against. I was pleased to discover that Reverse Rett came out on top in terms of the percentage of donated money going towards funding research.

Shortly after determining that Reverse Rett ticked all the boxes that were important to me, I contacted the people who run the charity, Andy and Rachael Stevenson, who are based in Manchester. With one child each diagnosed with Rett Syndrome (from previous relationships), they set up the charity in 2009, launching in 2010, to complement and endorse the work carried out by Rett UK, but to firmly place their focus on treatment and cure.

Chatting with Andy and Rachael, it was clear how passionate they were about their charity, organising several fundraising events and awareness raising campaigns over the course of the year, including an annual 10k, a gala in London and a *Big Give* event every Christmas. It's an incredible amount of work, proof of their devotion to the cause.

A year or so after contacting Andy and Rachael to express my desire to raise funds for Reverse Rett, I did the Glasgow 10k in their name, running with my big pal and former Kilmarnock and St Mirren teammate, Kevin McGowne. Andy ran it too, which allowed me to meet him and Rachael in person. The personalities that came across via email very much reflected those I interacted with in the offline world, enhanced by hearing their enthusiasm and gratitude.

Ever since I began doing stuff on behalf of Reverse Rett, I've raised approximately £60,000, which includes £24,000 for the Three Peaks Challenge I completed in 2012 and a little over £21,000 for the Marathon des Sables nine years later. I'm absolutely delighted to have raised this much money for a cause that's close to my heart, but I do find it uncomfortable asking people for money. Everyone responds brilliantly though, and it's not just financial support they provide; many also offer psychological, emotional, mental and even spiritual support. I have no doubt that this kind of support contributed to me developing the mindset necessary to run the Marathon des Sables.

In the build up to a charity event I did prior to the Marathon des Sables, celebrities such as Martin Compston and personalities from the footballing world such as Ally McCoist, Jack Grealish and Steve Clarke posted videos on social media about what I was about to take on. Getting support from household names gave me such a lift but, more importantly, it helped spread awareness to thousands, possibly millions of people. When the going gets tough, as it did several times during the Marathon des Sables, there's no stronger motivator than thinking about the number and the calibre of people who have put their hands in their pockets and/or promoted my venture.

Looking back to when I first contacted Andy and Rachael and comparing how I was then to how I was after the Marathon des Sables, my personal development and self-improvement has been astonishing. I've been to places – physically and mentally – that I never dreamt I'd go. I've pushed myself to my absolute limits, and then pushed some more. Completing these challenges in the name of Reverse Rett has led me down many paths of self-discovery, where I've learned about the power of the mind; not just learned about, but learned to appreciate it and respect it as the most adaptable and trainable muscle in the human body. I've developed endurance and resilience I never thought possible and experienced the joy of meeting difficult, long term goals, coming out the other side stronger, better, wiser, fitter, more determined, and with a smile on my face. And it's all because of Dionne.

FOOTBALL DAFT

I can't remember any part of my childhood that didn't involve kicking a ball around for as long as daylight would allow. Of course, this was the early 70s, a time when there were far fewer distractions than there are today. Back then, Sky TV was no more than a twinkle in Rupert Murdoch's eye and Xbox sounded like an episode of *Doctor Who*. In all honesty though, even if there were games consoles, smartphones and hundreds of TV channels to choose from, I reckon I'd still be outside from dawn until dusk, kicking a ball about with my pals. School was nothing more than something to do while the ball wasn't moving.

Thinking back to those days, I wonder if all that running around instead of sitting looking at screens had any influence on my ability to do the Marathon des Sables decades later. There probably is a link there. The desire to be regularly active as a child, the buzz I got getting in folks' faces on the football field during my time as a pro, my general love of the outdoors . . . these were likely precursors, along with Dionne of course, to developing the necessary mindset and endurance to spend the best part of a week running from one desolate part of the Sahara to the next.

Taking in all of primary school and first year of high school, I had a routine as soon as the bell rang to mark the end of the day, one I stuck to regardless of the weather. I'd run home, sling my schoolbag, get changed in a matter of seconds and be out kicking a ball while other pupils were still trundling home. Most of the time my pals would join me, but if it was raining and they chose to stay inside, I'd just play myself, booting the ball off walls or doing keepy-uppies. I was always first out and last in, squeezing as much daylight out of the sky as I could, especially in winter. This often meant my football time was topped and tailed with solo keepy-uppy sessions, which, as I soon discovered, would not be time wasted.

I was around 13 at the time when I saw an advert for a West of Scotland keepy-uppy competition, the first round taking place at Hamilton College, which wasn't too far from where I lived in Bellshill. I breezed the early rounds, which led to the finals, held at Parkhead at half-time during a Celtic v Hibs fixture. For the first part, I had to keep the ball up for five minutes, incorporating tricks like resting the ball for a few seconds between the back of my neck and my shoulders and then between ankle and instep. The second part involved travelling with the ball, navigating cones, and then volleying it into the net from 18 yards. It goes without saying that, during this whole process, disqualification would occur if the ball hit the ground, but the other stipulation was that the volley had to cross the line before making contact with the turf.

I came first, beating . . . well, everyone! . . . including future Scotland international and Champions' League winner, Paul Lambert, who came third. Not bad for a wee guy from Bellshill. I could say I was delighted, that it was a massive moment for me, but it all felt fairly pedestrian, which I mean in an honest rather than bigheaded way. All I did was replicate the stuff I was pulling off alone on a rainy Tuesday night, daylight fading by the second, while everyone else had gone in to do their homework, which I was delaying because the ball was still round and darkness was only threatening to fall. The only difference that day at Parkhead was that I was performing these well-rehearsed, fine-tuned skills in front of thousands of people instead of a row of recently switched on lampposts, a lock-up wall and a for sale sign. My composure under those circumstances only reinforced my aspirations to become a professional footballer. I'd heard about players buckling under the pressure of the occasion, especially if it was a significant game, but at that stage, it looked like I had the composure as well as the skill, at least at keepy-uppies.

Off the back of my first place achievement, I was invited to a national final at Hampden, to be held at half-time during the Scottish Cup Final between Rangers and Aberdeen. This featured all the top dogs from all over the country. I came third. It would have been great to get pole position again, but given around 500 kids entered, coming third is pretty damn good.

Things began progressing for me when I was playing for a variety of boys' clubs and attracted the attention of Alastair Stevenson, who at the time was a scout for Motherwell. He approached me one night after a match and suggested that I train at Fir Park. There was no pro-youth system in those days, but if a young player was deemed to have potential, they signed an S form, the S standing for schoolboy. So that's what happened: Alastair presented me with the form, I signed it, became part of Motherwell F.C. and trained with them a couple of times a week. I was only 13, but it felt like I was signing a proper contract. In a way I was, because an S form meant that no other team could sign me until I left school.

Alastair was the kind of coach who instilled a lot of confidence in me. Back then, it was fairly commonplace for coaches to be shouters, for negative reactions to be motivators to work harder, address weaknesses and prove worth. In contrast, Alastair was ahead of the game, opting instead to use encouragement, constructive criticism and patience as his tools to get the best out of his players. This style complemented his appearance: non-imposing, athletic-looking and of average build and height. I remember him as a dark-haired, good-looking average Joe, but one that knew what he was talking about and didn't have to shout to be listened to or taken seriously.

When schoolboy trials came up for the Scotland National Team, I expressed my interest in trying out as a midfielder, the position I'd always favoured and was currently playing for Motherwell. One of the coaches, though, told me that the competition for a place in the middle of the park would be fierce and suggested I try out as a left back. However, being based in the West of Scotland, I was only trying out for the team from that region. There were corresponding teams from the north, east and south of the country, the final team being made up of the best from each, decided after a four-way play-off of sorts, hosted at Inverclyde.

Channeling my success from the keepy-uppy competition, I went in all guns blazing, taking into consideration everything Alastair had taught and nurtured in me. And I made it! Another success and another feather in my footballing cap that I could be proud of.

Despite this though, there was a bitter taste in my mouth, because I didn't make it as a midfielder; I made it as a left back. I appreciate this might sound a little petty, but it's the equivalent of having a burning desire to be a pastry chef, having all the necessary skills a pastry chef requires, applying for a job as a pastry chef . . . and then getting the role of meat cook. To make that bitterness linger though, your work station is, crushingly, only a few metres away from the candidate who was appointed the role of pastry chef, the only role you've ever wanted.

I didn't hold onto the bitterness though. What would be the point in that? I had achieved great things for a lad my age, so I was delighted to be on the road to fulfilling my dream of becoming a professional footballer, and this ability to let things go after the initial disappointment wore off would be a character trait I'd find myself lucky to have later in life.

Unfortunately, I was pigeonholed as a left back from that point on, but I took solace in the knowledge that I was still young and had a lot of football ahead of me. Just because I wasn't a midfielder at that particular stage of my career, there was nothing to suggest I couldn't be in the future. I just needed the right opportunity or set of circumstances, or maybe just the right gaffer.

WELCOME TO MEN'S FITBA, WEE MAN

I put my heart and soul into training with Motherwell in my young teens – and one night all that effort paid off. I was 15 at the time, sitting at home watching TV because it was winter and darkness had fallen at about four o'clock. The phone rang. Bored by what was on TV (there were only four channels back then), I sprung from my seat and answered it. It was the Motherwell gaffer, Tommy McLean.

'There's a reserves game tomorrow night,' he said. 'Rangers at home. I want you to play.'

When I put the phone down, I was physically shaking, a little bit with apprehension, but mainly with excitement. This was going to be nothing like I'd experienced before in football. My heart was pounding against my rib cage, the grin on my face wide. It might have only been a reserve game, but to a 15-year-old Mark Reilly, it was everything.

Seasoned centre half Tom McAdam, who'd had a successful nine-year spell at Celtic, was on the books at Motherwell at that point. Having bags of experience, he was a fantastic guy to have around, especially since he showed great willingness to pass on his wisdom to young players like me, offering advice and encouragement at any opportunity. However, his brother, Colin, who played for Rangers, was a different story.

The following evening, having been unable to concentrate at school, I arrived at Fir Park. It was a cold winter's night with that drizzle that kind of dances in the sky, visible in front of the floodlights that illuminated the ground.

As we took up our positions at the beginning of the game, I looked at Colin McAdam. I would never class myself as a big guy, but even someone with seven inches on me would be shadowed by Colin. He was an absolute bear of a man: burly, broad, muscular and toned, standing at 6ft 1 with wild curly hair, his dark brown ringlets cupping a face and chiseled jaw that meant business. Despite my lack of physical presence though, at least in contrast to players like Colin, I was never afraid. Often I used my size to be nippy and smart, but just because I wasn't a bear, it didn't mean I would shy away from heavy tackles. I was always keen to get in and about things.

About 20-odd minutes into the first half, the Rangers goalie pumped a goal kick high and long towards the Motherwell box. It was coming my way, so I prepared myself to header it away from the danger zone. As the ball soared through the air, it was looking like it was going to be a routine clearance, but when I jumped, Colin McAdam, as if from nowhere, clattered into me, elbow first, the power and trajectory like a jet hitting a flock of birds.

When I hit the turf, blood poured from my nose, down my face and onto my shirt. Disorientated and dizzy, I looked at the sky, the drizzle falling towards me. If I was a cartoon, stars would be circling my head.

Then the silhouette of Colin's head appeared as he leaned over to assess the damage. 'Welcome to men's fitba, wee man,' he grunted, then walked away, making space for the arrival of the physio and his sponge.

It was a different world to what young players experience now. Currently, kids come through the pro-youth academy set-up, playing against boys their own age all the way through the ranks until they're 18 or 19. There are different opinions out there as to what's best, but that clattering from Colin McAdam allowed me to know what I was letting myself in for. Getting a taste for – as he put it – men's football, was important for my development. To be a real player, it was necessary to play against guys who were already there. In martial arts, green belts don't just spar with green belts, they also spar with white belts and black belts. They learn from the grades above them and can help develop the skills of the grades below them, through encouragement and advice, just like – in their own individual ways – Tom and Colin McAdam did with me and other keen young players. It's not like I enjoyed having blood streaming down my face and being mildly concussed, but the learning behind it was valuable. It stoked a fire that was already ignited and drew to my attention how important endurance was, weathering the storm to come out better, faster, stronger, more competent and more knowledgeable. Tom and Colin McAdam came at things from completely different perspectives, but between them, I learned valuable lessons that would remain with me not only for the remainder of my football career, but beyond it too.

A reserve team could include a whole cross-section of different players: those who had fallen out of the first team and wanted to prove themselves to the gaffer, key players coming back from injury, and 15-year-olds bursting with energy, just like that 15-year-old Mark Reilly. To me, putting those guys together on a field is much more beneficial to a young player than two teams made up entirely of 15-year-olds. Another perk was getting games at grounds steeped in history: Pittodrie, Parkhead, Tannadice, Ibrox, Tynecastle, Easter Road, and so on. With the current pro-youth system, the games are played on training pitches, so youth players don't get a feel for the grounds they'll be playing at if they become successful.

There are pros and cons to most things, but I think getting the young lads playing with players of experience is something that's sorely missing in the contemporary game. Even considering things from a manager's perspective, surely it'd be easier to assess a young player's ability, resilience and decision making when he's up against battle-hardened pros rather than boys his own age?

I'm not sure if I'd have become the player I did if it wasn't for Tommy McLean getting me involved in those reserve matches. And it's not as if it was only the Old Firm that had strength and depth and were able to field strong reserve teams. Playing against the likes of Aberdeen and Dundee United's second strings was equally as physical and challenging. They had some top-drawer players who, in my opinion anyway, were good enough to compete in the first team and play important matches. And all those sides would have players like Tom McAdam, who'd take the young guys under their wings, helping them along the way, talking them through the game, giving praise where it's warranted and criticism where necessary. I consider myself lucky to have experienced reserve football in the form it took when I was coming through the ranks, as things changed not too long after, possibly down to teams having smaller squads for financial reasons.

I was fortunate to have had such a great football apprenticeship, but it wasn't without its frustrations, the main one being that I never got a chance to play in midfield. As far as everyone else was concerned, I was a left back, and that was deeply disheartening.

Despite this, Tommy McLean was an excellent coach and had a great double act going with his assistant manager, Tom Forsyth, who was as hard as nails. In their playing days, they'd been teammates at Rangers, so they'd known each other for a long time and, despite having entirely different personalities, they had great chemistry, which Motherwell benefitted from.

It would be an understatement to say that Tommy McLean might not have come across as the most effervescent of characters. A bit like the consultant who arranged Dionne's diagnosis, his tone remained the same regardless of what he was talking about. But whilst that consultant was polite and friendly, Tommy was fearsome and strict, focussed to the point of obsession, meticulous in his approach to the beautiful game. That said, beauty wasn't something he considered, preferring to look at the game from more of a mathematical perspective: angles, velocity, height, weight, precision of movement, timing of runs, etc. – and if the sums added up correctly, the ball would be in the net.

Although not big in stature, he was someone who demanded respect purely by the way he conducted himself. It wouldn't be inaccurate to say that he lacked people skills – the way he saw it was that his way was the right way, end of. Everyone applied his tactics and philosophy, because if they didn't, they'd know about it. He didn't seem to have any appreciation of different approaches; if people wanted to do things their way or put their stamp on things, they had no place in Motherwell Football Club. As the old saying goes, he didn't suffer fools gladly and he'd be quick to dish out criticism, but there was no praise to balance things out. Getting no grief was his way of letting players know they were doing their jobs. He'd be there when the reserves were playing midweek and I'd worry what he was going to say at half-time. Everyone did.

What you've just read might make you think that those days at Motherwell back in the 1980s were steeped in negativity and that the atmosphere was nothing but doom and gloom, but that wasn't the case. Somehow, Tommy's clinical approach worked. I reckon the players worked their socks off because gaining his respect meant so much to them. He may not have been the most charismatic manager and you won't find his name in any books about positive affirmations or motivational speeches, but he got the job done, something he no doubt put quite a bit pressure on himself to do, covertly of course. I'll certainly always hold him in high regard, and the facts don't lie, namely winning the Scottish Cup in 1991 against Dundee United and taking Motherwell to Europe.

Tom Forsyth was different kettle of fish entirely. The best way to describe him is . . . well, put it this way, he'd kick the head off his granny to win a football match. He was a tank of a man who revelled in his reputation for being hard, so players had to put in a hefty shift to win his favour. There was a softer side hidden deep underneath his armour, but it took a lot of work to get there. The combination of Tom's tough guy approach and Tommy's scrupulous tactician approach brought out the best in the players and provided me with a solid platform to progress from – albeit at bloody left back!

Following a good few years of training with Motherwell, my senior debut came in October 1989, aged 20. Tommy McLean had educated me extensively not only in terms of the physical side of the game, but the tactical side too. I'd built up a great awareness of other players' positions, both on my own and opposing sides. I was geed up and fervent, my body fit and agile, mind focussed and alert, ready to read the game like Tommy had taught me and to use my strength, both physical and mental, to shine on that field. The field in question was Easter Road, away to Hibs in the Scottish capital. Their winger at that time was Mickey Weir, so it wasn't the easiest start. Mickey was nimble and sharp with a low centre of gravity. His quick feet could see him nipping past many a left back and delivering a killer cross in the blink of an eye. So I knew I had my work cut out for me.

My saving grace – in that game and in many others – was the guy playing in front of me, our left winger, Davie Cooper. Davie had a sensational career, clocking up an impressive 376 appearances for Rangers and 22 caps for Scotland during his peak, with 157 for Motherwell in his twilight years. Davie had great awareness and decision making, along with an uncanny ability to predict what was going to happen next. Off the pitch, he was a quiet, unassuming type, but on it he was a genius with a wand of a left foot. He had more strength and power than he did pace or height, but this made him difficult to tackle, which often allowed him to work his way through defences and make carefully executed passes or inch perfect crosses into the paths or onto the heads of centre forwards or attacking midfielders.

That day against Hibs, Davie was a shield for me and it was great to have that comfort. I noticed, though, that Hibs were playing a lot of balls on the other side, no doubt desperate to keep Davie quiet, despite the fact they could've tried to exploit the new kid making his debut at left back, even though said kid was, in his opinion anyway, playing out of position!

When Hibs did choose to play down the right, or if I was helping tidy up after a futile attack, all I had to do was find Davie and he'd take the pressure off me by taking the ball for a walk. I remember in training how difficult it was getting the ball off him; it was like his aura and stature gave off the message *This ball is mine, don't waste your time*. It was an honour to have played with him, even though we only featured together in senior games a handful of times. Unfortunately, Hibs won 3-2 that day, but I can safely say that none of the goals were down to any errors by me.

Following that debut at Easter Road, I played in the following three fixtures, but after that I was dropped – so like any kid who'd had a taste of the big time, I became frustrated that I wasn't getting more opportunities. Rather than bottle up my feelings and let the frustration fester, I decided to go and speak to the gaffer. Tommy had his own wee office at Fir Park, so after training one day I psyched myself up and knocked on his door. I had to play this right. It was important to me to let him know my feelings, but by the same token I wasn't going to march in there, slam my fist down on his desk and demand that I get a first team jersey every week.

Wearing a tracksuit but adopting the professional, clinical demeanour we had all become used to, Tommy answered the door and invited me in. As I sat down, I felt nervous, but not to the extent that it would have any effect on what I planned to say. Agents weren't really a thing in those days, especially for players my age, so I had no choice other than to represent myself.

Sitting up straight and looking him in the eye, I explained that Fraser Wishart and Tommy Boyd getting selected to play in the full back positions week in, week out was limiting my chances for progression. I can't remember the exact words I used, but I found the confidence to say something along the lines of 'What can we do about this?'

With no changes in his expression as I spoke (fully expected, to be fair), Tommy said he understood where I was coming from. After all, it wasn't like I was the first young player itching to play that he'd had on his books. He told me he'd ask about to see if anyone would be interested. I won't lie, a small part of me that day hoped he would say 'Well, how about we try you in midfield?', but that was wishful thinking.

One thing I didn't expect though was his willingness to offer me another contract at Motherwell if he couldn't find me a club I would be happy signing for. Looking back on it, I was a young player representing myself in front of a fearsome manager renowned for dishing out criticism rather than praise, yet his offer of finding me a new club combined with his offer of another contract at Motherwell if a suitable club wasn't found gave me all the positive feedback I needed. It didn't bother me that it was delivered in a covert kind of way, in monotone, and with a facial expression that didn't alter in the slightest, so much so that it looked like he was wearing a mask of his own face. What was important was that I walked away from that office knowing I was valued. If I hadn't bitten the bullet and decided to knock Tommy's door that day, my future might have ended up considerably different. What a tremendous outcome, and one that, writing about it now, I can align with other key moments in my life, notably when speaking to the American consultant about Dionne and the doctor at checkpoint three on the fourth day of the Marathon des Sables.

A week later, Tommy called me to his office and explained that Kilmarnock gaffer Jim Fleeting was interested in me and had invited me down to Rugby Park for a chat. During that chat, he offered to sign me there and then, the likelihood of featuring me in the first team on a reasonably regular basis mentioned during the exchange. I signed the contract quickly, excited about my new footballing home, eager to help them in their push to win promotion back into the top flight. Guess what, though? I was played at left back, which continued to drive me up the wall!

As the campaign progressed, I flitted in and out of the first team. I put this down to playing out of position, but it's not like it was a position I was new to. The truth was I didn't think I was good enough to be a full back, so I became unsettled and wracked with self-doubt, not helped by the irregularity of being in the starting 11.

Things then took a strange turn. Much to my surprise, Jim Fleeting was sacked by Kilmarnock's chairman, Bobby Fleeting. You might be wondering if there's a family link due to them sharing the same surname – and you'd be right to wonder. Yip, Jim was sacked by his own brother! I never found out what was behind that sacking, but I can only assume it had something to do with the premiership push strategy.

At the time, midfielder and former Celtic legend Tommy Burns was my teammate, but he was nearing the end of his playing days so, following Jim's departure, he took up the position of caretaker manager, later securing the role officially on a permanent contract. He must have seen something in me that made him think I could play in midfield.

During my time at Motherwell and the early stages of my time at Kilmarnock, it felt like every second person was called either Tommy or Tom. There was Tom McAdam, Tom Forsyth, Tommy McLean, Tommy Boyd, and now Tommy Burns. But it was Tommy Burns, or Tam as I knew him, who would change everything for Mavis Reilly, a focussed young footballer determined to prove his worth, but stuck trying to put the brakes on flying wingers rather than being in the thick of the action where he knew he belonged.

DO YOU WANT TO BE A FOOTBALLER?

I f I had to pick one person who had the biggest influence both on my career and the way I approached things on a day-to-day basis, it would be Tam Burns. I say 'approached things', but that should really read 'approach things' as, from beyond the grave[*], his influence remains with me to this day.

One day at training, he pulled me aside onto the running track that frames the pitch and, straight down the barrel, came out with, 'Do you want to be a footballer?'

I was taken aback. 'What do you mean?' I asked.

'Be honest with me,' he said, the look in his eyes telling me in no uncertain terms that this wasn't a wind-up. 'And not just with me, be honest with yourself as well,' he added, pointing at my chest. 'Do you want to be a footballer?'

I opened my mouth to answer, but before anything came out, he interjected with words that were music to my ears.

'I'm going to give you an opportunity to play midfield, because I think you've got the attributes to play there.' He glanced away for a split second, then came right back

---

[*] Sadly, Tam died from skin cancer in May 2008, aged 51

to me. 'You see, I don't think you're a left back and – more importantly – neither do you.'

I didn't know what to say. I was delighted he recognised this in me, but being someone who was never too high or low, even at the young age of 22, all I managed was, 'I agree.' As soon as I'd said those words, almost Tommy McLean style, I wondered if he'd interpreted them as arrogance. Whether he did or not, that certainly wasn't my intention. The truth was I was still curious about his opening question, which I was still to answer.

He glanced back at the guys on the field as a bullet of a shot pinged off the crossbar. 'Look, this is what I want you to do,' he said, looking back at me, the seriousness ever-present in his eyes. 'Go home tonight, have a good think, then come back tomorrow and tell me if you want to be a footballer.' I gave a little nod during his pause. 'And if you do, we'll have a go at making you into one.'

I went home and did what he said. After a shower and something to eat, I took myself up to my room and had a right good think. You might be wondering what I had to think about, why it was even necessary to go through the process of thinking about it. *Surely it was a no-brainer?* you must be thinking.

I'd wanted to be a footballer since as young as I can remember, but I didn't want the remainder of my career to be in a position I wasn't comfortable with. I had perceived limitations of my abilities as a left back and knew I had more in the tank to give, but as a midfielder. Tam was giving me an opportunity to play in midfield, but if that didn't work out, I could end up back at left back, chasing wingers and heading away route one hoofs. But sitting there in my room, the magnitude of the opportunity became clear. The ball was in my court.

Everything I'd ever wanted was laid out for me, all I had to do was prove to myself and the gaffer than I could hold my own in the middle of the park, so much so that he'd have no option other than to name me in the first team line up for each and every fixture.

That was probably the first time I realised how powerful the mind could be, at least in terms of motivation and positive self-talk. These moments seemed less significant at the time but, looking back, that night was a turning point. I gave myself full belief and full control of my future. The only person who could screw up being a mainstay midfielder for Kilmarnock F.C. was me, and I was prepared, physically and mentally, to ensure that didn't happen.

The next day, I knocked on Tam's office door at Rugby Park. 'I want to be a footballer,' I said as soon as he opened it.

With a nod and a toothless smile, he invited me in and sat me down. 'Okay then,' he said. 'This is what I want you to do. Every morning, look in the mirror and say to yourself, "You're going to do the best you can today", and at night, before you go to bed, look in the same mirror and ask yourself, "Did you give 100 percent?" I want you to do that every day, no exceptions.'

I carried out that routine for the best part of a year. I'd stand in front of the mirror and talk to myself first thing in the morning and last thing at night, often elaborating, sometimes raising my voice to ignite the inner warrior. Whilst it was a bit weird at first, it soon became habit-forming, a ritual as commonplace as brushing my teeth, and one that has remained with me ever since. Okay, I gave up the mirror routine less than a year after I started it, but that's because the positive self-talk became ingrained. The mirror was merely a vehicle.

Tam's instructions that day, coupled with my own enthusiasm and love for the game, gave me the baseline I needed to blossom and flourish as a midfielder.

Of course, this didn't mean everything was rosy from then on in, but even when things didn't go to plan, like a heavy defeat or a last minute winner for the opposition, I could still sleep knowing I'd given my best. This applied (and still applies) to everything I did, irrespective of the circumstances or cards I was dealt. Nobody gets everything right all of the time, that's obviously impossible, but as Tam advocated, what is possible is giving your all.

With Tam's routine embedded as an everyday activity, I was soon up and running as a midfielder for Killie, playing every match – including training – like it was a cup final. I treated training like this because of the old cliché, failing to prepare is preparing to fail. These things become clichés for good reason – because they're true.

Tam Burns was an inspiration to me, football wise and also in general. He could be tough when he wanted to be, but he had a great work ethic, was considerate and personable, and had a dry sense of humour that created many side-splitting laughs over the years. He was the kind of guy who'd never do anyone a bad turn and would always look for the good in people, which was particularly effective at training and on game days. If you knew he recognised your potential, you'd use everything in your tank to shine for him. He was a one-off and sadly missed in the football world. I loved him to bits.

I said there that he had a dry sense of humour. Whilst this is true, I'm underplaying it a bit. When he was in the mood, he could be as mad as a hatter. In 1993, we won promotion to the top flight, and early on in the new campaign, we were playing Rangers at Ibrox. All our strips were hanging up in the dressing room as expected, but Tam had gone round and put nappies in everyone's shorts! He then asked us to simmer down so he could deliver his team talk.

'You're on your own today, boys,' he said, climbing into the empty kit hamper and pulling the lid over on himself. The dressing room erupted in laughter, lifting any tension anyone might've had about taking on one of the big guns. It was a carry-on, but a well-timed, well-executed carry-on that had purpose behind it. He was full of this kind of stuff, and most of the time it'd come out of the blue or directly after he'd been saying something deadly serious. He kept you on your toes, which I thought was a great attribute to have. There were a number of occasions when I thought he was building up to a punchline, but it never came, and there were other times when he'd throw in a joke when I least expected it.

Like any football manager though, it was possible to get on the wrong side of him. Thankfully, I never did, but I witnessed a few instances when he was less than pleased with members of his squad. That same season, 1993/94, we travelled to Stark's Park in Kirkcaldy to play Raith Rovers, who were punching above their weight that season, fielding players like Gordon Dalziel and Peter Hetherston, led by player-manager Jimmy Nicholl.

The first half hadn't gone well for us and we slumped off at half-time 2-0 down. The away dressing room at Stark's Park was quite small, barely two metres squared (I'm guessing it's still the same, unless there's been an upgrade), so it was a tight space for a full squad of pissed off players. I ended up sitting between our two centre forwards, Bobby Williamson, a senior player who'd happily break the legs of every defender of the opposition to score a goal, and George McCluskey, who, in contrast, was levelheaded, controlled and deadly in front of goal, only for the past 45 minutes, he'd been feeding on scraps. Remaining quiet, but with disappointment swirling in my gut, I sat and breathed in through my nose and out through my mouth, occasionally taking a swig of water.

George leaned into me. 'Lecter's here,' he said. He knew Tam better than any of us and any time he was in a rage, he referred to him as Lecter, as in Hannibal Lecter. According to George, this was because his face would go red and the veins on his neck would protrude. It made no sense to me, because Hannibal Lecter was always cool, calm and collected, common traits of a psychopath. He did chew the face off people though, so maybe that's what George meant, only with the additional of a Hulk-esque bulging neck and beetroot face.

Anyway, entirely unlike Hannibal Lecter, Tam was livid, and livid at one man in particular: Bobby Williamson. Some managers would resist having a go at senior players, but not Tam. Bobby's seniority was immaterial to him, especially in the heat of that moment. He was in such a rage that Billy Stark had to hold him back. It was the kind of build-up you'd expect to snowball into a full-blown fist fight, but if Billy hadn't held Tam back, I don't think it would have come to that, but there would have been plenty shouting into each other's faces and a bit of grappling and pushing.

'You're hopeless, Williamson,' Tam boomed, wriggling free from Billy. 'Your touch is murder! Terrible!'

Bobby stood up to show he was willing to give as good as he got. He was one of the most aggressive players I ever shared a pitch with and the look on his face in that moment was like something out of a horror film, one far more terrifying than *The Silence of the Lambs*.

'And you lot should know he's hopeless,' Tam continued, gesturing to the rest of the dressing room, still raging, face the colour of a cross between a Hearts and an Aberdeen jersey. 'You're playing into his feet and his touch is rubbish! Just play it into the corners for him, because all he can do is run!'

Bobby bit back and about half the team did what they could to try and calm things down, while the other half had to deal with Andy Millen, who was visibly shaking with the cold, his skin a light blue colour as if he was a character in a comic who had fallen into a pool of ice. He was the leanest member of the squad, carrying somewhere in the region of six percent body fat, not a level that's in any way comfortable – or safe – on a bitterly cold day on the east coast of Scotland. He obviously didn't want to be seen to be disrespecting or not listening to Tam, but if he sat there any longer, he was going to get hypothermia.

It was a half-time like no other I had experienced. A claustrophobic, tight space, a gaffer and a striker trying to rip each other apart, and a defender nearly freezing to death, despite it being only October! Utter carnage, but between the rage and managing to get Andy a quick hot shower, it must've done something, because we piled back out for the second half and battled back to earn ourselves a 2-2 draw and a point to take back down the M77. And guess who scored one of the goals? Yup, Bobby Williamson.

When we returned to the dressing room at full-time, Tam was bouncing, the smile on his face like something out of a kids' TV show.

'Boabby, it was all down to you, big man,' he gushed. 'You were fantastic in that second half. What a player!' He did a quick scan of the rest of us. 'Some player, eh, lads?'

A few nodded and smiled, while others just looked knackered. It was a hard shift out there, but we dug deep and managed to salvage a point. I had expected the dressing room to reek of sweat, given the exertion and effort, but the seriously low temperature must've frozen it all to our skin, rendering it largely odourless. Bobby wasn't buying Tam's performance. He sat there wearing an expression more akin to waiting for a bus than getting praised by his gaffer for scoring a really important goal.

'Honestly, I can't speak highly enough of you, Boabby,' Tam went on, hamming it up. 'You were magnificent in that second half. Wonderful!'

Some of the guys were stifling laughs, conscious of the awkwardness of the situation. They wanted to relish the moment, but given that Bobby maintained his waiting-for-a-bus expression, fanning the flames wasn't a good idea, so they opted instead to be subtle in their enjoyment of Tam's jubilant performance. No disrespect to Raith Rovers, but most of the lads in that dressing room wouldn't be considering a 2-2 draw as something to celebrate anyway, so there would be plenty self-reflection going on while Tam was centre stage, pouring out his admiration for Bobby.

Once Tam had finished, still looking as elated as he did when he began, Bobby stormed off to the showers, clearly seething. Once he was under the water and out of earshot, Tam turned to me with the biggest, cheesiest smile I'd ever seen grace his face and said, 'What about that for man management, eh? Brilliant, wee man.'

To this day, I still don't know if Tam's half-time rant was designed to rile Bobby into proving his worth, or if he had genuinely lost the plot. Part of me wants to believe that it was all just an act; after all, the half-time and full-time reactions were so extreme, so polarised, that there had to be at least some pre-design going on – but then everything seemed so spontaneous, it was difficult to believe any of it was planned. Whichever it was though, it worked.

A match many a Kilmarnock fan will hold dear in their heart is the 1997 Scottish Cup final, where we won 1-0 to see off Falkirk and lift the trophy. Don't get me wrong, this was a great moment for the club, but getting to the quarter finals in 1994 under Tam Burns has always stuck with me, when we played Dundee at Rugby Park. The reason this particular game is lodged in my mind is, again, because of Tam's team talk. I'd never heard one like it before, nor did I hear anything like it again, from that day in 1994 until the day I hung up my boots.

Normally, the 18-man squad would be in the dressing room and the gaffer would name the starting 11 and then have a chat about tactics, set pieces, opposition players to look out for and how to deal with them, etc. This time though, Tam invited *everybody* in, including all the youth players, the physio and the kit man. The dressing room at Rugby Park was a decent size – certainly far bigger than the away dressing room at Stark's Park – but once everyone was in, we was bordering on sardines, folk jostling for space, wondering what was going on.

Once we settled in and everyone found their own pizza-box-sized area to stand or sit on, Tam addressed everyone individually, bigging us up in front of our peers and teammates, making us feel ten feet tall.

'If I had a player of the year trophy in my office, I'd bring it out and present it to you right here and now, Mavis,' he said to me, with no hint of sarcasm. It was honest, earnest and from the heart. It's the kind of thing that, in other circumstances, might have been cringeworthy, even embarrassing, but because everyone was receiving praise and plaudits from him that day, it blended in, but the detail registered. They were only words, but what he'd said made me want to run through a brick wall for him.

'We're all in this together,' he said to his cast, making it clear that Kilmarnock was made up of lots of individuals, but was collectively a single unit, and that unit was going to shine on the field that day. Which we did. It ended only 1-0, but in my mind, losing was never an option in a match I don't actually remember too much about. You can't get much better than a clean sheet and a victory though, so we held our heads up high as we came off at full-time, if it was at all possible to hold them any higher after Tam's rousing team talk.

That victory took us to Hampden for a semi-final against Rangers.

YOU'LL BE VITAL FOR THIS, MAVIS

Before the big game against Rangers, Tam Burns took us to Seamill Hydro Hotel in Ayrshire to prepare. I always shared a room with Big George McCluskey, who by this point was a veteran, having had a great career, including playing alongside Tam at Celtic.

There are two types of people in the world, larks and night owls. Big George was very much a night owl and could regularly be found watching TV in the small hours of the morning while I slept (or tried to sleep). The night before the semi-final, he was doing just that when the hotel room's phone rang (this was the 90s, so only rich businessmen had mobiles). I stirred in my bed and glanced at the alarm clock on the bedside cabinet. It was 20 to one in the morning! Big George answered the phone.

'Hello? . . . Alright, gaffer . . . Aye, he's here . . . Mavis?'

I rubbed my face, yawning, wondering what the hell was going on. 'Uh-huh?'

'Tam wants to see you in his room.'

Bewildered and half asleep, I pulled a t-shirt over my head, stepped into a pair of shorts and slipped my bare feet into a pair of trainers. It wasn't the time for faffing about with socks.

As I padded along the corridor towards Tam's room, various thoughts fluttered through my mind. First off, I hoped there wasn't any bad news from the family. Given it was pre mobile phones, maybe someone had contacted the gaffer and he had something bad to tell me.

It then crossed my mind that I could be getting dropped from the team. Maybe Tam had been thinking about formations and didn't want to hit the hay before telling me I was no longer in his plans. Without blowing my own trumpet, I didn't think this would be the case, but it *had* to be something important. No-one would summon a player at 20 to one in the morning for no reason. But then I reminded myself it was Tam Burns I was dealing with, not your average gaffer, or human being for that matter.

I wondered if he was going to play a joke on me, that this was some sort of wind-up, his way to ease the tension of the challenge awaiting us at Hampden the following afternoon. Maybe he would look confused at me turning up at such a crazy hour, deny summoning me in the first place and send me off with words to the tune of, 'What are you playing at, Mavis? I'm trying to sleep here. We've got a big game tomorrow, remember?'

As I continued walking along the corridor, conscious that it was deadly silent with no sign of life, like an establishing scene in a horror film, I remembered a joke he played on defender Steven Hamilton, back when Hammy, as he was known, was a youth player.

The story goes that the youth players were training at the back park, which was a park that sat – as you might imagine – at the back of Rugby Park. At one point during training, Hammy gave the ball away, so Tam ordered him to sprint a lap of the park as punishment, which he duly did. Breathless, Hammy joined back in with training once he'd completed his lap, but soon after gave the ball away for a second time. Tam issued the same punishment, leading to an even more knackered

81

Hammy rejoining training on his return, sweat dripping down his temples towards his chin. Unbelievably, he managed to give the ball away for a third time.

'Right, get off the pitch,' Tam snapped, pointing towards the changing rooms.

After training, Hammy was summoned to the gaffer's office for a word. When he arrived, Tam and Billy Stark were sitting reading newspapers.

'Sit down, Hammy,' Tam said, neither him nor Billy making eye contact, continuing to read their newspapers. Hammy sat down, awaiting a telling off. But then nothing happened. Apart from the sound of Tam and Billy turning the pages of their newspapers, the room was silent. Hammy sat patiently, but once a good few minutes of silence and no eye contact was reached, he decided to say something.

'Gaffer, are you wanting a word with me?' he said tentatively.

'Aye, I am,' Tam replied, still not looking up from his paper. The silence then continued for another five excruciating minutes.

Eventually, Billy put his newspaper down, stood up and walked out the office. As soon as the door closed behind him, Tam also stood up, folding his newspaper and placing it on his desk. 'Wait there till I come back,' he said to Hammy, still without making any eye contact, and then left.

A full hour later, Tam returned to find an obedient Steven Hamilton still sitting where he left him. He sat down across the desk from Hammy, picked up his newspaper and began to read again, ignoring Hammy completely.

'Gaffer, are you wanting a word with me?' Hammy asked again.

'Aye, I am,' Tam replied, again, still refusing to look at him . . . 'What did you learn today?'

'Not to give the ball away,' Hammy said, after a slight pause.

'That's right,' Tam said, matter-of-factly, still not looking at him. 'Okay, off ye go, see ye later.'

As I approached Tam's hotel room door, I wondered if he had something similar in store for me, an obedience, mental endurance or loyalty test of sorts but, as far as I was aware, I hadn't done anything wrong. I certainly hadn't given the ball away three times in training, so I reckoned I was safe from the silent treatment. But with Tam, you just never knew. Anything could happen!

With some trepidation, I knocked on his door.

When it swung open, Tam stood there wearing tracksuit bottoms and a navy blue T-shirt with a Kilmarnock crest on it. Sitting above the two legendary squirrels, I was drawn to the word 'Confidemus', a Latin term meaning 'We trust'. Conscious that I wear the same crest regularly, although I wasn't at that particular moment, I was reminded that Tam and I had a trusting relationship, which gave me a few threads of comfort.

'Come in, Mavis,' he said, brightly.

I followed him into his tidy, well-kept room, in which there were three chairs and a table at the far end, by the window.

'Take a seat there,' he said, pointing. Next to the table, propped up on the third chair, was an A3-sized green metal clipboard with white lines marked out as an aerial view of a football pitch. Magnets stuck to it, representing both teams' players and their positions. You've likely seen larger versions of these on football documentaries when a manager is talking through tactics with his squad.

This was Tam's portable version, but instead of a full squad of players sitting before him, it was just me in my shorts, at quarter to one in the morning. *He's not going to talk tactics, is he?* I thought to myself.

And then he did.

'Right, this is how we're going to play it. Three at the back initially, with the full backs pushing forward, so we'll need to be aggressive.' His tone was serious, his face business-like. I'm waiting for the gag. 'You'll be vital for this, Mavis, cos you're a combative player who gets into players' faces, so don't hold back with that, alright? I need you to get in there and make sure . . .'

He went on for a bit, moving the occasional player on his clipboard and then looking back at me, making sure I was absorbing what he was saying. And if I'm honest, I wasn't. I was nodding to keep him sweet, adding in the occasion 'uh-huh' or 'mm-hmm', but I wasn't giving him my full attention, distracted by trying to fathom the madness, wondering a) when the gag was coming, but also b) if there was a gag at all. He clearly hadn't picked up on my stony-faced, expressionless and tired face.

He was on a roll, animated and passionate, so I had to look for the slightest of gaps to get a word in edgeways.

'Gaffer,' I said, having finally found one. He stopped like he was an audiotape someone had paused. 'It's nearly one o'clock in the morning.'

He looked at me as if I was stupid. 'I know,' he shrugged. 'I cannae sleep.'

Not picking up on the obvious cue, or perhaps intentionally disregarding it, he rattled on for another five minutes or so, demeanour the same throughout: focused and serious. At no point did he ask for my opinion on anything, he just needed a sounding board. Maybe the only way he was going to get any sleep was to get this stuff of his chest, and I guess he saw me as someone who would sit and listen.

When he wrapped things up, he looked reasonably satisfied, like I had fulfilled my purpose. I gave him a smile and wished him goodnight before heading back into the silent corridor of the hotel, like a ghost from *Scooby-Doo* or something.

Baffled by what I'd just experienced, I padded towards my room, but that bafflement soon dissipated, making way for a different emotion altogether: honour. Of all the people he could have chosen to talk tactics to at nearly one in the morning, he chose me. I got a sudden adrenaline rush as I realised the faith he must have in me, something that had passed me by in the moment. Honour then made way for relief. I hadn't been dropped! That was evident when he told me he wanted me to get in people's faces – he obviously wouldn't be giving me such instructions if I was getting binned – but it had flown over my head because of how bizarre the while situation was.

Once I got back to my room, I was buzzing, never the best state to be in when it's time for sleep and recovery. Tam couldn't sleep, but at least he didn't have to run about on the turf for 90+ minutes in less than 14 hours' time.

George was still up watching TV, as if the only things he had in his diary for the following day were a long lie and a leisurely breakfast. I told him what had happened along in Tam's room.

'Ha ha, that's Tam for ye,' he laughed, finally turning off the TV.

As I lay in my bed, a smile came across my face. I loved the fact that I'd had no idea what to expect in there tonight. After all, Tam was a guy – certainly the only guy I knew of – who sometimes made his players practise singing the national anthem at training, his face dead pan the whole time.

Unable to drift off, I remembered another story that involved Hammy, but this time he wasn't the only one at the end of Tam's unique approach to coaching . . .

One Monday morning, Tam gathered all the youth players and grounds staff together in the dressing room for a chat. He then went round them one by one and asked 'Were you out on the sauce at the weekend?'

Everyone said no.

'Don't lie to me,' Tam said, sternly, swooping a finger round his audience. Silence.

'Right, I'll ask yous again,' he said, and proceeded to go round everyone individually for the second time, asking the same question, 'Were you out on the sauce at the weekend?'

This time, everyone admitted they had been out and had had a drink, although no quantities were revealed or asked for.

'Okay,' Tam said, no change in his expression. He then went round everyone for a third time, but this time with a new question: 'Did you get a bird when you were out drinking?'

Everyone said no, apart from goalkeeper Colin Meldrum.

'Right, Colin, you can leave,' Tam said, pointing at the door.

As soon as Colin had left, Tam proceeded to give everyone pelters, a) for drinking at the weekend when they were supposed to be athletes, and b) for not even being able to pull a bird.

George's breathing had become deep, a surefire sign he had entered the land of nod, whatever he had watched on TV having no impact at all on his ability to sleep. I lay for a while, doing my best not to think about the upcoming game or Tam's post-midnight tactics chat. And eventually, I fell asleep.

I WANT YOU TO
SMASH STUART MCCALL

The Kilmarnock and Rangers buses swept into Hampden at exactly the same time, their windows literally a few centimetres apart. The Killie bus was quiet, the anticipation and magnitude of the game evident, players and staff alike mentally preparing themselves for the challenge that lay ahead. It was our first year back in the Premier League, so to get to the semi-final of the Scottish Cup was a big deal, as the butterflies in our stomachs confirmed.

The Rangers bus contained a number of big hitters, including Mark Hateley, Ally McCoist, Duncan Ferguson, Richard Gough and Stuart McCall. It was difficult not to look at them, given the buses were so close together. As we did, it was clear they were entirely unfazed by the whole situation as they sat playing cards, smiles on their faces and shoulders relaxed, like they were on a caravanning holiday killing time between coming in from a walk and dinner being ready. It was just another game for them, it seemed.

Breaking the silence, Tam Burns stood up at the front of the bus and launched into a team talk. 'We're not here just to make up the numbers,' he boomed, 'and if I see anyone getting off this bus without their head held high and their chest puffed out, then they won't be playing, alright?'

After Tam had delivered more messages to that tune, Alan McInally (known as Big Jake* to players and staff, and Big Rambo to the fans) stood up. The 6ft 1 striker had come to Killie after successful spells at Celtic, Aston Villa and Bayern Munich, or 'The Munchen' as he called it. As anyone who's seen him on Sky's *Soccer Saturday* will confirm, he could never be described as the shy, retiring type. He was forever going on about playing for The Munchen, how big a hero he was in Germany, and that he wore one-off Versace gear. Anyway, he clocked Mark Hateley through the windows, whipped off his Versace jacket, pressed the Versace logo up against it and banged against the glass with the hammer of his hand. 'I wear one-off Versace,' he mouthed, thumbing to his chest.

Everyone erupted in laughter, including the Rangers boys. Playing cards still in hands, they were howling, throwing their heads back, most laughing with Big Jake, but probably a handful laughing at him as well. Not that that would have bothered Big Jake in the slightest. He was some character, never with a smile far from his face.

Between Tam's team talk and Big Jake's antics, the tension was eliminated, at least for a couple of minutes. If I could have captured that scene in a photograph, you'd never have thought the two teams either side of their respective windows were about to face off and go into battle.

'Mavis, come down here a minute!' Tam shouted, beckoning me with a hand. I was at the back of the bus and he was right down the front, so it was an impressive shout, given that the one-off Versace laughter was still

---

* He was called Big Jake by players and staff because his dad, Jackie McInally, played over 200 games for Kilmarnock

fading. Curious as to what he wanted, I walked down the length of the bus and sat next to him. 'Right, Mavis,' he said. 'Rangers need to know they're in a game and they need to know early.'

'Okay, gaffer,' I said, unsure of what else to say.

He tilted his hips so he could face me better. 'I want you to smash Stuart McCall,' he said, his tone deadly serious, but volume low in case anyone overheard. 'First chance you get, ideally in the first five minutes of the game. In fact, I want you to start a fight with him. We'll get a few of the boys round you to back you up. Rangers need to know they're up against a team who're all in it together.'

I breathed in, trying to think of a response to the instructions I'd just received.

Tam then stuck out a finger. 'But you better not get sent off, cos we can't afford to go down to ten men.' He glanced away for a split second. 'Oh, and don't do it where they can get a free kick at goal.'

I shifted in my seat and then looked at him. 'So, let me get this straight, gaffer,' I said. 'You want me to smash Stuart McCall and then start a fight with him, but don't get sent off and don't do it near our goal.'

'Aye, that's it,' Tam said, patting me on the shoulder. Mental, but typical, Tam Burns!

When it came to the game, I felt obliged to follow the gaffer's instructions. After all, I was only playing in my favoured position of midfield in the semi-final of the Scottish Cup, against Rangers at Hampden no less, because of the man who had issued those instructions. Stuart McCall was duly smashed and a melee followed involving a handful of players from each side. I never got sent off and the free kick awarded to Rangers for my trouble came to nothing. Mission accomplished. But it was Rangers who had the last laugh. The hard-fought game finished 0-0, but they went on to win the midweek replay and make the final, although they did suffer a 1-0 defeat at the hands of Dundee United to miss out on lifting the trophy.

1994 was also the year that, in order to allow league reconstruction to take place, three teams faced relegation. Despite missing out on the Scottish Cup, Rangers had secured the league title with a couple of games to play, the penultimate fixture being against Killie at Rugby Park, which was the last game before the stadium was rebuilt. There was a five-team relegation battle taking place, in which Kilmarnock featured, alongside Raith Rovers, Partick Thistle, Dundee, and St Johnstone. We managed to beat Rangers 1-0 in that penultimate game, meaning we only needed a draw in our final game to stay up, which was at Easter Road against a mid-table, nothing-to-play-for Hibs.

Prior to that critical fixture, Tam took the squad away to a hotel in North Berwick. On the morning of the game, we were instructed to take a walk along the seafront together, followed by breakfast in the hotel. We were a collective made up of individuals who represented a single force, all playing for the same badge with the same goal. Based on this, he felt it was important for us to begin the day together, to find confidence in each other and support each other in the task that lay ahead. Staying in the Premier League would mean so much to the fans, the players, the staff, and, of course, the financial stability of the club. We only needed one point, but getting it would be monumental.

After our walk along the beach, I ended up sitting next to Tam at breakfast. Big Jake was at the head of the table, unusually quiet for a man who was always the life and soul of the party. I glanced over at his plate to learn why; he had what must have been about three full English breakfasts piled up on a single plate, a tower of toast next to it, the foil of used individual butter potions littered around his feast.

In contrast, Tam had a tiny wee bowl of muesli, his appetite clearly impacted by the pressure of what was before us. 'I'm really nervous,' he whispered, resting his spoon on the table. 'I didn't get a wink of sleep last night.' He was breathing heavily, leg twitching. 'I've played in cup finals and played for Scotland, but I've never been as nervous as this.' He let out a big sigh, picked his spoon up and tried to get a little bit more muesli in his system. He was going to need all the fuel he could get.

Just then, Big Jake began banging his knife and fork off the table, causing crockery and other cutlery to clink and rattle. 'Big Jake played in the European Cup semi-final for The Munchen against AC Milan,' he announced, speaking about himself in the third person. 'Two hours before kick-off, he had a breakfast like this and then went out and destroyed Franco Baresi!'

The mood was lightened once again by the big striker, who had returned his attention back to his feast.

The game against Hibs was a nerve-wracking, tense affair. Those were the days when grounds still had terracing and Easter Road was packed to capacity, which created a fantastic atmosphere. Killie always brought a strong travelling support, so our 12th man was very much with us, sharing every kick of the ball. The excitement and tension was building in equal measure as the minutes ticked by and the scoresheet remained clean. Fans and players alike knew that one minor error or one moment of brilliance could change the outcome in a heartbeat.

I may be biased, but I thought Killie were the better side that day. We created the most chances, but frustratingly couldn't manage to convert them, despite Big Jake's three full English breakfasts. Tam Burns had put himself in the starting 11 as player-manager, pushing his sleep deprivation to one side like an unwanted second bowl of muesli, firm in his belief that, as a team, we had what it took to win the game. We played out of our skins, 11 men but one Kilmarnock – but we couldn't get the ball in the net.

The amount of time between the end of the 89th minute and the moment the referee decided to blow the final whistle felt like someone must have been fiddling with a time machine. But when it came, it was music to our ears. The final score was 0-0, meaning Kilmarnock would play in the Premier League for another season, much to the players' relief and the fans' elation. What a moment!

Results elsewhere meant that Dundee, Raith Rovers and St Johnstone were relegated to what was then the Scottish First Division. I felt sorry for St Johnstone, because they finished with the same number of points as Killie and Partick Thistle (40), but got relegated on goal difference. That must've been a sore one to take, especially since it was an anomaly of a year. Finishing third bottom had never meant automatic relegation in Scotland before, but moving from a 12-team to a ten-team league meant it was a necessary evil. More annoyingly – for St Johnstone anyway – the league reverted back to 12 teams six years later! Interestingly, Manchester United won the Premier League that day and when Alex Ferguson attended the obligatory press conference, the first thing he said was, 'Before I answer any questions, can anyone tell me the Kilmarnock score?'

It was quite the honour learning of interest from such a high profile figure as Fergie.

Arguably, the last two fixtures of that 93/94 season – the 1-0 victory over Rangers and the 0-0 stalemate against Hibs – were the most important games of football I played in a Killie shirt. If relegation had been the outcome on that final day, it would've been difficult to come back up again. The stalemate with Hibs allowed the club to maintain the good work it had done and continue to build as a top flight side. On a personal level, contributing to the club's success in staying up led to me securing my place in the middle of the park for the following season and for many seasons to come. I was delighted for Tam, delighted for the club, and delighted that I'd made the Killie centre-mid position, one that belonged exclusively to me.

Tam moved on the following season, taking up his dream job as Celtic manager. I was gutted to see him go, but he had helped me achieve my dream, so it was heartening to see him achieve his too.

SCOTTISH TALENT DOWN SOUTH

After three years, Celtic and Tam Burns parted ways and he was appointed as manager at Reading. Managing Celtic may have been his dream job but, as is still the case in today's game, a move from the top flight in Scotland to the second tier in England is seen as a step up. Reading were impressed with what Tam had done at Kilmarnock and Celtic, so when the opportunity presented itself, he took it as the next natural step in his career. It was clear from the off, though, that he was keen to show the English second tier that Scottish footballers were of a higher standard than some English football fans might give them credit for. He'd established a lot of trust and built lifelong friendships with many Scottish players, so now that he could, he wanted to give them an opportunity to shine south of the border. A certain Mavis Reilly was one of those players.

It was 1998 and I'd been at Killie for seven years by that point. I was perfectly happy where I was, especially since I'd played in centre midfield for four full seasons, but my contract was up, so I knew chats would be had and decisions would have to be made.

In the lead up to the time my contract expired, the end of the 97/98 season, Pat Nevin had been playing for us, finishing his playing career off if you like, after highly successful spells down south at Chelsea and Everton. Having learned of Tam's interest in signing me for

Reading, Pat brought it to my attention that the contracts Sky TV had established with the English leagues meant there was decent money flowing through the game down there.

This knowledge, coupled with the interest from Reading, made me think carefully about how to negotiate a potential new contract with Killie. It's not that playing for Reading was off-putting in any way – especially since I'd be playing under Tam again – but I had a sense of loyalty to Kilmarnock. The fans liked me, I always made the starting line-up and I was holding my own in the position I loved to play. Would I be able to replicate this contentment at Reading? Also, moving 420 miles* south would mean uprooting, looking for somewhere to live and distancing myself from family and friends in Scotland – so I had a lot of thinking to do.

I was on £400 a week during the 97/98 season, so I decided, when the time came, I'd be asking for more. I'm not pushy when it comes to these things, but there was interest in me elsewhere and the fans would want me to stay, so I figured there was no harm in determining my own value to the club, especially considering what Pat Nevin had told me. I'd also heard that Killie were in talks with Ally McCoist and Ian Durrant, neither of whom would sign for a £400 a week wage, and that French International Christophe Cocard was also being negotiated with. Given that he had played with Auxerre and, at that time, was playing in midfield for Lyon, he wouldn't be considering signing for £400 a week either, far from it.

I thought, too, about the decent number of Player of the Year awards I'd won over the past few seasons, confirmation that both fans and players appreciated my

* 675.9km

contribution to the club and the team. I had never had a signing on fee and had been giving 100 percent for Killie, week in, week out. I wasn't bitter, not in the slightest; I had my dream job and was loving my football, but I certainly wasn't as rich as the general football-attending public would assume. Given my age and experience at this stage, I classed the imminent conversation to be my last real opportunity to earn myself a decent contract.

I asked for £800 a week and was turned down.

A little bit of to and fro followed, but an agreement couldn't be reached. I phoned Tam, who was dumfounded when I told him what had been going on, although he was probably secretly pleased (not that he showed it) because I knew he wanted me on his squad. This was all happening at the tail end of April, shortly before an end-of-season encounter with Rangers (yes, them again) at Ibrox, where victory for the Gers would play a huge part in them winning ten league titles in a row, while victory for Kilmarnock would significantly increase their chances of securing a European spot. I'll cover this fixture a little later in the book, but let's just say it was memorable for a number of reasons. Anyway, it was the day after this match that Tam flew me down to Reading to discuss how I might fit into his team, as well as remuneration, terms and conditions and all that official stuff. During that visit, the strength of my attachment to Tam was enough for me to verbally agree to sign for Reading, accompanied by a firm handshake.

On my return, I made Bobby Williamson, who was manager at the time, aware of what had been going on. Interestingly, Bill Costley, the Killie chairman, phoned me and promised he would sort something out for me, but I told him in no uncertain terms that it was too late. I had shaken hands with Tam Burns and verbally accepted his offer so, as far as I was concerned, that was as good as my signature being scrawled on a line on a piece of paper. Bill tried to negotiate, saying that an attractive deal could be struck, but there was no way I was backing out on Tam.

It was all a bit confusing if I'm honest; if Killie were so keen on keeping me, the deal Bill referred to surely could have been struck when I first suggested a wage of £800 a week. Maybe something changed during that short period I was down south visiting Tam. Maybe my performance at Ibrox, still giving 100 percent despite knowing the club I played for didn't think I was worth £800 a week, changed their thinking. I suppose I'll never know. To be honest, I could probably find out, but it's all water under the bridge now, and it's not like it keeps me awake at night. It was, however, my introduction into how crazy financial football decisions can be, as subsequent pages will attest.

Unfortunately, things didn't pan out particularly well at Reading. Early on in the season, I suffered an ankle knock that kept me out for a couple of weeks. It's a dreadful time to sustain an injury, especially when a new team and a new manager are looking to prove themselves. If Tam was still around today, he'd probably admit that he brought in too many players who didn't know that league. There was a significant Scottish contingent which, as well as me, included Jim McIntyre, Robert Fleck, Stuart Gray and Grant Brebner. Brebner was signed from Manchester United, but the others came from Scottish clubs. Maybe it was too much, too soon.

Phil Parkinson, who later managed Bradford and subsequently Wrexham, was also in the squad at Reading that season. Unfortunately for me, he was a competent midfielder and shone in the centre of the park while I was off with my strained ankle ligament. To add insult to injury, he had been at Reading for a number of years and had become a fans' favourite. The parallel between him at Reading and me at Kilmarnock was obvious, which naturally led to him cementing his place in midfield and Tam looking for a new role for me. Although I found this frustrating, credit has to be given where it's due: Phil was an excellent midfielder and very much deserved to play where he played.

Tam tried me at left mid, which meant I regularly played the part of a winger, whizzing up the left wing and throwing in crosses. I did the best I could, but it just wasn't my position. The only place for me was smack in the centre. Not unexpectedly, Tam quickly recognised this and knew things weren't working out. It was a pity. The idea was good, but between my injury, Phil's competence in the middle of the park and a bunch of Scottish players trying to adjust to playing in England, I knew my time was limited. I was pleased I'd given it a shot though. If I'd stayed in Scotland, I might have ended up thinking, *What if?*

It didn't happen instantly, and I still gave 100 percent on the field when I was played, but when Tam asked to speak to me, I knew what it was going to be about.

'I'm not being fair with you,' he admitted. 'I brought you down here to develop your career and I'm playing you out of position. But I've got news for you. Motherwell are interested, and so are Kilmarnock.'

It was a bit bizarre. Killie could have had me, but weren't willing to reach an agreement when my contract was up. Maybe, like that Joni Mitchell song 'Big Yellow Taxi', they didn't know what they had until it was gone. This is not me bigging myself up, more a reflection on what they might have been thinking. I had a great relationship with the club and its fans, so I was interested in what they had to say. I hadn't taken being declined £800 a week personally, that's just football – even though it's a beautiful game, it's very much a business when all is said and done. I decided I would speak to both clubs, see what was offered and take it from there. I was at the stage in my career where I had to be playing. And playing in the centre of the park. I didn't want to sign for any club and play out of position or keep their bench warm. Tam agreed with my vision, expressed his regret that things hadn't quite worked out as planned at Reading, and wished me all the best with whatever decision I made.

Before any words were exchanged with either club, I was already veering towards Kilmarnock, but it'd be rude not to consider what Motherwell might offer. Also, Pat Nevin, who had played alongside me at Killie in the 97/98 season, had become Player/Chief Executive at Motherwell. This alone meant I would listen to what they had to say, and I reckoned Pat being there was a contributing factor to them showing interest in me. During our time together at Killie, I had got on brilliantly with Pat, one of the most appealing things about him being that, despite having a successful spell down south with one of the biggest teams in the country, there wasn't a shred of Billy Big Time about him. You got Pat the same way every time, which I admired, possibly because that's how I'm known by a lot of people too. Researchers and academics have theories on this I'm sure: that you're more likely to have respect for people who mirror your demeanour, beliefs, attitudes and attributes, sometimes consciously, but often subconsciously.

Another thing I admired about Pat was that he had no qualms whatsoever about being different to other footballers. In the dressing room and on the pitch, he was like any other player and fitted in really well, but on end of season trips, he would be far more interested in seeking out the nearest museum or art gallery rather than the best pub or biggest swimming pool. He took being somewhere new as an opportunity to learn about its culture and history rather than to learn only about its pubs and local beers. Not that he never had a pint with his teammates, it just wasn't his priority, which everyone respected. He talks about not being the archetypal footballer in his autobiography, *The Accidental Footballer*, which is definitely worth a read. I remember laughing at the title when I first heard about it. Even in the closing days of his playing career, he was a dazzling winger who lit up many a game in a Killie shirt, so it's hilarious to think such talent could be accidental.

To my disappointment though, when I went to Fir Park to see what Motherwell had to offer me, Pat wasn't there. Instead, it was Billy Davies, the gaffer at the time. Put it this way, his words didn't exactly have me fishing in my inside pocket for a pen to sign the contract. To give Billy his due, he'd done his homework on me and acknowledged my competence as a professional footballer, but he made it clear – or clear to me anyway – that he was indifferent and that it was Pat who wanted him to sign me. There was no busting a gut, no motivational speech and no charisma, so there was no way I was going to sign for Motherwell, despite Pat's interest and belief in me. They were offering a £40,000 signing on fee and approximately £80,000 per annum before win bonuses, which was great money, but even if it was double that, I don't think I would have signed. I needed to play for a gaffer who believed in me and who wanted me in his starting line-up each and every match day. Maybe it was my relationship with Tam Burns that instilled this in me, or maybe working with Tam had merely reinforced that value. Regardless, despite turning down a substantial sum that day, it's not a decision I've ever regretted.

When I went to Kilmarnock, it was like déjà vu sitting there with Bobby Williamson. The club's Chief Executive, Ian Welsh, had done all the negotiating to get me in the seat, but I wondered if chairman Bill Costley might have had an influence too, given his eagerness to sort something out for me last time round. Regardless, this time, Bobby clearly wanted me back. In order to secure the deal, I was offered the same wage I was on at Reading, which was around £1800 a week before win bonuses. There was no signing on fee like Motherwell had offered, possibly so they could afford to pay Reading £45,000 to release me, but I wasn't bothered. I was on a grand a week more than I'd been offered when my contract was up only a matter of months ago, but, more importantly, I was home.

Thinking about this now, it's crazy. No wonder some clubs end up in financial difficulty. Taking the Reading fee into consideration, Killie had to spend somewhere in the region of £140,000 to keep me for another season, and the contract was for three years. If they'd just said yes when I suggested £800 a week, another season would have cost them only £42,000! Money aside though, I felt wanted by the club that had already given me so much, plus Ally McCoist and Ian Durrant had signed, so I couldn't wait to get my boots on my feet, the squirrels on my jersey and feed balls to these seasoned pros. And, of course, 98/99 was the season I found a pal for life in McCoist.

BACK IN A KILLIE SHIRT

One of my first games back in a Killie shirt was at home against Aberdeen, and even if I say so myself, some of the football we played was top-drawer; the kind of stuff TV pundits would gush about if we were a top flight English team being featured on *Match of the Day*. Durrant was incredible, an utter joy to watch, made all the better by being on the same field and wearing the same strip as him. I always knew he was good as I'd played against him quite a bit when he was at Rangers, but a bit like Tam Burns in a way, I didn't realise just how good he was until I saw him day in, day out at training and subsequently on the field at the weekend, where he maintained and even sometimes exceeded his own high standards.

Some of the passes he made left members of the squad dumbstruck, not just because of the execution, but because he could identify the opportunity and then have the vision and confidence to pull it off. He played directly in front of me, so while I'd play a holding role, he'd float about, sometimes attacking, taking pops at goal, but also tracking back and helping me out during counter attacks. Having Durrant as a fellow midfielder gave me a great boost. I was always confident on the park, but knowing he was there offered an extra bit of security that made playing all the more enjoyable.

A lot of people talk about the formidable talent Durrant had around the time he sustained a horrendous knee injury at Aberdeen when he was just 21. The tackle, made by Dons midfielder Neil Simpson, tore both cruciate ligaments in Durrant's right knee and sparked a rivalry between Rangers and Aberdeen almost as intense as their rivalry with Celtic, which remains to this very day. The tackle put Durrant out of action for three years, during which time he received knee surgery, yet – remarkably – he picked his football career up again once he was fit enough to do so. Who knows how deadly he would have been in those three years if Neil Simpson hadn't made that tackle . . . As far as I was concerned though, he was deadly in his twilight years, proficient and clean, loving his football and causing a whole host of problems for opposing teams.

We beat Aberdeen 4-0 in that fixture. Maybe the Dons being the opposition gave Durrant an extra bit of incentive to ensure a comfortable win and a clean sheet. I didn't ask him, so I'll never know, but I'm guessing there was probably a part of him imagining his shirt was blue and white in a different sort of way that day.

What I find interesting is how Durrant, after returning to football after three years out, had to change the way he played. Not because of fitness levels or because he wanted to, but because he *had* to, due to the damage he'd sustained in his right knee. This change, whether down to his coach, personal choice, intuition, or all three, led him to become a playmaker. He nurtured a talent he likely had before, but became an expert in it. It was the one thing he could do to an exceptionally high standard whilst protecting what he had to protect. He went on to become a fans' favourite at Rangers and subsequently at Kilmarnock, so as far as stories of bouncing back are concerned, this is up there.

Writing about Durrant for this book has made me reflect on how much inspiration I took from him, subconsciously and perhaps even unconsciously, years later during the Marathon des Sables. When things go wrong, whether it's your own doing or otherwise, the only option is to keep going and bounce back. During day four, when I was running on empty, dehydrated and regularly spewing my load despite having only consumed a couple of fruit pastilles, I kept going. It may have been foolish, but I didn't see any other option. After Durrant's knee was destroyed by Neil Simpson, many a pundit, fan and fellow player assumed his football days were over, just like many people assume my life is exceptionally difficult because Dionne requires 24/7 care – but these are nothing more than other people's perceptions. The truth lies with the individual. Durrant made it happen. I doubt it was easy, but he did it. He bent to the circumstances he found himself in, weighed things up, accepted that he couldn't un-ring the bell, and made the best of what was available to him. And then that day at the beginning of the 98/99 season, he walked off the field with a smile on his face having played a key role in hammering Aberdeen. Brilliant.

And while Durrant was fantastic on the pitch, he was also sharp as a tack in the dressing room and a perfect foil for McCoist, who never failed to have a cheeky smile on his face and a twinkle in his eye. They were partners in crime, but Durrant was the more stylish partner because he was sponsored by Nike, so he was always decked out in the best of gear, including trainers, tracksuits, caps, sweatbands and, of course, football boots. My sponsorship – or sponsorship of sorts – had come to an end just before I headed south for my short spell at Reading, which was fortuitous timing as I wouldn't have heard the end of it with Durrant and McCoist in the squad. It wasn't a sports brand, or anything to do with sport really. Think instead of a something sweet that's called a cake but the only place it can be found is in the biscuit aisle.

THE SECRET
BEHIND THE PERFORMANCE

B ack in the late 90s, sports science was in its infancy, or at least that was the case when it came to professional football in Scotland. A heart rate monitor may be a fairly standard piece of kit for football players at any level in the modern day, but back then no-one had even heard of such a thing.

However, one afternoon, during the 97/98 season, a nutritionist came to Rugby Park to give the squad a talk about what we should eat and what we should avoid, in order to ensure we were sufficiently fueled and nourished to perform to the best of our abilities on match days. As he was talking, covering the various food groups and the impact they have on energy levels and such like, I couldn't help thinking about Dylan Kerr and the day he got his nutrition from a 15-year-old bottle of single malt whisky.

One of the things the nutritionist advised us to avoid was biscuits, due to their high fat and sugar content, including those the general public might refer to as plain, such as the Digestive, Ginger Nut or Rich Tea.

'If you *have* to eat biscuits though,' he said, which made it sound forced rather than personal choice, 'make sure it's Jaffa Cakes you eat because, in contrast to other biscuits, they're low in fat but high in energy.'

I looked around the faces of the squad, anticipating someone bringing up the point that a Jaffa Cake isn't actually a biscuit, the clue being in the name. If they were biscuits, surely they'd be called Jaffa Biscuits? It's a debate that's being going on for many years, but Digestives go soft once they've gone out of date, whereas Jaffa Cakes go hard, much like a Victoria Sponge or Red Velvet Cake would. This alone tells me that – despite being found in the biscuit aisle and referred to regularly as biscuits (which I have no problem with), a Jaffa Cake is a cake, in the same way a black forest gateau is a gateau.

No-one brought it up though. There were a few smiles, maybe because the nutritionist had said '*make sure it's Jaffa Cakes*', I don't know. Regardless, being someone with a sweet tooth, I took his advice on board and packed a couple of boxes of Jaffa Cakes for the away trip to Aberdeen that coming weekend. On the Friday night, I shared a hotel room with Robert Connor, who was known to everyone as Roger, although I have no idea why and – for some reason – I never asked. There are probably plenty people out there who call me Mavis without knowing where the nickname came from. I suppose when it comes to nicknames, it's not that important how they came about, at least that's what I'm telling myself. I called him Roger for years without knowing why, so I've decided I don't ever want to find out how it came about. Anyway, that night in Aberdeen, I asked Roger, who used to play for the Dons, if he fancied a cup of tea and some Jaffa Cakes. He said yes, so I boiled the kettle, made the brews, and we sat and munched our way through the best part of a packet of Jaffa Cakes each. They go down far too easily.

The following day, we beat Aberdeen and took three points back down the road. I played well, but Roger played a blinder, so much so that he was awarded man of the match. Because of this, he was asked to attend the post-match press conference.

'Robert, that was quite a performance today,' a reporter said. 'Did the extra motivation and drive come from playing against your former club at all?'

'No,' Roger replied. 'Last night, Wee Mavis made me a cup of tea and gave me a packet of Jaffa Cakes. That was the secret behind the performance!'

When I turned up for training the following Monday, the girls in the office said that someone from McVitie's in London had been on the phone looking to speak to me. It turned out they had a PR company that sends them press cuttings, and the sports pages of the Sunday papers had been full of headlines like 'Jaffa Cakes Inspire Killie Victory'.

When I phoned them back, the girl I spoke to from McVitie's said they were delighted with the publicity and offered to sponsor me. I say sponsor, but it wasn't like a traditional sponsorship deal. They didn't pay the club any money, nor did I turn up to training or attend any media events wearing a Jaffa Cakes cap or McVitie's sweatbands. Instead, for two full years, I was sent up boxes of Jaffa Cakes every week! Who knows, maybe those little cakes disguised as biscuits were the secret to me holding my position in the middle of the park at Killie for all those years. Stranger things have happened.

Unfortunately, my deal came to an end when my contact from McVitie's asked me if I could get her tickets for any England game in the France '98 World Cup. Why she thought a Kilmarnock midfielder had access to tickets for a game being played by a national side from a different country, playing in a tournament taking place in a different country again, is beyond me. Maybe she assumed all professional footballers get first dibs when it comes to these things, regardless of the country they play in or for. Realistically though, she might as well have asked me if I could get her tickets for Paraguay versus Bulgaria. The phone conversation seemed pleasant enough, but her disappointment was demonstrated by calling time on sending me complementary boxes of Jaffa Cakes. It was great while it lasted though, and I do still enjoy a Jaffa Cake from time to time now, even though I have to pay for them.

COISTY, THE NEW KING IN TOWN

Despite being on either side of the Old Firm, Ally McCoist and Tam Burns were the best of pals. Naturally, they had great passion for their respective clubs, but friendship was more important to them than kicking a ball would ever be. Their personalities and sense of decency allowed them to transcend the prevalent and often ugly football and religious rivalries that are rife in Glasgow and the West of Scotland, but which also exist in all other parts of the country as well.

Regardless of football or religious persuasion though, people who met them liked them. It was impossible not to, because they shared that ability – that natural gift – to make whoever they were talking to feel like the most important person in the world. I have no doubt that being around Tam Burns and Ally McCoist during my football career impacted me in ways that benefitted my frame of mind, decision making and my overall level of contentment. I consider myself to be a positive person, but regardless of who you are or how content you feel, being around people who radiate positivity can only be beneficial.

Sadly, Tam Burns is no longer with us, but Coisty's positivity, charisma and infectious sense of humour lives on in abundance. It's no surprise that he has become one of the country's favourite broadcasters on talkSPORT Radio and arguably one of the best co-commentators during significant televised tournaments like the World Cup and the Euros. His unbridled love for the beautiful game spills out of the screen and into the living rooms and bedrooms of thousands of football fans, making it feel like he's sitting next to you chatting away about the match. I might be biased, but in my eyes, he has become the John Peel of football commentary and broadcast journalism.

Coisty was an absolute star on the pitch and the life and soul of the party off it. Everyone loved him at Kilmarnock, not just because of his skill with a ball, but because no-one had a clue what he was going to do next, the only certainty being that it would be funny. When he first came to Killie, he burst into the changing room and said, 'Right, where's the number 9 peg?' Paul Wright, known to everyone as Bunion, was our number 9 at that time and his shirt was hanging up where he would expect it to be when he returned from the gym. Coisty marched over, swiftly swiped it off its peg and chucked it in the bin. When Bunion showed up, Coisty threw him a cheeky grin and said, 'Sorry, Bunion, there's a new king in town!' followed of course by the heartiest of belly laughs. Everyone was in stitches, and thankfully Bunion saw the funny side too.

Another thing Coisty would do is turn up to training without any toiletries and steal everyone else's shampoo, shower gel and deodorant.

'What's this rubbish?' he would say, rifling through someone's stuff. 'I'm used to Ray Wilkins stuff and now I've got to put up with this rubbish. I'll tell ye, lads, I've come down in the world!'

During the Marathon des Sables, I met a guy called Jack Fleckney (mentioned in the prologue), who'd turned 30 a couple of month previous. As an ex-Marine who joined the corps at the tender young age of 17, Jack had endurance as default and positivity deeply engrained in his factory settings. I took advantage of this, drawing on his energy to help me through the toughest patches in that never-to-be-forgotten week. His engaging personality and smiley-laughy face, despite the conditions we found ourselves in, provided much-needed mental nourishment.

As we battled the conditions with smiles on our faces, I told him his positive demeanour and ability to find a joke in anything   reminded me of Coisty. I'm not sure if he was flattered or not – sand was blowing in our faces at the time, so it was difficult to read his expression – but he said it was something he was taught in the Marines: always smile and be happy, because even in times of great adversity, it makes you and the people around you feel better. It's a fantastic mantra for life, one that's much easier to buy into when you're around the right people. I consider myself to have been exceptionally fortunate in this regard. I've worked hard and pushed myself, but rubbing shoulders with positive people makes the world of difference.

Jack claimed he got his positive attitude from being a Marine, but positivity was very likely part of his make-up, brought to the fore by the environments he exposed himself to and the people he mixed with and learned from. In contrast, Coisty was never in the Marines, but I always assumed it was something similar – an upbeat and enthusiastic outlook, amplified by the fulfilment of ambitions and working hard to be where he wanted to be. I remember, after a few drinks one night, our faces sore with laughing, I, for some reason, became suspicious and decided we were close enough by then to warrant me quizzing him on the matter.

'Is this an act?' I asked him. 'You always seem so happy, but there must be times when you feel down. You're only human after all . . . aren't you?'

After a few more laughs and sips of our pints, he adopted his seldom-seen serious face.

'Aye, there are times,' he said, 'but I try not to show them.' And then he told me about a period when his son was really ill in hospital. He'd visit him every opportunity he could, laughing, joking and smiling for the duration of visiting hours, using positivity as medicine as much as he possibly could. Then, just before leaving, he'd pull the curtains around the bed and cry his eyes out for a couple of minutes, before slapping the smile back on and returning to the persona he'd created and nurtured over many years. For someone like Coisty, all that's required is the occasional release, a short burst of emotion, the regularity dependent on the extent and severity of the challenges life throws him at any given time.

Speaking of hospitals, Killie were playing Rangers at home one Saturday in 1999, during which Coisty was putting a bit of pressure on Lorenzo Amoruso, trying to cause him problems. At one point, Amoruso had the ball and Coisty was giving chase, when he suddenly fell to the ground, landing in a heap. He was stretchered off and, while the game continued, was taken to hospital with a suspected broken leg. Despite losing one of our key players with more than half the match still to go, we held our own and – as far as I was concerned – should have gone on to win against a strong Rangers side. However, despite creating some decent chances and defending well, it was all square when the full-time whistle sounded. A goal and a point to each side.

The combination of failing to find the winner and Coisty being stretchered off and taken to hospital meant the dressing room was quiet and subdued. Some players might have been concerned about Coisty, others disappointed at the result, possibly going through a period of self and team reflection and analysis in their heads, processing things so they could dust themselves down and look to go again in a week's time.

Muttered conversations bounced between a handful of players, while others fiddled with toiletries and faffed with towels in preparation for the showers. The downcast atmosphere was then flipped on its head in the blink of an eye as Coisty burst through the dressing room door on crutches, the proverbial Cheshire cat grin on his face.

'Brilliant, boys!' he rejoiced. 'Here was me thinking I was slowing up, but look, it's only a broken leg, so we're alright!'

Laughter filled the dressing room, instantly putting a plaster over the disappointment of the draw. Only Coisty could leave a hospital on crutches and see the bright side. Brilliant!

Thankfully, the leg break wasn't severe and healed reasonably quickly, so much so that Coisty ended up making his film debut later that year in *A Shot at Glory*, playing the part of an ex-Celtic player trying to help a Second Division side win the Scottish Cup. I couldn't help laughing when I heard about this; an ex-Rangers player playing the part of an ex-Celtic player. Let's face it, while the Old Firm means a lot to a huge number of people and generates interest in Scottish football from all corners of the world – not to mention money – it can also be grim. Sectarianism, abuse, racism, assault and bullying (including cyber bullying) are all by-products of the Old Firm rivalry. That's not to say these behaviours and attitudes don't exist in other rivalries, but as far as

Scotland is concerned, it's predominately where the darkness lies. Strong, historic rivalries can generate some fantastic football of course, but it's sad that these rivalries can't exist without hatred being part of the picture. Football should be about football, not about religion, race, hair colour or anything other than a leather sphere on a field.

Because of how strong this rivalry is (and continues to be), I was proud of Coisty for taking on such a role. I don't know if playing an ex-Celtic player was part of the attraction of the role, to show that such trivial things can be put aside in the interest of the project at hand, but I thought it was admirable that a player seen by Rangers fans as a true club legend happily played a part that involved being associated with their biggest rivals. I've heard of Celtic fans who refuse to travel in blue cars, and in the Rangers-supporting town of Larkhall, protective grates cover green traffic lights to prevent them being smashed by locals. If this is how some fans behave, I think any football legend, regardless of which club they're associated with, should get credit for trying to bridge the divide, and I say this despite the fact Coisty wore a Rangers top under the Celtic one during filming! My guess is this was a clever media stunt to ensure Rangers fans continued to hold him in high regard.

Around the same time Coisty was involved with *A Shot at Glory*, the *Daily Record* was running a weekend supplement that featured snaps of celebrities (or so-called celebrities) in and around Glasgow. One weekend they had a double page spread of several Celtic players going into Archaos, a nightclub in Glasgow city centre that closed down in 2007. They were clearly on some sort of VIP list and getting priority treatment. However, unfortunately for me and my teammate John Hendry, known as Zippy, we featured in the background, queuing to get in along with the general public, emphasising our lack of VIP status.

When Zippy and I turned up for training on Monday morning, enlarged prints of the photograph were pinned up all over the dressing room, our faces circled, just in case it wasn't obvious that Mavis and Zippy weren't VIPs, unlike the Celtic elite. We then received total dogs abuse off our teammates, who, for some reason, revelled in the fact that we weren't considered big time enough to be given special treatment. And who was in among it all, pointing and laughing until his face was rosy pink? Yip, Coisty.

It was water off ducks' backs for me and Zippy though; we just laughed along, taking the ribbing in the spirit it was intended. When you're a footballer and folk like Coisty are in your dressing room, you don't have any other option really!

The following week, we had a midweek team night out in Glasgow, during which there was there was still plenty reference to what happened at the weekend. Zippy and I just smiled along, enjoying our night out and brushing away the dregs of old, recycled jokes.

'Here, lads,' Coisty said, leaning over to me and Zippy. 'My mate has just messaged me asking if I fancy meeting him for a drink at the Rogano. Do you two want to come and we'll catch up with the boys again later on?'

'Aye,' Zippy and I said in unison. If anything, at least it would allow us to be exposed to some different banter for a bit. So, we made our excuses and the three of us headed off to Glasgow's famous Rogano restaurant and bar.

'There's my mate there,' Coisty said, pointing at . . . Robert Duvall! 'Come and say hello, lads.'

Robert Duvall, star of classic films like *The Godfather*, *Apocalypse Now*, *To Kill a Mockingbird* and *True Grit* had played the part of the manager of a fictional Scottish Second Division team in *A Shot at Glory* and, unsurprisingly, had totally hit it off with Coisty. Although he'd been back in the States since the film's completion, he'd returned to Scotland and was as keen as mustard to hook up with his co-star again.

Zippy and I couldn't believe it. Coisty's "mate" was Robert Duvall! He was sitting with a couple of other guys, who turned out to be film directors. I wasn't expecting this at all. Coisty was always full of surprises.

'Robert, this is Mark. Mark, this is Robert,' Coisty said, opting for the traditional formal introduction. That wasn't like him, but maybe the film directors' presence made a difference; either that or he thought it might be weird introducing one of his teammates as Mavis!

'Call me Bobby,' Duvall said with a smile, 'all my friends call me Bobby.' We shook hands and I sat down. I'll be honest, I was dumbfounded. For one, it was a massive surprise to be sitting in Robert Duvall's company, but more importantly, it was heartening to get such a warm welcome. I suppose it can be easy to assume that highly successful, internationally recognisable actors are prima donnas prone to being standoffish and cold, exasperated with ceaseless uninvited attention. But Duvall wasn't like this in the slightest. Instead, he was all smiles and, before even speaking to me properly, had decided that if I was a friend of Coisty's, I was a friend of his – so much so, that I could call him Bobby.

'Call me Mavis,' I said with a smile. 'All my friends call me Mavis.'

I loved Duvall's reaction to this. Most people laugh and ask why, while others look at me like I'm on the wind-up. Duvall had barely any reaction – a little nod to let me know he'd received the message was all I got. Maybe in his line of work there were no surprises anymore.

We hit it off instantly, the conversation flowing naturally with no awkwardness or preconceptions. We discovered we had a mutual love of boxing and spent ages chatting about various fighters and the bouts we'd seen. As the drinks flowed, he told me stories about growing up in San Diego, including his dad being away for lengthy periods serving in the military. Being Scottish, the name Bobby doesn't come naturally, so oiled by a few pints of premium lager, I ended up calling him Boabby a few times. Again, he just smiled, making no comment, but hopefully he saw it as affectionate. With the extent to which we were hitting it off, I doubt he would have seen it any other way.

At one point, it was obvious there were only a few sips left in each of our glasses, so it was time to charge the glasses, as they say. Duvall could easily have used his status and/or money to get table service, or at least for someone to be responsible for trips to the bar, but being the kind of guy I knew him to be, even in such a short time, it was no surprise that he took his turn. Despite it being midweek, the bar was rammed, shoulder-to-shoulder stuff. Chatting back and forth with Zippy, Coisty and the two film directors, I kept glancing over to see Duvall in among a bunch of Glaswegians like the proverbial sardine, slowly edging his way to the front of the bar. I noticed a couple of people do a double-take, but opting not to say anything, possibly assuming there would be no chance Robert Duvall would be out drinking in Glasgow and that they should maybe consider a less lethal cocktail next round.

I was saying something to Zippy when I heard this loud American accent coming from the bar. 'Mavis! Hey, Mavis! What is it you're drinking again?'

It was one of the most surreal moments of my life. I stood up and, over the heads of the crowded, bustling bar, I shouted, 'Pint of Peroni please, Boabby. Cheers, pal!'

I haven't seen him since and I don't know if I'll ever see him again, but that was the night Boabby and Mavis were the best of drinking buddies in the heart of the city of Glasgow.

When I sat down, I leaned over to Zippy. 'A week's a long time in fitba, eh, Zippy? Where's that *Daily Record* photographer now when we need him?'

Zippy and Coisty burst out laughing, the film directors laughing along despite not knowing the full story, although I'm pretty sure Coisty filled them in once my pal Boabby came back from the bar and we recommenced our chat about boxing.

That night is one I'll never forget, but it would never have come about if it wasn't for Coisty noticing Zippy and me tiring of the constant ribbing the lads were dishing out. Zippy and I were laughing along, perfectly aware that these things happen in football and that it would be someone else's turn to be the butt of the joke soon enough, but Coisty – despite being all over it the previous week – had decided enough was enough. But, instead of dealing with it in a negative way, like getting on the lads' cases and suggesting they calm it, he opted instead to remove Zippy and me from that environment and treat us to a night with Hollywood royalty.

I'm putting Coisty on a pedestal here (which I'm sure he'll be happy about), but it's a valuable message. Think about how many instances you've seen where people fight fire with fire, generating nothing more than flame after flame of resentment, animosity, blame, jealousy, and desire for retribution. It can be difficult, and I appreciate everyone has their own strengths and weaknesses, but there is always a positive option. The night out with Boabby Duvall was nine years before Dionne was born, but when that time came, I could have dealt with the reality of her having Rett Syndrome negatively, but I chose not to. Similarly, I could have dealt with having that horrendous stomach bug during the Marathon des Sables by pulling out and resting, but I chose not to. Because there's always a positive. It may not always be obvious, but if you develop the right mindset, you'll find it, and the more you train your brain to pick out the positive, the easier it will become, regardless of the circumstances you find yourself in.

That night in Glasgow in 1999, Coisty could easily have slipped off to the Rogano without me and Zippy, keeping his Hollywood pals all to himself, but he read the situation and chose not to. The outcome was a great night for me and Zippy, with the lads we left behind continuing to have a great night too. In the modern world, we're often fed messages, through the media in all its contemporary guises, that it's lose/lose, but with developing the right mindset, you have the power to change that to win/lose and even win/win.

I'm not claiming to be an expert in this area, I'm merely looking at my own experiences and the influence of specific people to highlight how exciting, fruitful and satisfying life can be if you view the cards you've been dealt from a different perspective.

Coisty is certainly a character, as anyone who has met him will attest, but when it came to training, he would never be found wanting. This was what Killie expected of him of course, and of Durrant, but given they were a pair of jokers, full of mischief and carry-on most of the day, it was great to see they could turn that switch off and get their game faces on. When it came to match days, they were deadly serious about their roles and how to maximise their abilities in the interests of the team and getting the ball in the net.

Many years after that night out at the Rogano, Monica and I were sitting on the sofa watching the Tom Cruise crime thriller *Jack Reacher*, which also happens to star my good pal, Boabby Duvall. When he first appeared on screen, I tapped Monica on the arm.

'Look, it's Boabby Duvall,' I said, casually. 'I had a night out with him once. He's a lovely guy, knows a lot about boxing.'

Eyebrow raised, Monica looked at my grinning face like I was losing the plot.

Cheers, Coisty.

A 15-YEAR-OLD
V
BRIAN LAUDRUP

I consider myself fortunate to have been a professional footballer during the 90s and early noughties, playing alongside and against household names like Coisty, Tam Burns and Paul Gascoigne. In the eyes of the public, players like these were classed as 'big characters', whether that be down to their sense of humour, their general approach to the game, showing or not showing emotion, the stuff they got up to off the park, or the way they interacted with and responded to the relentless media attention that comes with being a professional sportsperson.

Of course, there were plenty other big characters in the game at that time, and many a story that managed to escape media attention. It was a period when mobile phones were nowhere near as common as they are now, and those who had one didn't have particularly good (or any) video functionality. This, along with social media behemoths like Facebook and Twitter yet to exist, meant not everyone considered themselves to be a reporter and/or filmmaker. The story I'm about to tell is about another of the game's big characters, Dylan Kerr, and it's one that managed to slip under the radar of the media and popular press. I do, however, have full permission from Dylan to tell this story, so big thanks to him, as it's a cracker!

Born in Malta but brought up in Sheffield, Dylan began his football career in England, playing initially for Sheffield Wednesday and then Leeds United, where he played a fundamental role in Leeds winning the English First Division in 1992, the final season before the league was rebranded as the Premier League. During that period, he was close friends with one of the guys from Heaven 17 and dated one of the girls from The Human League. You can probably surmise from this that he enjoyed a party. A bit like Coisty, his personality was infectious; you knew when he was around as he brought a noticeable energy to the room, whether that room was a dressing room or a nightclub.

A bit like me, he too had a spell at Reading (pre-Tam Burns), the difference being his was lengthier and more successful. However, not unlike me, he also sustained an injury (must be a Reading thing), which led to him losing his place on the starting line-up. After a period of recovery in 1996, he headed north and joined Kilmarnock. He found a nice house in Troon and settled in quickly, engaging with the local community and making friends effortlessly. His personality mirrored the way he played football – vibrant, enthusiastic and full of energy. I class him as one of the first players to consider a full back's role as playing near enough the entire side of the park. He was always zipping up the left wing and throwing in crosses, then using his speed to track back and defend. The attacking full back was a role that suited him to a tee, rather than never straying far beyond the halfway line and existing mainly to defend.

In March 1997, Killie travelled to Ibrox to take on a rampant Rangers side that were winning the league year after year and had become accustomed to success. They had some fantastic players in that era, none more so than the Great Dane, Brian Laudrup, a powerful, fast and competent winger who barely put a foot wrong and was a danger to any opposing team when he had the ball at his feet. With Dylan as our full back, he was going to have his hands full marking the Great Dane for 90 minutes.

The Killie squad arrived at Ibrox around 2pm and Bobby Williamson named the starting 11, which included Dylan at left back and me in centre midfield, as we expected. At half past two, we headed out to the pitch to commence our warm-up in preparation for the regular 3pm kick-off. To save the goalmouth from getting damaged before the game, the Rangers ground staff had put a portable goal half way up the pitch on the touchline. I jogged across the pitch to sample the atmosphere before the team warm-up began. As I turned at the opposite side of the pitch and headed back towards the main stand, I couldn't believe what I was seeing.

Goalie gloves on his hands, Dylan was in the goal, diving about the place, saving shots from the subs. What the hell kind of way was that to warm-up for facing an in-form, at-the-top-of-his-game Brian Laudrup. As someone who doesn't get angry often, I have to admit I was furious with him. I ran over to the goalmouth.

'Dylan, what are you playing at?' I shouted, shaking my head, looking at him incredulously. It was then that I smelt the booze. He smelt like a distillery. How Bobby hadn't noticed, I'll never know. 'You're reeking of bevvy, mate,' I added, screwing up my face.

'She cheated on me,' Dylan said, dropping the ball he had in his hands. Then he told me the full story, his eyes bleary and his heart clearly broken.

It was 10pm the previous night when he found out, and the only coping mechanism he had was to reach for the bottle, the bottle in question being a 15-year-old Balvenie single malt. He had cracked it open shortly after learning of his wife's infidelity, hoping it would help him get off to sleep, but it didn't, so he got up and kept drinking, finishing the bottle around 5am. Knowing it was highly likely he'd be in the starting 11 for the Rangers game, he decided going to bed would be a bad idea, so he chose to stay up, drunk and hurt, yet his loyalty and commitment to Killie seemed to be unwavering.

It was impossible to be angry at Dylan. My burst of anger dissipated almost instantly after learning what was going on. He was clearly still half-cut and inside he'd be hurting, but it looked like the game had come around at the perfect time – his drunkenness had gone full circle and he was back at the stage where he felt giddy and invincible, as if nothing had happened the previous night and he'd just knocked back a couple of shots before jogging out for the warm-up. To complement this, his circadian rhythms would've been confused with the lack of sleep, but must've been communicating to his body that daylight and a stadium full of effervescent football fans means wakey-wakey time, generating adrenaline and providing him with a much-needed second wind. Dylan would crash soon, that was for sure, but we could only hope that was at least three hours away.

'I'm feeling great!' he said, kicking a ball out to one of the subs. 'I'm totally fine for the game, Mavis, trust me.'

I patted him on the back, non-verbally demonstrating sympathy and confirming I trusted him at the same time. I didn't vocalise it, but I decided to look out for him during the match. If he was struggling with Laudrup, I would make every effort to get over there and give him as much cover as possible.

But there was no need.

Dylan played an absolute blinder, keeping Laudrup quiet for the full 90. Not only that, we came out 2-1 winners, away to Rangers, a team who, at the time, seemed incapable of losing anything. What a day. The Ibrox crowd wasn't happy at all, but the Killie corner was in raptures.

As we were walking off the pitch at the end of the game, I clocked Dylan.

'Hey, Dylan, you needing any Balvenie for next week?' I shouted at him.

He just smiled.

Bobby Williamson – sometime between naming the starting 11 and the end of the game – discovered Dylan was half-cut. Unsurprisingly, he told him he wanted to see him first thing on Monday morning.

Whilst working half-cut after a night of no sleep is not something that tends to be tolerated in the workplace, Bobby, once he heard the story, showed understanding and let it go. Heartbreak, especially if it's the result of something completely out of the blue, can lead to unwise decision making. Dylan, of course, picked himself up and soon got on with the rest of his life. He's currently (at the time of writing) living in South Africa, managing Marumo Gallants F.C., a professional football team based in Limpopo Province. And he no longer drinks Balvenie – or so he tells me!

Any time I think of Dylan's whisky story, I wonder if Bobby Williamson would have been as understanding if Rangers beat us 5-0 and Laudrup got a hat-trick . . .

NICE ONE

D ylan's triumphant, alcohol-fuelled performance against Brian Laudrup came a year and a bit before Coisty and Durrant joined Killie, but Dylan didn't leave the club until 2000, so there was a period where they played together, along with other powerhouses such as Kevin McGowne, Gary Holt and Gordon Marshall. With that kind of talent on the pitch and Bobby Williamson, Gerry McCabe and Jimmy Clark working hard to develop our defensive shape, it allowed the team's creative players the liberty to express themselves, confident their holding midfielder and back four were solid.

At the beginning of this period, about a year before Coisty and Durrant joined, we drew a two-leg fixture against OGC Nice after qualifying for Europe as a result of winning the Scottish Cup in 1997. We travelled to France first, but came home deflated after a 3-1 defeat, a converted Paul Wright penalty giving us at least a little bit of hope. I saw it as 2-0 at half-time in a 180-minute game, so there was plenty opportunity to redeem ourselves.

Believe it or not, when Nice visited Rugby Park, yours truly put us ahead. This meant, due to the away goals rule that applied in that competition, we only needed one more goal to win and advance to the next stage. We gave it our best shot, the Killie fans behind us 100 percent, but it wasn't to be . . . Nice equalised and the game petered out. It was an incredible experience though, made all the sweeter by getting on the scoresheet. Apart from that short period at Reading, I played 11 seasons with Killie and scored 11 goals; the fact that one of them was against a tough European side is something I'll always be proud of.

My time at Kilmarnock came to a natural end in 2002. During that 11th season, I sustained an ankle injury, so understandably I was being rested and was receiving treatment from the club physio. Once I had recovered, I was put out on loan to Airdrieonians to get my fitness up. Owen Coyle was playing there at the time and Ian McCall was the gaffer, so the standard was decent. I played half a dozen games for them during their push to win the old First Division, which I really enjoyed. They were a great bunch of guys and the training and game time meant I was fully fit again and therefore ready to return to Kilmarnock.

However, during my time with Airdrieonians, Bobby Williamson had moved on to be the gaffer at Hibs, and was replaced by Jim Jeffries. I didn't get the impression that Jim had anything against me, but the impression he did give me was that he wanted to make his own mark on the team and a 33-year-old Mavis Reilly, not long back from injury, didn't fit into his masterplan, especially since he had signed Steve Fulton to play in the middle of the park.

I wasn't bitter in the slightest though. To coin a few clichés, nothing lasts forever and all good things must come to an end. I walked out of Rugby Park as a Killie player for the last time with my head held high, delighted at what I'd experienced and achieved. I'd played with, and been managed by, Tam Burns. I'd played against and alongside Ally McCoist and Ian Durrant. I'd scored a goal against OGC Nice. I'd played shoulder-to-shoulder with Paul Gascoigne. I'd been in the team that won the Scottish Cup in 1997. And I'd been given my nickname: Mavis. The fans would often sing, 'One Mavis Reilly! There's only one Mavis Reilly!' They wouldn't be singing that again though, because it was time for that one Mavis Reilly to kiss goodbye to the squirrels on his shirt and, with a smile, take a step into whatever was coming next.

Me and Ian Durrant holding our own against Celtic's Colin Healy

Back when we were rivals: Durrant taking me out during a Rangers v Kilmarnock encounter at Ibrox

Me and Dionne with Graeme Souness

The day of the Chain Carousel

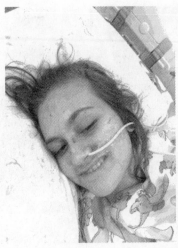

Despite the miseries of Rett Syndrome, Dionne still manages a smile

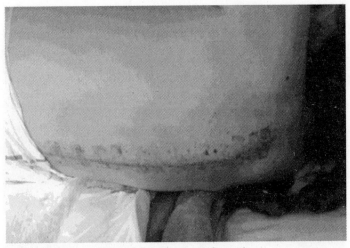

Dionne resting up after major surgery on her spine

Smiling and laughing: Dionne as a young kid, her infectious spirit shining through

With her best pals, Manny (L) and Milo (R)

Definitely not a left back! Me netting against Hibs and receiving praise from the new king in town!

Player, gaffer and legend: the formidable Tam Burns

Tam showing his appreciation to the Killie faithful

Hitting the gym with (L-R) Coisty, Bunion and Gordon Marshall

THE TWO SAINTS

I wasn't done. My time at Kilmarnock had come to an end and the club would always hold a place in my heart, but I knew I still had more football in me. It wouldn't be in blue and white stripes, but I was keen to squeeze as much football out of myself as I could. I was 33, but I was still fit and knew I could hold my own in the middle of the park. All I needed was a club looking for someone with experience who could bring something to their squad. That came in the shape of Perth outfit, St Johnstone. Billy Stark was the gaffer there, so having been with him at Killie, we knew each other well and he knew what I could bring to the St Johnstone squad. Having always had lots of respect for him, I was thrilled to be able to continue my career with him at the helm, both for his amiability as a person and his proficiency and prowess as a coach.

At that time, St Johnstone were in tier two and I was determined to help the club win promotion to the top flight, because I knew it would mean the world to Billy. Unfortunately, though, that didn't quite happen, with the team finishing third behind Falkirk and Clyde. We went again the following season, frustratingly finishing third again, this time behind Inverness Caley Thistle and Clyde.

Because he failed to win the team promotion after two attempts, Billy was sacked in April 2004 and replaced by John Connolly. League positions don't lie, so the club decided change was the way forward. Understandably, John wanted to shake things up, so I wasn't too surprised to hear that I didn't feature in his plans. It was time to move on again, this time with a degree of sadness. I enjoyed my time at St Johnstone very much, but sometimes things don't pan out as you hope. That's football, of course, a game that will – for eternity – provide players, fans and managers with cocktails of elation, celebration, disappointment and despair, sometimes in equal measure and sometimes not, depending on the circumstances the club in question finds itself in at that given time.

Andy Millen had let the St Mirren gaffer, Gus McPherson, know that I was available, so that was a good lead. Soon after, the phone rang. I picked it up, hopeful that it'd be Gus.

'Hello,' I said.

'Mavis, it's DC here,' said the voice on the other end of the line, DC being Dick Campbell, the gaffer at Brechin City.

'Dick, how are you doing?' I said, smiling.

'Brilliant, Brilliant,' he replied, and with no hesitation, he cut straight to the chase. 'Mavis, this is what's happening. I'm gonnae give you five minutes to convince me to sign you for next season.'

I burst out laughing, not because he wanted to sign me, but at the way he conducted business. Dick had been in the game for many years and had a reputation for being a character. I think he knew I wouldn't be biting his hand off to play and train up in Angus, but his approach of turning the tables was refreshing and memorable. I was tempted to play his game and convince him to sign me, purely because of the way he went about it. I wonder how long he would've let me talk if I'd started listing my strengths and attributes.

'Only if you ground share with Motherwell,' I said, still laughing. He joined in with the laughter and then cut the conversation short, telling me I'd declined the biggest opportunity of my life but wishing me well for the future. DC: what a guy.

As I'd hoped, Gus McPherson did make contact and offered me two years at St Mirren. There were a number of senior pros there that season, including Kevin McGowne, Hugh Murray, Andy Millen, and my former St Johnstone teammate, Mixu Paatelainen. Charlie Adam was there too, on loan from Rangers. Even as a young player at the time, he had some talent, later going on to play in the English Premiership with Blackpool, Liverpool and Stoke City. John Sutton and Kirk Broadfoot were also on the squad, providing competence and quality up front and in defence. Similar to St Johnstone, St Mirren were a tier two team, but were building a squad that would be up there, challenging for the league title. Although finishing second to Falkirk in the 2004/2005 season, Gus McPherson's recruitment and tactics proved to be effective in the long term, with the team not only winning the league and promotion to the top flight in 2006, but also the Bell's Cup (now known as the Challenge Cup).

I loved my time at St Mirren, especially since I helped the club win two trophies, but more importantly because I proved to myself I still had it. After leaving Kilmarnock, and the St Johnstone years not quite going to plan, my career could easily have petered out, but belief, determination and the right contacts let me finish in style, my official last kick of the ball taking place with a team top of their league, soon to be playing back in Scotland's top flight.

Writing, albeit briefly, about those last two years of my football career brings home, once again, the importance of mindset, not just in competitive sport but in all walks of life. After my two years at St Johnstone, I was 35 and the most recent entry on my football CV was failure to win promotion after two consecutive attempts. I could've let these facts persuade me that it was time to hang up my boots and crack open a beer, but I didn't let those disappointments fester. Instead, I brushed them to one side and looked for new opportunities. Both head and heart were telling me that – even at 35 – my time wasn't up. Opportunity surrounds us on a daily basis, but some become blind to it through disappointment or setbacks, or in more severe cases, through trauma and/or poor mental health. I'm not trying to sound like a guru here, but if you can swipe away the cloud of disappointment, opportunities will become more visible.

Dionne being diagnosed with Rett Syndrome was a setback. The Marathon des Sables in 2021 being the hottest on record (despite it being October!) was a setback. Getting a stomach bug whilst running the world's most gruelling footrace while raising funds for Reverse Rett was a setback. But I kept going and, as much as possible, looked for the positives and opportunities. Looking back to when I was a teenager, kicking a ball against a wall and doing keepy-uppies on my own in the rain because everyone else was indoors, dry, warm and watching telly – that could be seen as an example of brushing disappointment to one side (having no-one to play with) and seeking out opportunities for development (improving my keepy-uppy skills and target accuracy). If you look at rise and fall stories, there's often a turning point where disappointment spirals into lack of self-belief, in turn perpetuating a mediocre or substandard performance, at least in the eyes of the media and fans. Disappointment can be exceptionally powerful, but only if you let it. Instead, you can use it positively to bounce back.

Of course, what's equally important is knowing when it's time up. When it comes to sport that requires a high level of physical fitness, it's never a good idea to keep going until your knees pop or your muscles are so tight, you need two days of hot baths and massage to feel human again. So, despite St Mirren offering me a one-year extension on my contract, I knew in my heart of hearts that, at 37, playing in the Scottish Premiership would be too taxing for me. I didn't want to let the club down, but nor did I want to warm their bench for most of a season. It also wouldn't be fair on Michelle as she was pregnant with our son, Dean, at the time, plus I already had plans in place for how I would support myself and my family after I'd kicked my last professional ball. So, that season – 2005/2006 – was my last, but as far as I was concerned, I'd finished on the ultimate high.

When I was kicking the ball about on dark, rainy nights as a kid, if someone told me that I'd play professional, full-time football at a good level for more than two decades, I'd have bitten their hand off for it. It may sound clichéd or corny, but I loved every minute. I didn't have a Plan B and I got there, through turning belief into reality. I considered myself fortunate to be able to fulfil my Plan A, seeing playing football never as a job, only an honour. It was knowing how fortunate I was, and being grateful for the opportunity, that made me always give 100 percent.

During my prime, when I was at Killie, I remember chatting to people at parties, events or on holiday, and they'd ask me what I do for a living. It was great to never dread that question, and equally as great being able to reply that I played professional football. I'd then ask them what they do and they'd say things like bus driver, accountant, IT technician or sous chef. *I'd hate that*, I'd say in my head as we continued to chat. Of course, as long as they don't hate what they do, that's fine. Someone might love being an accountant as much as I loved being a footballer. I'm not being judgemental, but from reading body language and listening to tone of voice, it's obvious when people are doing what they do because it's their job rather than their passion.

Unless there's a specific physical requirement, it's never too late to make your dreams a reality, or at least to try. If you keep telling yourself the same story, eventually you'll believe it. When I was a kid, I believed that football would be my destiny, so I gave the game the love it warranted. And it worked. There's a great comfort in looking back and knowing I gave 100 percent.

During my final week with St Mirren, I phoned Tam Burns to thank him for everything he'd done for me. He was no doubt the biggest influence on my career and without his guidance and belief, my football career could have just have petered out or ceased to be full-time.

During the call, Tam invited me over to his house in Newton Mearns for a bite to eat and a proper catch-up. I accepted and made my way over. When he opened his front door, he looked down and pointed at my shoes.

'Come on in, Mavis,' he said, 'but take your shoes off first.'

'No worries,' I said, thinking nothing of it. I bent down, unlaced my shoes, left them at the door, and walked into his hallway in my socks.

'Rosemary!' Tam shouted to his wife. 'That's his shoes off. You can steal them now!'

Despite the circumstances, I really should have expected something like that from someone who was always on the wind-up, the circumstances being the skin cancer diagnosis that, tragically, would take his life less than two years later. Obviously, at that point, I didn't know how long he had left, but it was still an emotional meeting for me. The facts didn't lie, and even the thought of him being taken early stirred emotions in me, affecting my level state. However – not that it was a surprise – he didn't show an ounce of self-pity. All he wanted to do was talk about football, me, and what I was going to do for the rest of my life.

I've shone a lot of light on Tam Burns, but he wasn't someone you'd want to get on the wrong side of. I remember a game against Morton: I had the ball and Tam shouted for it, his instructions loud and clear as he ran into space, but I decided to play it elsewhere. When I glanced over to him, his expression said, 'I'm going to kill you.' He went through me, there on the pitch and again in the dressing room after the match. Thing was, once it was out of his system, it was as if someone had pressed a reset button on his back. Next day of training, he was hugging me like a bear in the dressing room. What a man!

YOU HAVE A NICE DAY NOW, SIR

This may come as a surprise (unless you're someone who knows me well), but I don't show much interest in football these days. I'll take a glance at *Match of the Day* or *Sportscene* if I happen to stumble upon either during a channel hop, and I'll watch the occasional World Cup or Euros match, but I never have football in my diary. For someone who lived and breathed football from the day I could kick a ball right up to that final season with St Mirren, I appreciate that this sounds odd, bizarre even. A lot of people ask if something happened, like a horrible injury when playing five-a-sides or something – but no, nothing like that happened. To be entirely honest, it was a bit of a surprise to me too, but I can explain.

After that final season with St Mirren, I was offered a coaching role with the Under 19s. At first, I was stoked. It meant I could still be involved in football, stay with the club and use my experience to train and nurture the future of Scottish footballing talent. I threw myself into the role with gusto, adopting my no-less-than-100-percent approach that had served me so well during my years on the pitch. But, after a while, I just wasn't feeling it. I realised I was embracing every opportunity to coach on the pitch rather than from the sidelines. Being actively involved in a game whilst shouting out instructions, advice and feedback was the only time I properly enjoyed what I was doing.

That's when it occurred to me: my love of and obsession with football came from *playing* it. If I wasn't part of the game, in amongst everything, affecting what was going on, I wasn't interested. The love and passion wasn't there. Maybe that's why playing in the middle of the park was so important to me – because I was literally at the centre of everything. There was no adrenaline rush from the sidelines. Don't get me wrong, it was great to see some of the Under 19s come on, but all I wanted to do was put a strip on and join them.

I suppose if a pilot, who lived and breathed being a pilot and liked nothing more than flying a plane, had to take early retirement for health reasons, the last thing they might want to do is teach at pilot school, visit airports and watch *Pilot of the Day* on TV on a Saturday night. I didn't retire for health reasons of course, just age reasons. I could still play football, but would have struggled to play in the top flight at 37.

I played five and six-a-sides for a little while after the end of my professional career and competed in official, televised tournaments for Motherwell and Kilmarnock respectively. It was a good way to keep fit, but I packed it in after about 18 months. Sure, I had the ball at my feet and was actively involved in what was going on, but there was no opportunity to excel, no league to win and no fans singing and cheering. I had had my time in the limelight, which was all I could ever have wished for, but I quickly realised that coaching wasn't for me, and neither was five-a-sides.

I keep fit these days by – surprise, surprise – running, and as far as watching sport is concerned, I'm into boxing and mixed martial arts. I'm not sure if it's because they're individual rather than team sports, or because I've had no active involvement in either, but I'll watch boxing or mixed martial arts before I'll watch football. The mindset, focus, self-belief, dedication and resilience boxers and fighters exude has always inspired me. There's a whole lot more to it that throwing punches and kicks. Fitness and strength has to be at an incredible level, but it's all for nothing if timing, strategy or concentration are lacking.

During the year I was coaching the Under 19s, Michelle and I opened a Subway franchise in Coatbridge (yes, the sandwich shop with the sandwich artists). I was conscious of how difficult it can be for professional footballers to adjust to the real world after retirement, with many ending up depressed, turning to drink, or disappearing into obscurity. Of course, some become coaches, pundits, columnists, commentators or broadcasters, but not everyone has talent in those areas, or indeed the desire to follow those paths, whether they're capable or otherwise. Conscious of all this, I was determined to find something I could transfer my focus to.

A Subway shop in Coatbridge might sound like a bizarre decision, but the opportunity was there, so we took it. I figured I could co-run the shop and work on attaining my coaching badges at the same time. As you know, I discovered coaching wasn't for me, but I soon discovered that running a Subway shop wasn't for me either!

I hated working in that shop. It was a world apart from being in a dressing room with a squad of guys, laughing and joking. I certainly didn't get the same sense of camaraderie and togetherness from members of the sandwich-buying public! Likewise, our staff, whilst most of them were perfectly nice, spoke about soaps and celebrity scandals, which was a far cry from the dressing room banter I'd enjoyed for over 20 years. It was me who had to adjust though.

Whilst most people will have worked with a mix of men and women over their careers, I was working with women for the first time in my life at the age of 37. I won't lie, I found this difficult. Between the attitudes of the general public, the gossip in the shop and the long days, turning to drink suddenly seemed like an attractive option!

Joking aside, footballers are advised to 'plan for retirement' at the age of 25, just before their peak and around ten years from when they're likely to retire. It's like a 25-year-old guitarist being told to prepare for not being able to play guitar in ten years' time. Some listen and chew over a few ideas, but no-one has it as a priority. Most are looking forward only as far as the next game, or even the next training session. But, before they know it, BAM!, they're 35, have kicked their last professional ball and have no idea what to do next. It's weird – you can be a professional footballer on Tuesday, then not a professional footballer on Wednesday. Periods of adjustment, acceptance, planning and the seeking out of a new calling/role/purpose should therefore naturally follow.

Of course, rather than acceptance, some footballers fall into periods of denial, which can lead to poor self-esteem and/or issues with drink, drugs or both. A lot of the time, too, the public show no sympathy, adopting the attitude that the player has had 'the dream job' and 'got paid to kick a ball about.' Many also say things like, 'What have they got to be miserable about?' and 'They don't know how lucky they are.' Yes, absolutely, we've been fortunate, but that doesn't mean walking away from it when time's up is easy. And while the wages are good, most Scottish players aren't paid anywhere near the same amount as players in the English Premiership. As far as remuneration is concerned, a midfielder at Dundee United's wages is a world apart from a midfielder at Arsenal's.

Despite not liking it, I persevered with the Subway shop until just after the credit crunch hit in 2008. To be transparent, I stuck at it because it was making good money. Fast food is popular in Scotland, so there was always someone asking for a sandwich. This reinforced the thought process I'd gone through after retiring from football. It was either going to be a REMAX estate agents' shop or a Subway, and we went with Subway on the basis that people need food every day, but people don't need to move house every day.

Some days were tough, though. Occasionally, we'd get homeless people coming in asking for free coffee, which could cause other patrons to leave. We also had some staff steal from us – not big amounts, but enough for us to notice. On one occasion, I found a member of staff sitting in the fridge because she was too warm! On another, a customer held down one of the fizzy drinks dispensers, letting his paper cup overfill and sticky pop flow over his hand, into the overflowing drip tray and onto the floor. When I asked him to stop what he was doing, he glared at me and said, 'What are you going to do about it, like?' No day was predictable, but not in a good way. I used to wake up in the morning thinking, *What the hell is in store for us today?* It was a challenge, but I wasn't a quitter, so I kept going, putting the winnings away for a rainy day.

It's well-known that Subway is an American franchise, so all the training and literature had an American feel to it. Although the shop was in Coatbridge, we were encouraged at one point to say 'Have a nice day' or similar to our customers. One morning, we had a chat with the staff about it and decided there was no harm in giving it a try, deducing that being pleasant and positive can only be a good thing, whether based in North Lanarkshire or North Dakota. Later that morning, I presented a customer with the foot long sandwich, coffee and donut he ordered.

'Thanks,' he said, lifting his order from the counter and turning to leave.

'You have a nice day now, sir,' I said.

He stopped in his tracks and turned back to me. 'What did you say?' he asked, a scowl on his face.

'I said, you have a nice day now, sir,' I repeated, adding a smile and a nod.

He leaned towards me. 'Are you taking the piss?'

'No,' I replied, no longer smiling. 'Just wishing you a nice day.'

'Well, don't bother,' he snapped and marched out the door, shaking his head.

Says it all really. What works in America doesn't always work in Coatbridge, no matter how much you sugarcoat it. I never saw that customer again, strangely enough!

Although I always knew it in my heart, the day I decided the Subway shop wasn't for me was when I nipped into Waterstone's after being at the bank. Regular visits to the bank were necessary back then, and I would usually return to the shop immediately, especially during busy periods. On this particular day though, I decided to do a bit of book browsing before heading back. I stood in the fiction section, reading a paperback, wondering what the hell I was doing with my life. *One more page*, I said to myself, until I'd been in there for over 20 minutes, a chapter and a half in, legs becoming uncomfortable from lack of movement. That was the moment it became clear I was no longer giving 100 percent, which wasn't me. I wasn't that guy. It was time to hang up my apron and cap, wish my Subway shop a nice day now, and hand everything over to Michelle. I had given it my best shot, had no regrets and learned a lot in the process. Although the credit crunch had a detrimental impact on sales, overall it was a decent venture financially – and from a personal development perspective, it's true what they say about there being no such thing as a bad experience. Those 'bad' days were merely learning days, and learning I could take forward into whatever was coming next.

The tail end of my time at Subway was the beginning of a period of instability for me. With business and enterprise being heavily bruised by the credit crunch and uncertainty hanging in the air, it wasn't the best time to have no job or purpose. As I pondered what to do next, I began running regularly. I had always enjoyed running, but when I was working at Subway, the opportunities were few and far between. Of course, as well as being known the world over for the credit crunch, 2008 was a very important year to me personally, as it was the year Dionne was born. Naturally, my running routine became patchy and irregular again, especially when Michelle and I became aware of Dionne's issues and subsequent diagnosis.

That short period of regular running prior to Dionne's birth ignited something in me though. It helped me focus, kept my legs moving and gave me a little bit of the adrenaline rush I experienced when I played football. Granted, it wasn't as intense, but I still got enjoyment from it and it laid the foundation for the running challenges and fundraising events I would plunge myself into in the coming years.

As much as I was enjoying having plenty running time and was delighted to be away from the day-to-day stresses of Subway, I did feel the pressure of having to find a new job – a new purpose; something I could get my teeth stuck into. I was going to be a dad again soon, so it was important that I was able to support my family, something that can't be achieved by running through the woods. I had savings, so there was no immediate panic, but I'd always seen work as more than just the generation of income. I suppose I was feeling like I lacked a degree of identity. I was Mavis Reilly, ex-professional footballer and ex-Subway manager, so I needed to find something to fill the next chapter.

I got chatting to my next-door neighbour, Russell, who was an inspector in the police at the time. After telling him about my quandary, he suggested I apply to be a police officer.

'You're still young and fit enough,' he said, pointing at my torso, 'and it's the kind of thing that'll suit you.'

'Do you think so?' I pondered. 'I've never thought about the police, to be honest.'

'Well, you like to get out and about, don't you?' he said, his question rhetorical. 'And that's what happens in the force – you get out and about all the time, and no two days are the same.'

His sales pitch piqued my interest, so I decided I'd look into it. As the idiom goes, timing is everything, and that chat with Russell just so happened to take place during a big recruitment drive. Being a dog lover, I thought I might be able to get involved with the dog branch, be a handler or trainer perhaps.

I applied and got through the first interview successfully, which was a confidence boost, given I didn't have much workplace interview experience. That's not to say football didn't involve interviews of sorts, but any time I sat in the equivalent of the interview chair at a club, it was because we were already interested in each other. Those 'interviews' were about terms and conditions rather than convincing a panel that I was suitable for the job.

The second interview, which was carried out by a Chief Inspector, will always stand out in my memory. The interview went well, but afterwards, the Chief Inspector in question told me he was surprised by my performance, on the grounds that football players he'd encountered in the past didn't have much life experience. I was tempted to burst out laughing. I'd never heard so much nonsense. I was 40-years-old at that interview; I had bags of life experience, some of which came purely from having been on the planet for 40 years, but a huge proportion came from my days as a footballer. He was miles off. I probably had a right to be offended when he said what he said, but all it deserved was a stifled laugh and an internal shake of the head.

Football had taught me the value of teamwork, the importance of resilience (physically and mentally), the need for patience, the power of communication, the impact of decision making (good and bad), the need for precise timing, and the ability to cope with exhilarating highs and crushing lows. With their astronomical wages, the top end players might not seem to live in the real world, but every footballer, whether they play for Dunipace Juniors or Manchester City has had to deal with setbacks.

My performance at interview – despite the Chief Inspector's assumptions about ex-footballers – earned me a place at Tulliallan Police College in Alloa, where I had to address superior officers as Ma'am and Sir. It reminded me of Army films, especially since marching also featured as part of my training. My fellow students and I were all in it together, though, all with the common goal of coming out the other side as a fully qualified police officer.

A lot of my classmates were in their 20s and had been to university, but this didn't put me off. At 40, studying for exams for the first time since high school was hard work, but it's not like that was a surprise. It would've been odd if everything was a walk in the park. I gave 100 percent and – more importantly – enjoyed giving 100 percent, unlike when I was at Subway.

The graft paid off and, in May 2009, I got through Police College successfully, getting a great mark for the final exam, and became PC Mavis Reilly! Or PC Mark Reilly, rather. Being notoriously difficult to get into, the dog branch route didn't come to fruition, but many years later, in 2021, I would win the Specialist Crime Division Making a Difference to People's Life Award for my charity work. When I became a fully-fledged police officer, Dionne was less than a year old, so she was yet to be diagnosed with Rett Syndrome. That subsequent diagnosis coupled with the maintenance of fitness through police training and running would form the foundation that would one day lead to me running the craziest, most treacherous, but ultimately rewarding, race of my life.

GAZZA HUGS

I doubt many people would be quick to see the similarities, but there are times my role as a police officer reminds me of being in the dressing room before a big match. There's the camaraderie between officers and the collective belief that results will come if everyone pulls in the same direction. Okay, the police force is probably a bit more politically correct than the average squad of football players is, but as someone who has been immersed in both environments, there are more similarities than I expected.

One thing I'm exceptionally grateful for is that my transition from football life to – as some might call it – 'normal' life was relatively straightforward. State of mind and personality certainly play a part in how smooth or otherwise the process can be, but I do consider myself one of the lucky ones as far as these things are concerned. For some players, it can be the biggest challenge of their life. I know a lot of guys who have struggled, some of whom found even talking about it challenging. They'd often look for a way to change the topic at the first possible opportunity, especially if they still had a season or two left in them.

I can see similarities between footballers and dogs, in that they both live in the moment. Footballers pull on their boots for training every day and then play in front of thousands of fans on match days, usually without giving any consideration whatsoever to what they might do when age catches up with them and they can no longer hold their own on the pitch. Similarly, a dog never thinks about that inevitable day when it'll be too tired, slow or uncomfortable to retrieve the ball its owner has just thrown most of the length of a football field. All it thinks about in that moment is getting to the ball as quickly as possible and fulfilling its role in tearing back to its owner as fast as its legs will allow, ball in mouth, tail wagging and loving life. But, the final whistle always comes. For the dog, this often means it's reaching the closing stages of its life, but for the footballer, there are many, many years ahead.

Without any planning or forethought, those looming years can be full of uncertainty. Some players may be asked to consider their post-football future at the age of 27, and I can totally understand why they might balk at such a suggestion. At that stage, they're likely to be in their prime, fighting fit and living their dream; the only thing that matters is the next game. The problem with being in your prime, though, is that once you reach your peak, downwards is the only way you can go. I say this in a realistic rather than a negative way, and a player at 27 might have only five years left in the game, depending on injuries, position, club they play for, etc.

During my time as a professional, I think the Professional Footballers' Association (PFA) could have done more. Strong links with the likes of careers advisers, life coaches and counselling services might've helped many a player who faced the abyss of the normal world with a concerned expression on his face, having given no thought as to what to do for the rest of his days. On a more positive note though, the PFA has rolled with the times and now runs courses that allow players hanging up their boots to become qualified tradesmen. There's also a lot more help out there in terms of mental health support, which wasn't there when my career came to an end. Luckily, I didn't need it, but if you look at a player like Paul Gascoigne, mental health support and career advice might have made quite a difference if it was made available to him. We'll never know for sure, but as someone who played against Gazza, I watched his well-documented troubles through my fingers, and often wondered if earlier intervention might have changed his path for the better.

For Gazza, football was *everything*. He thrived on the adulation he got from the fans – but imagine experiencing the buzz of having over 50,000 people sing your name one week, and then the following week . . . nothing. That's a hammer blow, one he didn't deal well with, unfortunately. A lot of people likely thought he was just having a good time, tapping into all the money he'd earned to let his hair down and party, free from the pressures of maintaining fitness and performing on match days. As is fairly common knowledge, things spiralled for him as the years went on, which, as someone who liked him, was horrible to see.

Guaranteed, there were people out there who had no sympathy for him, given the lifestyle and wage packets he enjoyed as a professional footballer for club and country. I understand those people's stances, but regardless, alcoholism is a deeply damaging affliction, irrespective of career and monetary worth. Like reporters said about COVID-19 during the pandemic, booze has no prejudice.

On a more upbeat note, Gazza was the best player I ever played against. There were some formidable midfielders around at the time, like Paul McStay and Lubo Moravcik, but Gazza was unplayable at times.

Strong, fast and ambidextrous, it was as if the ball stuck to his feet when he was dribbling. Whether we were playing at Rugby Park or Ibrox, I'd regularly get the job of man-marking him and, believe me, there were times when it would have been easier nailing jelly to a wall.

Early on in the match, I would always try to – how do I put this? – let him know he was in a game. I was never a dirty player, but when it came to Gazza, it was important to let him know that I was around, and that I wasn't a pushover, so I communicated this by leaving a little bit on him in the first tackle. On the days he reacted, I always knew I was in with a chance of holding my own. It was the days I got no reaction that were the hardest. It was his way of communicating to me that I was in for a tough ride.

On one occasion, a midweek fixture at Ibrox on a cold December night, I gave him my custom nibble on the first tackle and he went down. The free kick was taken quickly by one of his teammates and everyone's attention shifted to the left wing. As Rangers formed an attack, Gazza quickly got to his feet, clocked the referee following the play, and volleyed me full force, wiping me off my feet, leaving me in a heap on the turf.

I jumped to my feet as quickly as he did. 'What do you think you're doing?' I shouted in his face (or words to that effect). Then he hooked me. A full-blown haymaker, somehow missed by every official, but not enough to knock me to the ground.

When things like this happen, it's important to show that you can take it as much as you can give it out, so I checked my jaw wasn't broken, shrugged it off and got on with the game. About ten minutes later, while the ball was out of play, I heard a Geordie accent in my ear.

'Sorry about that,' he said with a smile, pulling me in for a quick hug.

At the time, I wasn't sure if he was being genuine, or if it was merely a continuation of the mind games we'd been playing. Regardless, while I appreciated his apology, it didn't mean I'd be holding back. The last thing I wanted was for him to think I could be silenced by an apology and a hug, especially since he was apologising for something that would have been a straight red if any of the officials had seen it. Luckily for Gazza, and many players of that era (including me), there was no such thing as VAR in those days.

At 1-1, Rangers got a penalty just before half-time, and when it was Gazza who placed the ball on the spot, I got right into his ear.

'You're missing this,' I told him. '100 percent.'

Without giving me a second glance, he took a few steps back and waited for the referee's whistle. Once it sounded, he ran towards the ball at speed and struck it with conviction – but Dragoje Leković dived low to his left and saved it!

'Told you!' I shouted, while he stood rubbing his face in disbelief. 'You're hopeless!'

That might sound a bit cruel or unreasonable, but it was just part of the game. Once we walked off at full-time, all would be forgotten, or that was certainly the case for me. The game has changed quite considerably since the 1990s of course, but the same kind of mind games definitely still go on, a key difference being that, in the modern day, bad feeling can continue on social media, more so between opposing fans rather than the players. Without sounding too nostalgic, it was a better game when I played it and it doesn't feel like the increased surveillance has reduced the number of bad tackles, injuries, divers or play-actors. If anything, all that stuff seems to have increased.

Gazza's penalty miss that day didn't change the outcome of the game, unfortunately – well, unfortunately for Killie anyway – with the final score being 4-2 to Rangers.

Rescheduled from earlier in the season, we had another midweek fixture against Rangers a month later, this time at Rugby Park. During the warm-up, Gazza ran over to me, gave me another hug and apologised again for the haymaker he dealt me during our last encounter. I took this to mean he was genuinely sorry, that it wasn't a mind game, and that he regretted reacting the way he did. I shrugged it off and we had a laugh about it. We both knew, though, that come kick-off, it would be back to business.

Once again, I left one on him first chance I got, just a lingering leg, nothing excessive or damaging in any way. One of those tackles that, if the ref has a word with you, you hold up a hand and say, 'Just a little late, sorry ref.' On this occasion, though, Gazza ignored me completely. Nightmare. He ran me ragged for 90 gruelling minutes, yet somehow we managed to salvage a point, the game ending 1-1. He was unbelievable, though. A brilliant footballer.

When his career finished, Gazza clearly had his struggles, proof that the transition from football life to non-football life can be difficult, emotionally, mentally and physically. Top end players can finish their careers with healthy bank balances, but without the demands of day-to-day training, their fitness can quickly suffer, while their lack of purpose can lead to a poor state of mind and subsequent emotional difficulties.

For me, as much as I enjoy my work, there's nothing to compare with playing football for a living, nor will there ever be. That's something I accepted early on and I think that helped a lot. I'll never get those halcyon football days back, but I feel honoured I was able to experience them in the first place. When my career ended, I was conscious of the gaping hole in my life, so I sought out things that would interest and challenge me, both physically and mentally. This is when I first got into fundraising challenges, knowing that they'd help me maintain my physical fitness and give me goals to focus on.

I've never been someone who watches much TV or binges box sets, preferring to be out and about doing something active or meeting new people and learning new skills. When there was a lull in fundraising activities, I took an online course in counselling. It was important to me to keep both brain and body active, conscious that many ex-footballers can quickly become bored. I didn't want to fall into that trap. Boredom can easily lead to hitting the bottle to find highs out of the humdrum. Not that I'm a big drinker, but I'd seen other ex-professionals end up on that slippery slope purely because there was no longer enough excitement or stimulation in their lives. It was important to me to maintain stimulation through any means necessary. My days as a footballer were over, but my legs still worked and my brain was hungry for new challenges.

After that chat with Tam Burns when I was 22, I placed a lot of focus on my physical fitness. In contrast to others, I had to work hard at it, but one thing I was naturally good at was press-ups. For the entirety of my 11-year tenure, I was press-up champion, even on a Christmas night out after drinking a nip of whisky after every set of 25, while my sneaky opponents weren't. The joke was on them though, as, despite having a belly full of whisky and a slightly fuzzy head, I still came out victorious! It was always the long game for me, though; I found 100m sprints exceptionally difficult, but I was always among the front-runners when it came to 800m.

Sometimes I'd see players on the pitch tanking it in the first 20 minutes, looking to make a big impact on the game early on. Of course, sometimes it worked and they'd get an assist or be a key part of a sequence of play that led to a goal – but if their early efforts were fruitless, they were potentially setting themselves up for a breathless second half or being subbed off with 25 still to play. If it was me who was marking them, I'd clock it, knowing that, at some point, I'd overtake them in terms of speed and stamina – and that would mean opportunities. Even if I suspected they'd be subbed, I'd push that little bit harder around that time. These little windows can easily affect the run of the game and, ultimately, the outcome.

This ability to maintain consistency throughout a game, coupled with the natural strength I had in my chest and arm muscles, got me to thinking that an extensive endurance challenge might – at some point in the future – be the ideal thing to focus my mind, test my resilience and prove to myself that almost anything is possible with the right approach. That manifested itself, many years later, as signing up for the 2021 Marathon des Sables in aid of Reverse Rett. As it transpired, I was going to need every last ounce of the fitness I'd built up over nearly 30 years, just to survive.

THE RUNNING MAN

After Dionne was diagnosed with Rett Syndrome, I decided to put any spare time I had into fundraising for Reverse Rett. Working as a police officer and responding to Dionne's needs certainly didn't mean I had quiet life, but the buzz I got from football, physically and mentally, had left a gap. It was a gap I wanted to fill. I was motivated to raise funds for Reverse Rett, but that motivation was topped up by an itch I had to step out of my comfort zone and do something that would push me to my limits.

I'd done a few 10ks and enjoyed them, but in June 2013, I decided to move things up a few notches by taking on the Three Peaks Challenge, which involves climbing the UK's three highest mountains – Ben Nevis in Lochaber, Scotland, Scafell Pike in England's Lake District, and Snowdon in Gwynedd, Wales – all within 24 hours.

As well as being a test for the legs, heart, lungs and mind, it also tests driving skills, time management and patience. With the significant distances between the three mountains, there's a fair amount of motoring involved – and whilst driving from A to B is as routine as it gets, the goalposts are moved when the clock is ticking, there are speed limits to stick to, and you have no control when it comes to other road users, roadworks, last-minute diversions, accidents, or unanticipated freakish weather.

When one foot is going in front of the other, the control lies exclusively with the person those feet are attached to. But the road is a different story altogether.

It wasn't a challenge I wanted to do solo, so I contacted a few of my former football mates and asked them if they'd be game. I ended up being accompanied by Jim Weir from St Johnstone and Ally Mitchell, Kevin McGowne and Andy Millen from Kilmarnock. They all knew about Dionne and signed up mainly to support me in my fundraising endeavours. They were all fit guys though, so I knew they'd be able to handle it. Having said that though, Andy Millen and Ally Mitchell were in bits by the end of it, despite being two of the fittest guys I'd ever seen play football. It turns out that running for 90 minutes on a football pitch is quite different to climbing the three highest mountains in the UK!

Participants can do the peaks in any order they wish, so naturally we started with Ben Nevis and finished with Snowden. We did Ben Nevis mid-afternoon, completing it as night was beginning to fall. For most, that would be the time to rest, recuperate, have a bite to eat and then sleep like a log, but for us, it was a minibus journey to the Lake District. It was permissible to sleep during the journey, but a minibus is a horrible place to try and get some kip at the best of times, let alone when it's full of ex-footballers taking part in a physical challenge. Thankfully, we had a driver, Cammy Moir, who was a police sergeant and former traffic cop (now retired), so he was no stranger to roads and – as you would expect – stuck to the speed limit for the duration. It was comforting having someone solid at the wheel. It meant we could put all our concentration into the task at hand. It also meant power naps wouldn't be interrupted by ropey driving or hard braking.

We were a third of the way through the challenge and I could already feel it in my legs. This was fine though, it just meant my body was going through the recovery process after the work I'd put it through. It was probably anticipating a comfy bed with freshly laundered linen and eight or so hours of shut-eye, but instead, it was going to be climbing the highest mountain in England – and the steepest of the three peaks – at half one in the morning in the pitch dark.

Endurance, resilience and positivity got us up and down Scafell Pike all in one piece. It was tough, but I was kept going by the camaraderie and togetherness, the cause always bubbling underneath. Even if Dionne wanted to do the Three Peaks Challenge, or any kind of hillwalking for that matter, it wouldn't be possible. I was doing it because she couldn't. Any time I felt fatigued or breathless, I thought about Dionne, which kept my legs moving and my lungs working. She wasn't there physically, and never would be, but she was always with me mentally and emotionally, metaphorically pushing me up that mountain.

Daylight had returned by the time we began our ascent of Snowdon. It was a novelty being able to see what was ahead of us without a torch, but that novelty was short-lived as, despite it being June, the sky was grey, the rain was pouring and the temperature was uncharacteristically low. It would have been easy to quit at this stage, but we kept going, tapping into that mental strength we seemed to possess as a group, like we were all on the same football team again, facing tough opponents but very much holding our own. *I thought it was meant to be warmer in the south,* I remember thinking to myself as we soldiered on up, the rain stinging our cold faces. It was peak three of three though, so every new step was one more towards the reward of completion.

When we reached the bottom of Snowdon within the 24-hour limit, it felt like we'd gubbed Real Madrid 3-0, every goal from open play, a fourth in stoppage time chalked off due to being a fraction offside. I'll always be grateful to Ally, Andy, Jim and Kevin for going on that crazy ride with me, all guys who were in the trenches with me during our football careers. A teammate can sometimes end up being nothing more than someone shooting in the same direction wearing the same colours and club crest. Likewise though, a teammate can become a friend for life, someone who shares a lot more than a dressing room and the occasional laugh. That applies to Ally, Andy, Jim and Kevin. Through loyalty and comradeship, these guys put themselves through the mill for me – and for Dionne. That's a special thing.

Another special thing was that we raised £24,000 for Reverse Rett, most of it donated by the average punter and friends we reached out to. I was blown away by this figure, and it inspired me to keep going and keep pushing the boundaries. Tough or unusual challenges attracted donations, so I kept my eyes peeled for something that would up the ante. That's when I learned about a footrace that took place in the Sahara: The Marathon des Sables.

MAVIS THE WATER RAT

In 2010, former Olympic rower James Cracknell took part in the Marathon des Sables and made a documentary about his experience. He had set himself the goal of becoming the highest placed Brit, which, testament to the strict, intense training regime he put himself through, he managed to achieve, finishing 12th. Despite his record being broken by Danny Kendall, who finished fifth in 2014, and subsequently by former Army Captain Tom Evans, who finished third in 2017, Cracknell's documentary ignited something in me. Following his story, I experienced a deep level of admiration I'd never had for anyone before (or since). At one point during the race, he was badly dehydrated and was offered an IV drip, but he refused on the grounds that it'd mean incurring a two-hour penalty. From a health perspective, it might seem like an unusual thing to admire, but it was his warrior spirit and unwavering dedication to his goal that I was in awe of.

The Marathon des Sables looked like the ultimate test of everything: character, fitness, endurance, resilience, fortitude, motivation, spirit, mindset and heart. I wanted in. I told myself I was meant to watch that documentary, as if fate had had a hand in the buttons I pressed on my TV remote that night. It was an awakening. *Well, you were looking for the ultimate challenge, Mavis*, I said to myself. *Looks like you've found it.*

Having made the decision that the Marathon des Sables was going to feature in my future, I began doing research in order to get a comprehensive understanding of what I was letting myself in for. I was conscious that I'd only done one regular marathon before, although I had done two Ironman events, which are made up of a 2.4-mile* open water swim, a 112-mile† cycle and a full 26.2-mile‡ marathon.

I knew the Marathon des Sables would be a big step up from an Ironman, but they were vital in my preparation, physically but especially mentally. They helped me develop the resilience I needed to believe I could take things to the next level. Due to its relentless heat and barren terrain, the Sahara is known as one of the most inhospitable places on Earth, so not the most natural place for a baldy, fair-skinned guy from Bellshill to be drawn to!

My first Ironman came about after I bumped into an old pal of mine, Gerry Seenan, in Hamilton Town Centre one midweek afternoon. I mentioned that I'd done a bit of fundraising for Reverse Rett.

'You should do an Ironman,' he said, casually. 'I've done a couple of them. I think it's the kind of thing you'd get your teeth stuck into.'

The longer we chatted, the more appealing the idea became, but there were a couple of obstacles standing in my way. First off, I hadn't ridden a bike since I was ten-years-old. Loads of kids I grew up with spent long hours scooting around on Choppers, Strikas and BMXs, but I always had the ball at my feet. As far as I was concerned, any time spent cutting about the streets on a bike was

---

* 3.9km
† 180.2km
‡ 42.2km

time I could've spent playing football or practising keepy-uppies. Since my childhood days, I've been on the occasional static bike in the gym, but certainly not for the equivalent of 112 miles!

Whilst I considered my lack of cycling over the years as an obstacle, it was something I knew I'd be able to overcome with the right mindset and putting the hours in on the saddle. The second obstacle was a little more significant though: I couldn't swim.

I don't know why I didn't learn to swim when I was a kid. The majority of kids at my school and in my area all learned, some becoming strong swimmers and taking it up as a regular leisure pursuit. It's classed by many as a fundamental life skill, part of a survival toolkit, but it was never something I was interested in. Again, anything that used up time I could have been spending playing football was pointless to me. I stuck with my passion, which paid off nicely for me in the long run, but to the detriment of developing some key life skills, like the ability to swim. I have no regrets about how I spent my time in childhood, but if an Ironman was going to happen, it was necessary to learn. *Do classes even exist for adult minnows?* I wondered. I would have to put pride to one side, do some searching and make some enquiries.

Having known Gerry for long time, I mentioned my problem.

'Aye, but Mavis,' he shrugged, 'what's the point of taking on a challenge you could do tomorrow?'

I loved his attitude, and he was spot on, so I knuckled down and began the lengthy process of turning myself into someone capable of completing an Ironman.

The next day, I joined the David Lloyd gym in Hamilton and asked if they happened to do swimming lessons for adults. As fate would have it, they did, so I signed up for six lessons with a fully qualified instructor, to take place once a week. Between lessons, I hit the pool nearly every day to work on what I'd been taught. I'd love to say I took to it like a duck to water, but the reality was I was out of my depth. I'm not sure if it was because of the decades of football, but my feet were like anchors due to the shape they naturally held. Adjusting them to help me cut through the water more easily was incredibly uncomfortable at first, but I worked away at it and made gradual improvement.

I was in my mid-40s at the time, sometimes sharing a pool with kids who could swim effortlessly, as if it was the most natural thing on Earth. I saw comparisons with learning a foreign language. A kid who has been exposed to two languages from birth or early childhood, perhaps due to having a Scottish dad and a German mum, can speak both languages – and chop and change between the two – without thinking about it. This is quite a contrast to someone in their mid-40s learning Hungarian for the first time. I had to concentrate on everything. Every stroke, movement and breath. For someone who hadn't learned to swim as a kid, and who had some sort of weird brake system going on in his feet, there's a lot I had to focus on and try to develop at the same time.

As well as the lessons with my instructor, there was also a club at the gym called the Water Rats! I was apprehensive to join at first due to being such a weak swimmer, but the banter was brilliant. It was run by Alan Kain and Jack Dickson, who loved a laugh, as did the guys and girls who regularly attended. It took me back to my days in the football dressing room, because there was plenty of stick flying about. No-one took anything to heart though, even those who were berated for being a regular attendee of the beginners' lane (i.e. me), often sharing the water with kids wearing armbands.

It's the kind of thing some people might be embarrassed about, but starting at the beginning was my only choice, so I embraced it, knowing I would eventually progress to the intermediate lane and – one day – the dizzy heights of the advanced lane. This Water Rat was well and truly out of his comfort zone, but I knew that was the ultimate place to be if I wanted to experience growth. And with every stroke, laugh and splutter, I was one tiny step further to being Ironman ready.

Despite having a lot to work on as far as the swimming was concerned, it was a warm, welcoming, supportive and often laughter-filled environment. This wasn't the case when it came to the cycling. People use the phrase, 'It's just like riding a bike' either to appease someone who might be concerned about taking on something new, or to highlight that something is straightforward. There's this assumption that riding a bike is some sort of inherent quality, merely a modern day equivalent to riding a horse before the motor car was invented. This wasn't the case for me. A lot had changed since I last had my feet on a set of bike pedals.

Back when I was ten, there was no such thing as cleats, or if there was, I was entirely in the dark. Cleats are the bits attached to the pedals that the rider's shoes are slotted into, so they're attached to the bike. All Ironman competitors have cleats, so it's not like they were an option, but they felt alien to me. I was taking things seriously though, so I had to embrace the modern kit with a smile. I bought myself a bike and all the kit: helmet, padded shorts, cleats, a tight Lycra top, a fancy water bottle, the lot. I reckoned that looking the part and having all the kit would make things smoother when I hit the tarmac, but the reality was I was all gear and no idea.

On my first day of training, I ended up injured only a few metres away from my house. The cleats were uncomfortable, so I was jigging around, trying to get a snugger fit. As a result, I was looking down at my feet rather than in front of me, lost my balance and landed in a heap on the road. I suffered a skinned hip and knee, and a dent to my pride. It felt humiliating at the time, but looking back on it now, it is quite funny. You must be wondering how I ever managed to complete an Ironman with this kind of start! Getting up off the road and dusting myself down, I thought about Dionne and how no end of things were a struggle for her, yet she never grumbled and always tried. I had to adopt that approach if I was ever going to be confident on a bike, so I gave myself a quick talking to, shook off the pain, stuck a smile on my face and got back on the horse.

I'll be honest, it was a slog, and it took me months to build up any sort of confidence. Like everything though, the more I hit the road, the more competent I became, and competence breeds confidence. It was gradual and I plateaued a few times, but I knew perseverance would see me through. I think the issue with the cycling over and above the running – and even the swimming – was that I felt at the mercy of the many variables that come with sharing the road with cars, vans, lorries, trucks and motorbikes. With running, I could run wherever I wanted and on any type of surface. If I chose to run on roadside paths, I felt a lot more in control than I did on the bike. And with swimming, I was in the water, very much in control of what I was doing (despite having brakes for feet) and all I had to do was make sure I didn't get in the way of other swimmers. That was all straightforward in comparison to cycling alongside other road users.

Despite being a positive person, I often felt apprehensive any time a car was behind me, looking for the right time to overtake. Most drivers were just being safe, but I always felt I was inconveniencing them, forcing them to go slower than the speed limit in order to stick to the rules. Some drivers came way too close though, narrowly missing me with their wing mirror. They weren't in the majority, but I had trouble suppressing that apprehension no matter who was behind me.

On a bike, being on the road and keeping up with the flow of traffic is a deafening place to be, a world apart from being in the car with the radio on, cruising along at 40 mph. There's little more intimidating than a lorry driver dropping a gear and flooring it to overtake you on a narrow road, especially when they're clearly not leaving the recommended amount of room. Those booming diesel engines whizzing past, often throwing up road spray and dirt, were the most perilous moments of any training I've done for any event, including the Marathon des Sables.

Interestingly, whilst being overtaken by angry lorry drivers running late with deliveries was terrifying, the silence of an approaching electric car was equally as bad. On one occasion, I had no idea whatsoever that a car was sitting behind me, and nearly jumped out of my cycling shorts when it passed me like a stealth ninja, albeit keeping a safe distance this time.

I don't know if I was just unlucky with some of the routes I chose to take, but I found myself constantly avoiding potholes too. This sometimes meant choosing between clipping the kerb or moving out into the road a bit more. When I did the latter, I'd sometimes get horns beeped at me or windows wound down and abuse hurled at me. Sometimes – and I don't know if this is a Scottish thing – abuse would be shouted at me even if I was sticking to the Highway Code 100 percent. It was usually young guys having a carry-on, but I didn't find it funny in the slightest. I just kept my head down and ignored them, but sometimes it'd keep coming. With football, altercations were over in an instant, but this stuff was constant. I don't mean it happened with every vehicle that passed me, but the anticipation of it was always there, so I always prepared for it, or for something to be thrown at me, which happened a couple of times as well. I can only assume the morons who did these things wanted me to lose my balance and fall off the bike. The first time it happened, the fright nearly sent me flying, so I was conscious not to show any weakness thereafter, because that's what they wanted.

For a while, I went out on the bike early in the morning. There was far less traffic around at that time, so it was a bit more relaxing and I could focus more, but I wouldn't go so far as to say I enjoyed it. One of those mornings, my old St Mirren teammate Kevin McGowne came out with me. Because the roads were pretty quiet, we were riding parallel and building up decent speed, giving our legs a right good workout. I was on the outside and Kevin was on the inside, sandwiched between me and the kerb. We were both focussed on the task at hand, but occasionally spoke. It was during a brief exchange about our route that our handlebars clipped, causing my bike to buckle, throwing me onto the opposite side of the road. Conscious of where I was, I got to my feet as quickly as I could and limped out of the path of danger. If a car had been coming, even at 20 or

30 mph, I could've ended up in serious trouble. I had scrapes, scratches and cuts all over me, but at least I was alive and all my bones were intact.

As if that wasn't enough, that incident knocked the confidence I had managed to build up . . . but I kept going. I had to. The whole point was doing things Dionne couldn't, and doing them *for* her, to better her life and/or the lives of other Rett Syndrome sufferers as much as I possibly could. The experiences I had on the bike helped me build resilience, increase my fitness and develop my mindset, each of which were fundamental for what was to come years later in the Sahara. I'll be upfront though, once the bike had served its purpose, I got rid of it. Cycling just wasn't for me. If I'd decided to keep it, I doubt I'd use it for much more than nipping to the shop for a pint of milk on a nice day.

My first Ironman was in Bolton in 2015. With sheer determination, I had persevered with the swimming and cycling training, which gave birth to one of the most satisfying feelings any human being can experience: belief. It's not that I didn't believe in myself; I wouldn't have signed up for an Ironman if I didn't believe I would be capable of it in time – but when that belief is full and uncompromised, it glows, and mine even managed to glow during the 2.4 mile swim I did in brown, murky, ice-cold water with zero on the visibility scale. As each stroke advanced me closer to my goal, I kept three things in mind: everything I'd learned from my swimming instructor and the Water Rats gang; Dionne; and Gerry Seenan saying 'What's the point of taking on a challenge you could do tomorrow?'

Once I got on the bike, it was a better experience than going out onto the roads of Lanarkshire, maybe because everyone had the same goal. Safety in numbers, as the old saying goes. I wouldn't go as far as to say I enjoyed it, but I got into a groove and kept my focus. Every turn of the pedals, cleats attached safely and snugly, was another step towards achieving a massive life goal.

My legs were aching when I got off the bike, but I had mentally prepared myself for the marathon at the end to be like a dessert. It was the leg I was most comfortable with in training, and whilst 26.2 miles is a long way, especially after a 112-mile cycle, I knew I had it in me to cross the finish line. It's difficult to describe the feelings I experienced when that time inevitably came. Relief was in there, as was pride and elation, but one of the first things that crossed my mind when my legs finally stopped moving was that the Marathon des Sables had become that little bit more doable, especially since it didn't feature swimming or cycling!

Energised by my achievement in Bolton, I decided to continue my trajectory towards the Marathon des Sables by signing up for another Ironman, this time in Barcelona in early October 2016. Although I like to get my teeth stuck into new challenges, there's reassurance in familiarity, so the Barcelona Ironman, despite it not exactly being a walk in the park, was more enjoyable. I was in peak condition by that point and had become a (slightly) more competent swimmer and a less nervous cyclist, although the cycle was still my least favourite leg by far. In contrast to Bolton, the Barcelona swim was a pure delight. At one point, the water was so clear that I became mesmerised by all the colourful fish darting back and forth underneath me, to the extent that it slipped my mind I was taking part in a competitive race. That leg was as relaxing and tranquil as an Ironman swim can be, testament that my perseverance in the pool, alongside my lessons and the sessions with the Water Rats got me to a place where I could swim without thinking about it.

In-between the Bolton and Barcelona Ironman, I did the Nice Marathon with a few of the guys from the gym, completing it in three hours and 16 minutes. I enjoyed that race immensely, and was pleased to get a 'regular', stand-alone marathon under my belt. I did it again in 2017, this time with Monica. She wanted to mark her 50th birthday by doing something she hadn't done before, so I suggested the Nice Marathon. She had played tennis over the years, so had a decent level of fitness, but she'd never done any long-distance running before. She had obviously seen me develop a passion for it, so she thought there was no reason not to find out what all the fuss was about.

I was impressed with the dedication Monica showed when it came to training. Most of us probably know someone who's signed up for a marathon or half marathon, started training with a month to go and ended up totally knackered after the first five or six miles*. Monica, in contrast, began doing short runs as soon as the decision was made, and later signed up for a structured four-month training programme to ensure she was fully prepped. She put heart and soul into it, performed brilliantly on the day and thoroughly enjoyed the experience. The reason I'd suggested the Nice Marathon over and above any other marathon was because of the route. It starts at the Promenade des Anglais and finishes in Cannes, so it hugs the spellbinding French Riviera the whole way. As scenic routes go, it really doesn't get much better than that.

We went on to do the Amsterdam Marathon in 2018 together, Monica the half and me the full. It was another

---

* 8 - 9.7km

great experience to share together, drinking in the Dutch culture and landmarks as we ran. By this stage in my prep for the Marathon des Sables, I felt like I was becoming more and more confident, a well-oiled machine that could find its rhythm and pace without much difficulty. There was something immensely satisfying about that. My brain was sending the messages to my muscles and legs to keep me moving, but at times it was like there was a disconnect, but in a good way, my contact with the ground smooth and controlled to the extent I could place my focus on breathing the air and enjoying everything that was going on around me. Of course, in time I would find out that the Nice and Amsterdam Marathons, and the Bolton and Barcelona Ironman triathlons were a walk in the park compared to what was waiting for me in the Sahara a few years down the line.

LIGHT DRAWN FROM DARK

Although I had told myself – on numerous occasions – that the Marathon des Sables would feature in my future, these things are all just talk until an application and entry fee are submitted to the powers that be. It's not that I was in any doubt; after all, the two Ironman triathlons, along with the Nice and Amsterdam Marathons and umpteen other smaller local and national races, were a significant part of preparing myself for the toughest test of my life. I desperately wanted not only to do it, but to do it well. It ticked every box. Massive personal challenge that would push me to my limits? Check. Raise awareness of Rett Syndrome? Check. Attract much-needed funds for Reverse Rett? Check.

After a discussion with Monica, in which I made clear my unwavering desire to sign up, we agreed as a couple that I should go for it. So, on Sunday, January 26th, 2020, I submitted my application to compete in the 2021 Marathon des Sables, due to take place in April, a mere 15 months away. I was buzzing.

As far as big life decisions go, this wasn't one that was exclusively about the race. The fee was in the region of £4,500, but once all the gear is added, that figure can be topped up by a good few grand. You might think people are off their heads for parting with thousands of pounds to run in a boiling hot desert for six days, but they do it because they thrive by stepping outside their comfort zones, and events organisers are aware of how big that market is. Although I was buzzing and very much up for the challenge, I'd be lying if I said I wasn't apprehensive, scared even. Alongside the charity aspect, these are major drivers though. Fears are there to be faced head on, to test fortitude and character, and to foster personal growth. The comfort zone is a nice place to be from time to time, but growth and development can only occur by stepping outside that comfort zone, embracing the unknown, welcoming the new and unfamiliar with a smile, and getting in about it with gritted teeth. These things, as far as I'm concerned, are priceless.

Very kindly, Reverse Rett offered to cover my fee, or rather offered that it come out of monies raised, but I politely refused. Monica and I had been putting money aside for a good while, so we had it covered. Regardless, it was important to me that every penny handed over by anyone kind enough to sponsor me went to Reverse Rett.

I was keen to build up my training and continue to push myself, but on the day I signed up, there were a few murmurings on the news about a deadly virus taking hold in the Chinese city of Wuhan, but given that the news and social media can be guilty of fearmongering, it wasn't really registering in the consciousness of people in the UK. There had been items about viruses in the past, but nothing catastrophic had happened. COVID-19, of course, was a different story and only two months later, the country was in full lockdown, changing our everyday lives for what turned out to be much longer than we initially expected.

At this point, my training was significantly disrupted, but that wasn't important in the grand scheme of things; not important at all. People were dying; others were seriously ill, while doctors, nurses and the wider health professional community battled a virus whose behaviour they were pretty much learning about in real time. Uncertainty bred throughout the nation; throughout the world. Marathons of any sort were no longer a priority and, naturally, any event that involved people congregating in the same place was cancelled. This of course included the 35th edition of the Marathon des Sables, which was scheduled to take place in April 2020, less than a month after lockdown was enforced. My priority at that time was to protect myself and my family, especially Dionne. Her disability may have meant she was more vulnerable but, due to the nature of the situation, we weren't sure if that was true and if it was, to what extent.

April 2021 was still a long way off though; over a year at that point, so I was hopeful that COVID-19 would be a thing of the past by then and that the 35th edition would go ahead as planned. It was a minor setback. I would have to up the intensity of my training once I was allowed more than one hour of exercise per day, but I was up for that. All it did was make the challenge that little bit more challenging.

However, as you'll know, COVID-19 outstayed its welcome, causing no end of devastation to people's lives and careers. By the end of 2020, things hadn't improved, so it was no great surprise that I received notification that the 35th edition of the Marathon des Sables was postponed until further notice. Gutted didn't cut it. I'd received a tremendous, overwhelming amount of support through sponsorship, but there was nothing I could do. It's not that I was surprised, just massively disappointed. The world was still closed, so it follows that a sporting event, fund generating for charity or otherwise, would not be honoured any exemption.

There are proverbs out there, some of them religious in their tone or intention, that say – and I'm paraphrasing – that bad things can present new opportunities; that light can be drawn from dark; that the unfortunate or inconceivable can encourage fresh thought and new perspective. As the streets remained emptier than usual, the cogs in my head were turning and before long, I had a Plan B.

ONE HUNDRED MILES

Since the Marathon des Sables had been postponed and it being anybody's guess when it'd be rescheduled for (if at all), I felt I had to do something to keep me focussed and to maintain my commitment to raising funds for Reverse Rett. It had to be something more challenging than an Ironman but not as challenging as the Marathon des Sables. I needed something that would sit between the two and generate a bit of interest from the public and press. With this brief in mind, I did a bit of thinking and decided that a 24-hour or less 100-mile* run between the four football grounds I'd spent my career fit the bill.

Starting in Perth and finishing in Kilmarnock, with Paisley and Motherwell in-between, I worked out it'd entail 5,500 feet of incline. This, combined with the challenge of completing it in a single day, led me to become a little concerned. It was almost four marathons back-to-back! That concern was short-lived though, quashed by reminding myself that if it was easy, there'd be no point in doing it.

With plans in place and publicity building, I was raring to go, but COVID-19 once again had different ideas. Due to cases remaining high in Greater Glasgow and Clyde, the Scottish Government announced that the level classification would continue to be at a higher level

---

* 160.9km

than most of the rest of the country, meaning it wouldn't be possible for me to run through the city to get from Motherwell to Paisley. Regrettably, this meant that I had to change my plans and miss St Mirren out, which was really disappointing, but I managed to find a way of maintaining the integrity of the challenge and keeping it a 100-mile road race.

Bending to the cards I'd been dealt, I mapped out a route from Perth to Motherwell and then on to Kilmarnock, which left me 12 miles[*] shy of 100. To make up this shortfall, I included a lap of Strathclyde Park and a few extra streets in Kilmarnock. I was sorted.

When the day came, the support I received was incredible, so much so that I never ran a single step of those 100 miles alone. There were loads of people with me at the start, including Andy and Rachael Stevenson from Reverse Rett, and Kevin McGowne, who did about 70 miles[†] alongside me on the bike. At times, it looked like the race was tougher on Kev than it was on me, because the bike he was riding was too small for him and he was only wearing a t-shirt, a pair of football shorts and a pair of trainers. Football shorts don't have the extra padding cycle shorts have, so he ended up pretty uncomfortable, suffering from chaffing as well as muscle strain due to being too big for the bike.

My support crew was made up of Monica and my daughter, Nicole, who drove a van the whole distance, providing me with food and water when it was needed. The stuff I ate on the way started off reasonably healthy: bananas, peanut butter sandwiches and oat bars to give me slow release energy. That all went out the window later on though, when all I yearned for was fuel in its

---

[*] 19.3km
[†] 112.7km

basic form, which came in the shape of a KFC and 12 Krispy Kreme doughnuts! Not exactly the finest cuisine, but they served their purpose and kept me going.

One of the (many) things I thought about during the run was the literature I'd read saying that a 100-miler should not be attempted unless you've got four or five 50-milers[*] under your belt. The most I had run in one sitting was 32 miles[†], and I'd only done that once – so a little bit of concern started creeping in. Sometimes running is a peaceful, cleansing and revitalising activity; being out in the fresh air, getting the heart rate up and feeling the breeze on your face can allow for periods of reflection, contemplation and contentment. On the flipside though, it can also be a time where your brain talks to you a bit too much, which can lead to self-doubt or negative thinking. I'm not someone who lets the latter happen very much though.

Any time I feel negative thought creeping in, I make a point of putting a stop to it, catching it in time before it manifests into anything that might impact my focus or mood. As I continued to run, I told myself that those articles were just that: articles. Published material that contained recommendations – but recommendations from what? There must be loads of variables, like age, gender, fitness level, background, occupation, genetics, maybe even blood type, skin type, height, cultural heritage, and so on. If I was Thomas Edison and the articles were suggesting that 150 was the maximum number of times a human being should attempt to make a light bulb, would I accept that and throw in the towel? No, I'd try to prove them wrong. In fact, it'd give me more determination to do just that. So, while I'm sure

[*] 80.5km
[†] 51.5km

those running articles weren't based on nothing, I decided to disregard them as assumed truths and use them positively to sharpen my focus and strengthen my resolve. I turned red, negative thinking into green, positive thinking and, as I gulped down a mouthful of chocolate-glazed doughnut, I swore I felt myself increase in speed a little bit.

Another positive I had running with me, albeit not in person, was the training regime I'd been following from Rory Coleman, someone who had completed the Marathon des Sables an astounding 15 times. Long before I'd gone for broke and committed to it through signing up and paying the fee, I'd sought Rory out because I knew he knew everything there was to know about the race. Although based in Wales, he emailed me heaps of stuff and we spoke regularly via videocall, where he imparted invaluable advice on all things running. It was, of course, with the Marathon des Sables in mind, but many of the same principles apply to any form of long-distance running, of which my ambitious 100-miler was one.

Rory's programme facilitated my physical training, but he also advised me on what food I should eat and the basic kit I should carry on my person. This advice was for the Marathon des Sables, but it was equally as useful for the 100-miler. One thing was for sure, though – in the desert, I wouldn't have Kevin McGowne cycling alongside me or my wife and daughter following me in a van!

During those times of great uncertainty, when no-one had any idea how long COVID-19 was going to hang around for, or how extensive its destructive hold would be, I signed up for an online counselling diploma. I was conscious of how fragile some people had become, not necessarily physically, but mentally. We are social animals after all, designed to interact and move rather than be confined to specific spaces, sitting on our backsides, denied interaction with other members of our race. The uncertainty about everything was leading to increases in anxiety, depression and a general decline in mental health. I wanted to protect myself – and those dear to me – from these forces as much as I could. I'd always considered myself as someone with mental strength, but no-one predicted how extensive and crippling COVID-19 would be on an international scale. The course helped me maintain my mental strength, but also educated me on how to recognise and respond to the mental health needs of others. I've always been fascinated in the power of the mind and how even the slightest shift in mindset and change in habits can make such an incredible difference. I'd read a number of books on self-development, self-improvement and life coaching, so it was worthwhile taking all of that, adding to it and gaining a qualification. It was a suitable and useful distraction to what was going on elsewhere.

So, with my mind in the right place and the physical training side of things aligning with someone who had done the Marathon des Sables 15 times, you might be thinking that my 100-mile run was just a formality. I wish I could say it was, but that'd be a big lie. I enjoyed it and was pleased I had decided to do it, but it was incredibly tough. Humans are built to move, but I'm not sure the design extends to 23 hours of near constant running. In football, you change direction regularly, working different muscle groups. There are short, sharp bursts of acceleration, jogging, walking, jumping, sidestepping, and occasional moments of standing still. With the 100-miler, it was relentless pounding of the same muscle group, which in time became a form of mild torture, especially given the route was often hilly and the terrain was a mix of tarmac roads, hills and, at one point, a dual carriageway.

Naturally, once I got to the time when it was becoming dark, my body told me it was time to stop and rest, rather than continuing to run through the night when I should be fast asleep. There are studies out there that talk about the damage that can be caused doing physical exercise at night when the body and mind should be repairing, recuperating and resetting itself for the coming day. This period was one of the toughest. It was very much a case of mind over matter, my mind convincing my body that it not only *should* continue running, but it *had* to. This point was the crossover between it being a predominantly physical challenge to a mental one. This is where the self-help, motivation and mindset stuff really kicked in. People are capable of pushing themselves physically, but can end up giving up due to the mental side.

When I was toiling, one of the things I avoided was asking questions like 'How long to go?' or 'How much have I done?' Questions like that can easily lead to the beginning of a downward spiral, resulting in the challenge being aborted. I was determined not to let this happen to me. Of course, by saying to myself, *Don't think about how long you've got to go*, it's a bit like telling myself not to think about a purple and yellow zebra. To stave off the temptation, I kept my focus on the next lamppost. There are many proverbs and sayings that reference any journey of length beginning with one small step. Sure, 100 miles was a long, long way, but every lamppost I reached was another step towards achieving my goal.

You're not running 100 miles, Mavis, I said to myself. *You're only running to the next lamppost. You'll manage that, no bother.*

During the entire route, I only stopped twice, once at the Falkirk Stadium and once at Fir Park in Motherwell, each stop an hour long. It was necessary to recharge the batteries, but there were people there too, so it gave me an opportunity to chat to them and thank them for their support. Again, the mental side of the challenge kicked in when it was time to recommence after an hour's break. It would have been tempting to just jump in the van with Monica and Nicole and head off to my bed, but I had briefed myself to instantly terminate any thoughts of that nature.

Despite those two one-hour breaks, I completed the challenge in 23 hours and one minute, which I was absolutely delighted with. Mind and body had come together to allow me to achieve something the articles and books I'd read suggested wasn't possible. Not that it was my focus, but I'd thrown those stats back in their faces, attracted a little bit of media hype, prepped myself further for the Marathon des Sables and, most importantly, raised more awareness and funds for Reverse Rett. The whole experience gave me great confidence, despite the fact that what was waiting for me in the future made the 100-miler seem like a 5k* park run.

When the COVID-19 restrictions were eased further, I received the good news that the 35th edition of the Marathon des Sables had been rescheduled and was due to go ahead in October 2021. It was news I very much welcomed as it meant I had a new target. Motivation can sometimes waver if there's no set target. I certainly wasn't going to hold back with my training, but the new

---

* 3.1 miles

date gave me something to focus on. Rory Coleman put together detailed training plans that I could fit around my work and Dionne. This meant I was running between 70 and 100 miles* per week. It would occasionally vary, but my general weekly routine consisted of a 10k† on Monday, 14 miles‡ on Tuesday, seven§ on Wednesday and another 14 on Thursday. I dubbed Tuesdays and Thursdays my double days, running seven miles before work and seven after. On the weekends I didn't have Dionne, I'd do six miles‖ on a Friday and then tank it on a Saturday and Sunday, each day doing a minimum of a half marathon and sometimes as much as 30 miles¶.

As I've always loved running, I didn't consider any of my training a hardship as such, but there were times when I couldn't be bothered. I am only human after all, so it was romantic to assume that my early morning runs, which meant the alarm going off at 5am, always consisted of me leaping out of bed, clicking my heels, clapping my hands and singing 'Reach' by S Club 7. That's not to say there weren't mornings like that. Sometimes I'd have unadulterated enthusiasm and the boundless energy of a five-year-old on Christmas morning. In contrast, on other mornings, all I wanted to do was smash my alarm clock with a hammer, pull the duvet over my head and pretend there was no such thing as Rory Coleman or a marathon in the Sahara that went on for days.

The mornings I felt like staying in bed were because my body was telling me it hadn't had sufficient recovery

---

* Between 112.5 and 160.9km
† 6.2 miles
‡ 22.5km
§ 11.3km
‖ 9.7km
¶ 48.3km

time. I still got up and did what I had to do, despite feeling lethargic, but it was important I listened to my body. I had been doing the graft but wasn't giving enough consideration to recovery, which of course is exceptionally important. I put this down to running too fast when I first started Rory's training programme. Not only did I feel like I wasn't recovering in time, but I was also picking up minor injuries and niggles. Having been an athlete in some shape or form for so long, I knew that a niggle could develop into something more if it wasn't acknowledged and dealt with. Many a runner has ignored a niggling knee because it's not something debilitating, but often it's the body sending a message about the beginning of something that – if you don't do something about it – could end up being a major issue, sometimes to the extent of meaning that running is off the cards.

So, I slowed my pace. Covering the miles safely was more important than covering them quickly. No pun intended, but it was a marathon, not a race. It was important to protect and look after myself. No-one was bothered one way or the other if I was running super-fast before 6am on a Wednesday morning. My change in approach worked and the niggles began to abate and eventually disappeared. This, in turn, increased my motivation to get up, especially on rainy or cold mornings, and get out there.

After a while, it just became a habit, and whether I was oozing verve and gusto or fancying a few hours more kip, my legs hit the carpet automatically and off I'd go. As time went by, these runs, sometimes at what some people would call unsociable hours, became almost addictive. A lust for the release of those feel-good endorphins I'd get after each and every training session, whether six or 30 miles, and the satisfaction and sense of achievement that I'd done it rather than drink tea and watch telly. It became a daily buzz, meaning even if it was raining and cold, my niggle-free body began not only to look forward to it, but to crave it.

SKY BLUE ENERGY

As the months passed, my fitness and endurance continued to increase as October 2021 edged ever closer. Regardless of how much training I'd done though, or how fit I felt, I had to pass a medical within 30 days of the event, which, as well as getting an electrocardiograph (ECG) to make sure my heart health was suitable, involved my blood pressure being taken. I was a bit worried about this because, on and off over the years, I've had high blood pressure. This had nothing to do with my circumstances, stress levels or my football career, it was purely genetic, hence the concern. If I failed the medical, I wouldn't be allowed to compete and all the training and preparation I'd done would be for nothing. Well, maybe not nothing as I was in the shape of my life, but I would be gutted if the rug was pulled out from under me purely because of genetic blood pressure levels. Unfortunately, when the day of the medical came, I'd had a crazy-busy day at work and ended up finishing late, meaning I was rushing to make my appointment in time. I turned up about five minutes late, flustered and apologetic, not exactly a state associated with low blood pressure.

My luck was in though; the nurse wasn't irked by my lateness and accepted my apology – and reason – with a smile. Once I got myself settled, I then explained the reason for the medical and my concerns about my blood pressure. Seasoned when it comes to these things, she listened to my concerns and responded by talking about mindfulness. It was a relief to hear that word come out of her mouth as it confirmed to me that she appreciated and understood the link between mindset and physiology. She gave me time to sit and breathe and then gave me a technique to help me relax more and, hopefully, bring my blood pressure down. It was a straightforward technique that entailed closing my eyes and putting myself in a situation, preferably a recent one, where I've felt completely relaxed.

After a few minutes of carrying out the exercise, she took my blood pressure, which registered as 157/95! This wasn't good. Ideally, it should 120/80, so I was a fair bit off. At that very moment, there was no Marathon des Sables for Mavis Reilly and the first thing that popped into my head was how disappointed I'd be for Dionne and the good people at Reverse Rett. I took a few deep breaths and had a word with myself. I had successfully employed mind over matter techniques in my football career, in my 100-mile run, and in my training for the Marathon des Sables up to this point. I paid attention to my breathing and focussed on positive thought, bits of self-help stuff I'd read over the years fluttering through my mind. I had to get this under control and I convinced myself I had the power to do just that.

I asked the nurse if it'd be okay if I went away for ten minutes to practice her technique. Graciously, she agreed, so I took myself off to a quiet place in the clinic, knowing that the following ten minutes would be instrumental in terms of what my short-term future looked like. It was critical not to focus on the possible consequences and instead to employ mindfulness, concentrate on my breathing and think of something that relaxed me. A month earlier, Monica and I had been on holiday in Croatia, so I closed my eyes and thought about watching the sunset from the balcony of our hotel room. Following this, I employed another technique, which involves, for a count seven, breathing in a colour that represents positive energy and calmness, and then, for a count of 11, breathing out a colour that represents negativity and tension.

Sky blue is my positive colour, so I imagined filling my body with this blue, positive energy. I then breathed out a murky cloud of dark brown, part of which was made up of my genetic high blood pressure. I repeated this a number of times, sometimes combining it with my memory of Croatia and the feelings of contentment and serenity that sunset ignited. After about eight minutes, I headed back to the nurse's room to have my blood pressure retaken, continuing the techniques as she strapped on the equipment. It recorded 127/75, which was a marked improvement on the first reading and meant I had passed the medical. I let out a long sigh of relief, clear in the room but dark brown in my mind's eye. I was good to go!

With only a month before I set off for the Sahara, the next priority was sorting out my kit. This consisted of a backpack, a compass, a head torch plus spare batteries, a Swiss army knife, disinfectant, 200 Euros, a survival sheet and an anti-venom pump in case of a snake or scorpion bite. Gulp! You might be wondering – what good is 200 Euros is to anyone in the middle of the Sahara? And if I'm honest, I don't have an answer, but it was on the list of essentials, so I had to make sure they were there.

Rory recommended that I travel as light as possible, one reason being that I'm not that big a guy, coming in at 5ft 8 inches and 10.5 stone. It made sense – why weigh myself down with stuff I'm unlikely to need. I had planned on taking two pairs of trainers, but trainers take up a bit of space and I thought it was unlikely that I'd go through a full pair in a week, so I left the spare pair in my suitcase. To protect my one and only pair, I sent them off to a cobblers in London to have Velcro attached to them. This was so I could attach Desert Gaiters to them, which are covers that help keep sand out, minimising blisters. I still got blisters, but that was down to the amount of running rather than sand. I took only three pairs of socks, changing them once every few days. They were Injinji socks though, so essentially gloves for your feet, a section for each individual toe. Like the Desert Gaiters, they're designed to reduce blistering, emphasis on the word reduce rather than prevent. I can only wonder what kind of condition my feet would have been in if it wasn't for the Desert Gaiters and the Injinji socks, because at times it felt like even my blisters had blisters!

Rory also recommended that I wear black clothing, which came as a surprise, given the common belief that white clothing is better for staying cooler because it reflects the sun rather than absorbs it. Rory informed me that while light colours do reflect the sun, it's then reflected back onto your skin. I wasn't sure of the science behind it all, but I had no reason to contest it. After all, the Bedouin tribes, who spend almost all of their time in the desert, wear black, loose-fitting robes. They've had generations of exposure to the relentless desert sun, so there are no people better placed to make the call as to the most suitable colour to wear to keep core body temperature as low as possible. With no need to check or challenge, I went out and bought myself a black top I could split peas through, as well as a pair of black compression shorts designed to minimise chafing. Rory was advising from a position of experience, so it was important to listen to him in order to maximise comfort and minimise discomfort as much as possible.

Sunscreen was an essential. As a wee, Scottish bald guy, an industrial factor was required to protect my peely-wally complexion. I also packed obvious things like a small toothbrush and a mini tube of toothpaste, as well as wipes that I could douse in water and re-use to wash myself. Again, to minimise friction and chafing, I packed tape so I could tape up my shoulders and back so my backpack wasn't rubbing on my skin through my super-thin black top.

As far as food was concerned, there was a limit to the amount that could be taken, but each competitor had to ensure they had a minimum of 2000 calories per day. I packed a little bit more than that, as it seemed low. It wasn't loads more though, probably about 500 calories or thereabouts per day – well, that was until the stomach bug hit, which changed the landscape considerably. It was important to consider the type of food to take though, especially since it was fueling my body to carry out a task so alien to anything it had carried out before. On a typical day – before the stomach bug took hold – my supplies would typically consist of a protein bar, some granola, two energy gels, a packet of fruit pastilles, 60g of macadamia nuts, some beef jerky and two recovery shakes.

After checking my medical certificate, ECG and insurance were all in place – and going to great lengths to ensure I had all the necessary COVID-19 documentation – I was ready to go. I checked my kit about a dozen times, constantly questioning if I had everything I needed, but simultaneously making sure I wasn't taking anything I didn't need. It wasn't a trip for surplus; if something didn't serve a purpose, it had no place in my kit.

I class myself as a bit of a home bird so, in the build up to leaving, I had a lump in my throat. This was going to be the first time in my life that I'd be away from my family for any length of time. That was difficult to get my head around, especially since I'd have no way of contacting them. It's not like I could sit down on the sand, crack open a cold beer and send everyone updates via WhatsApp or Facebook. I was going to a place as far removed from Uddingston as anyone could imagine. No town centre or main strip, only sand as far as the eye could see; a largely unchanging landscape for mile after mile. I was up for the challenge, but being cut off from everyone important to me was emotionally taxing, especially the thought of seeing Dionne for the final time before leaving.

It's hard to know for certain, but I doubt she had any true understanding of what I was about to do. Not that that stopped me from telling her, of course. Part of me believes that she understands me fully, taking everything in and processing it no differently to any other member of my family, the only difference being that she can't show that understanding because of her impaired ability to communicate. Every time I spoke about what I was going to be doing in the Sahara, she looked at me, giving me her full attention, recognising me as her dad. If she understood, I hope she was as excited as I was at taking on the biggest challenge of my life, driven by my desire to make her life better.

Before departing for the Sahara, I knew the names of the guys I'd be sharing a tent with, because requesting tentmates in advance was allowed. I'd never met any of them before, but had picked them exclusively on the basis that they'd also trained under Rory Coleman. So we could get to know each other a bit, we decided to meet up for dinner at the airport hotel the night before flying out to Morocco. This came off the back of setting up a WhatsApp group a few days before departure, a modern day convenience soon to be taken away from us.

Meeting up for a bite to eat helped me a lot. As we ate and chatted, it transpired that none of us had done the Marathon des Sables before, despite everyone having taken on fairly major challenges. These, of course, were all training days for the biggie we were about to embrace, all as keen as mustard. Apart from Matt, who was 46 and had completed 19 Ironman events, we were all in our 50s. Six Englishmen, a Welshman and a Scotsman sitting round a table, which sounds like the start of a naff joke, but as we were about to find out, the joke ended there. The oldest member of the group, John, was 59 and had worked with England Athletics before taking early retirement. No stranger to long-distance running, his marathon personal best was an impressive three hours and nine minutes. The rest of the English contingent was made up of Mark, Chris, Terry, Matt and Aiden, with Sean as the solo Welshman and me as the solo Scot.

The banter flowed as we all got to know each other and I remember feeling a great sense of relief that the camaraderie was as instant as it was effortless. I was going to be sharing an incredible experience with these guys, a group whose collective age was likely higher than that of any of the other 86 tents that would soon be pitched in the desert. The hell we were about to expose ourselves to would've been all the more hellish if there were personality clashes in the group, or a sole idiot mouthing off and causing hassle. During that meal, there were plenty of laughs and daft stories, each story a glue that helped us bond. Once the meal was over, I felt like I'd known my future tentmates for much longer than a few hours. There was great comfort in knowing there would be no friction and that we all had each other's backs.

The camaraderie continued on the chartered flight to Morocco, but it's not as if the good vibes existed exclusively in our group; the whole plane was buzzing. There wasn't a kid in sight, but the atmosphere was akin to a soft play area on Christmas Eve.

Then, when we arrived at Errachidia Airport, we got our first taste of the heat we would be fighting against in the coming week. I didn't find out the exact temperature, but it was incredibly hot, like nothing I had ever experienced before. Sweating, we were bundled onto a coach and driven into the desert, arriving late Friday afternoon, ahead of the Sunday start.

We were camped in a Bivouac, the name given for a temporary encampment. Our tent was number 54, which was apt since it was representative of our average age. It was also easy to pick out from the rest due to the Welsh flag Sean had pinned to the top of it. This went down like a lead balloon with the English contingency (in a jocular sense) as none of them had thought to pack a Saint George's Cross. I hadn't thought to pack a Saltire either, but I thought the starkness of the red dragon of Wales was the most suitable for what we were about to take on. Dragons breathe fire, and it felt like there were hundreds of them in the sky, breathing fire down upon us. On a more positive note though, a dragon is strong, a force to be reckoned with, a mythical beast representing power, strength and dominance. These were traits we'd need for the race, so the Welsh flag aligned with this far better than a couple of crosses.

Our tent was basically a black canvas sheet held up with sticks that looked like branches, and held down with rocks. Low and wide to accommodate the eight bodies, it wasn't possible to stand up in – or not fully, even for someone short like me. Speaking of that, because I was the shortest, I ended up in the corner, closest to the hostile conditions on the other side of the canvas. Getting in and out of my space involved crawling, ensuring I avoided sticking a knee into anyone in my path.

The following day, the Marathon des Sables organisers fed us lunch and later dinner, our last supper before the race. We had Moroccan stew, which was tasty, but a few folk later raised concerns about the salad it was served with, suspicious that it could have been responsible for the stomach bug. In such high temperatures, the shelf life of salad must be significantly reduced, but I wasn't convinced it was at fault. It's not like the lettuce was brown or acrid, plus I'd had a headache for at least 24 hours by that point, so it was more likely that the bug made its first appearance on the flight or in one of the airports.

After all the admin stuff was taken care of, we were each given an SOS button in case we ran into difficulties, and allocated a race number, 710 in my case. While Sean and I were standing in the queue to get all this done, I was already feeling exhausted, despite not having run a single step of the race yet. I'd had interrupted sleep the previous night, which didn't help, but the main distraction was the heat. It was 50 degrees Celsius*, 20

* 122 Fahrenheit

degrees[†] higher than the average temperature in April, which is when the Marathon des Sables usually takes place. You might be wondering if October is traditionally hotter than April in Morocco, but that's not the case. Whilst the temperatures are never as low as what you'd expect in the UK in October, they are usually lower than April, so it goes to show just how uncharacteristically extreme the temperatures were for that time of year. Despite sweat pouring down my face, I managed to laugh it off, imagining the world specifically selected 2020 and 2021 to have a great big strop and punish its inhabitants for mistreating it over the preceding couple of thousand years.

My laugh didn't last for long though, thanks to my stomach doing cartwheels, the bug taking its toll. The headache I'd had since Friday, which I'd done my best to ignore, had progressed into nausea and then the runs, so I knew something wasn't right. Combining this with the absurd temperatures, I was struggling. It was a blow. Struggling at this stage was never in the script. All I was doing was the necessary preliminaries and standing about chatting. If I was finding that taxing, how was I going to fare running in the desert? I had to stay positive though, so I kept chatting away to Sean and looking for other things to distract myself from what was going on in my insides.

One welcome distraction came in the shape of Kevin Webber, the guy standing in front of Sean and me in the queue. We got chatting to him and learned that, six years ago, he'd been diagnosed with stage four prostate cancer and given two years to live! He'd defied all medical advice and had doctors and other health professionals scratching their heads. This alone was a triumph, but the

---

† 68 Fahrenheit

fact he had already run and completed the Marathon des Sables five times in that period was utterly astounding. Sean and I looked at each other, mouths agape. This was someone who – according to the medical world – should be dead, never mind queuing up to run the hardest footrace in the world for the sixth time. As we chatted, my stomach bug was still causing me discomfort, but if Kevin could run for nearly a week in the Sahara with stage four prostate cancer, surely I could manage it with a stomach bug. I kept telling myself that story and it helped take the focus off the bug and the heat and place it back where it belonged: on the race and Dionne.

Throughout my football career, I played numerous matches either injured or not feeling particularly great. I got through them though, and sometimes the intensity of the match and the job at hand took the focus away from my injury so much that I forgot it was there. I was hopeful I could do the same thing with the Marathon des Sables. Okay, it was going to last much longer than 90 minutes plus stoppage time, but I was hopeful the same principles would apply. There was no point worrying about it, that was for sure. I just had to take the cards I had been dealt and do my best.

Once everyone in our tent had had all their admin processed and race numbers allocated, we spent the rest of the day dodging the sun as much as we possibly could. Usually when British people go to sunny places, whether for business or pleasure, they seek out the sun and bask in its rays, a tan being the goal. In stark contrast, all we wanted at that stage was to keep out of it. We knew there would be no escape once the race was underway, so we took the opportunity to protect ourselves from it while we could.

For a little while, there was a slightly strange atmosphere in the tent. We'd all trained really hard for what we were about to take on, so we just wanted to get on with it. If it wasn't for the bug, it'd probably be impatience and nervous excitement, but the bug had added concern into that mix. I kept thinking about Kevin Webber though, and Dionne, the reason I was here in the first place, to stave off any negativity. My body was about to be put through the mill, so it was critical that I kept my mind strong and cancelled out any negativity with positive thinking.

The atmosphere lightened quickly when one of my tentmates, Matt, started telling funny stories, the best one being the night he got blind drunk on a night out in London and bought a donkey off a traveller.

'It seemed like a good idea at the time!' he laughed. 'Until I realised I was responsible for it and had to take it home.'

'What did you do?' I asked. 'Did you take it home?'

'I did, but I didn't live close to where I'd bought it, so I had to take it on the tube!'

The tent erupted in fits of laughter. It was unbelievable that he even managed to get it on the tube. Dogs aren't allowed on underground trains, so how he managed to get a donkey on board is anyone's guess.

'Somehow, I managed to get off at the right stop and stagger my way home,' Matt continued 'attracting plenty of looks on the way of course. When I got to my front door, I couldn't find my keys, so I knocked on the door. Needless to say, my wife were berserk and it was made clear that the newest addition to the family was not welcome!'

Again, laughter filled the tent, seven heads shaking with disbelief.

'What did folk say on the tube?' Sean asked.

'You've obviously not been to London much, mate,' Matt chuckled. 'Nobody speaks to each other on the tube, whether they've got a donkey or not!'

The laughs kept coming as more stories were shared, despite none eclipsing Matt's donkey story. Ever the tonic, the laughter helped us channel our nervous excitement in a positive way and took our minds off the furnace-like temperatures and the stomach bug that was doing its best to tear through the camp.

Later on, when I settled down for the night, I thought about Monica and Dionne. It was a wrench to be away from them, but in a way I was looking forward to being on my own out there in the desert. I had challenged myself in many ways over the years, but I was intrigued by the challenge of solitude the Marathon des Sables would offer me, almost as much as the running aspect.

How would I cope being alone, with no way of making contact with any of my loved ones? It was a fascinating concept. In the modern day, so many people are reliant on their devices, to the extent that they freak out if they misplace, lose or break them. For days, I was going to have none of these conveniences. No mobile phone; no computer; no car. It was me and whatever nature decided to throw at me. This might not sound particularly appealing, but appealing was exactly how I felt about it at that point in time. In theory, we are in control of our devices, free to break away from them whenever we wish, but as time passes and technology progresses, them controlling us is becoming more and more the reality. Taking on the Marathon des Sables meant forced separation and – for me – there was a fair degree of relief in that.

Having said that, text messages of support do help spur me on, especially if I'm lagging – but instead of receiving them, I'd just have to think about the messages I'd received prior to arrival. I'd fed off that need for purpose in the past, but this time, there'd be a total disconnect. It applied to every competitor of course, so while I'd be alone in the desert, I'd never be truly alone.

Mind buzzing, it was difficult to fall asleep and when it came, it was fitful and short-lived. Before I knew it, the blazing sun was up and the day I'd been looking forward to for years had finally arrived.

BECAUSE I CAN

As you would expect, before signing up for the Marathon des Sables, I had a look at their website. Underneath the heading 'An Extraordinary Race for Extraordinary People in an Extraordinary Place' a number of questions were posed, including 'Who could you be if you pushed yourself to your limits?' I was fascinated by this question. It suggested that taking on the Marathon des Sables and giving it 100 percent could lead to becoming a different person – a stronger, fitter, more resilient and more defiant individual, rewarded with new powers like a character from a video game.

Some of the blurb made me think of video games: 'multi-stage adventure', 'the stuff of legends', 'the ultimate challenge' and 'an experience like no other'. It was like I was going to be a Scottish, male version of Lara Croft, but instead of someone else controlling me, I'd be in full control of myself. Another part of the promotional blurb mentioned 'endless sand dunes', which isn't possible as they'd have to come to an end at some point – but those words were chosen for a reason, as I'd soon find out. My constant companions would be the glaring sun, an abundance of sand, and high temperatures. It sounded intimidating, which I'm sure was the point, but with the pay-off of experiencing 'exhilaration and joy' when crossing the finish line.

There has never been a Marathon des Sables where everyone who began the race has finished it, but I liked that the website – despite being honest about the magnitude of the race – pitched the crossing of the finish line as an achievable feat, given the right attitude and preparation.

My tentmates and I made our way to the inflatable arch that marked the start line in plenty time for the 9am kick-off. I'm not sure the beginning of a marathon isn't regularly referred to as a kick-off, but that's my footballing past sticking with me there. There wouldn't be a referee blowing a whistle on this occasion though, nor would I be having a shower and resting in a couple of hours' time.

Thanks to my mind buzzing, trying to get used to the rocky, uneven ground, and getting up a few times to the toilet thanks to the stomach bug, I wasn't well rested – not by a long shot – but there was nothing I could do about it. There was no going back now. The only way was forward with the sand beneath my feet, and despite the 50-degree temperature and room for improvement in the stomach department, I'd be lying if I said I wasn't excited.

To make things as comfortable for myself as possible, I'd made sure the softer items in my backpack were at the bottom so it'd be easier on my skin when it rubbed against my back. I'd also taped up my back and shoulders to minimise chafing from the straps. These were little things, but it was important to make things as comfortable as possible. I'd decided against taping up my feet, mainly because I didn't get any blisters during my 100-mile run, nor did I get any of any significance during my entire football career. A desert is a different ball game, but I had my Desert Gaiters on, so I reckoned I'd be okay.

Despite my stomach fighting against me, I'd managed to eat some granola for breakfast and keep it down. This may not sound like a major victory, but I was delighted I didn't instantly spew it back up. After all, I was going to need every ounce of energy to get my ill and under-rested body through a day of running in 50-degree heat.

I looked back to where our campsite was. The Berbers (Moroccans who work for the Marathon des Sables) had dismantled all the tents and were in the process of transporting them to where we'd be sleeping at the end of the day. Bizarrely, that helped increase my motivation to ignore the bug as best as I could and not only to get on with the race, but to enjoy it. Our tent wasn't comfy, but it was my bed, and that bed was the reward at the end of this part of the race.

As the minutes ticked down, there was a real carnival atmosphere in the air, which helped keep me focussed on the positives. Although soundless and invisible, I could feel the adrenaline surging through the hundreds of fellow competitors who stood alongside me, eagerly awaiting the sound of the starting klaxon.

The race director, Patrick Bauer, jumped up onto the bonnet of his Land Rover and then onto the roof, microphone in hand. He then proceeded to give a speech in French, which, chunk by chunk, was translated into English. With the translations, his speech was probably about 15 minutes long, but it felt like double that. That's no disrespect to him; his speech was engaging, it was just that my tentmates and I were all eager to get going and hadn't anticipated it lasting as long as it did.

Bauer is an interesting character to say the least. He spends a large proportion of his time working as a music and concert promoter, but has always had a taste for adventure and pushing himself to his limits. Back in the 1980s, this led him to traverse the Sahara on foot, alone, with no support or backup. He covered a remarkable 350km* in only 12 days. This experience planted the seed in his head that would one day become the Marathon des Sables. He'd been there, done it, made it official and was now welcoming us to the 35th version from the top of his Land Rover.

Once he'd finished his speech, 'Highway to Hell' by AC/DC blasted out of the PA. I looked round to see people's reactions. A few were shaking their heads, but most were smiling, laughing or running on the spot, the pounding beat and meaty riffs giving them an extra boost of energy, highlighting the power and influence music can have on physiology. My guess is that 'Highway to Hell' was selected, not just because of its presence and pulse, but also to intimidate or frighten even. It was like it was hitting home the reality of what we'd all signed up for: 156 miles† of running in a sandy furnace! Thinking about it this way, Hell seemed entirely appropriate! Regardless, the song had done its job, because the buzz in that desert on that Sunday morning in October was incredible.

'Here we go,' Sean said, nodding towards Patrick Bauer, who held aloft the starting klaxon. As its piercing sound filled the desert air, I took my first official step of the 35th version of the Marathon des Sables. We were off!

No doubt due to the adrenaline pulsing through them, some people actually started with a sprint. I'm all for healthy living and positive energy, but sprinting at that

---

* 217.5 miles
† 251.1km

stage was lunacy to me, although I must admit that I admired them in some way for their unbridled, almost child-like enthusiasm. The first leg of day one was 32.2km*, so they'd run out of steam soon enough, especially in 50 degree heat.

Our group had started somewhere in the middle of the pack and had vowed to stick together as much as possible. The intention was nice, but we all knew it was likely we'd spread out as the race progressed. We each had our own journeys to complete and our own reasons and motivations for embracing such a challenge.

After a while, I split away from my tentmates and became lost in my own little bubble, running (or jogging/walking) to the beat of my own drum. Despite the stomach bug and the lack of sleep, I managed to get into a decent rhythm. I was enjoying it, taking everything in, occasionally thinking about Dionne and the kindness so many people had shown me through their donations. Every step was for Reverse Rett and Dionne who – even if she desperately wanted to – would never be able to run in the desert, or on any terrain for that matter. I had only been running a short time, and I knew it was going to be tough, but my legs worked, so that was good enough for me.

In 1924, George Mallory was asked by reporters, 'Why would you want to climb Mount Everest?' 'Because it's there,' was his answer. So why would I, retired midfielder Mavis Reilly want to run 156 miles in the Sahara? Because I can.

---

* 20 miles

IMAGINARY LAMPPOSTS

Naturally, my backpack was heavier on day one because I was carrying all the food I'd need for the entire race. It was nice to know that it'd become lighter and rub against me less as the week wore on. As far as route and distance were concerned, day one was known as the most straightforward. Maybe this was to ease competitors in gently, or because the organisers knew it was the day backpacks would be their most full. Regardless, it wasn't gentle – not because of the route or distance, but because of the heat. I'd never experienced anything like it.

The sand dunes on day one were only about 20 feet in height (about six metres). Not to be sniffed at, but I'd heard these were tiny in comparison to what to expect on day two. For me, the height was manageable, but the terrain between each dune was rocky, which was difficult on the feet. I found myself altering my gait, weaving my way round them again as if in a video game, but inevitably I ended up stepping on quite a few rocks, which didn't do my feet any favours. If there was one part of me that I wanted to keep in as good a condition as possible, it was my feet. They're pretty much an essential part of any marathon!

Prior to the sound of the starting klaxon, I'd had a chat with myself and decided I would run as much of day one as possible. I maybe wouldn't use the word 'run' to describe what I ended up doing, but it could certainly be called a steady, consistent jog. It was this that helped me get into a decent rhythm and enjoy what I was doing. In training, and when I was doing the Ironman events and the 100-miler, there were periods – sometimes extensive periods – when I'd be on automatic pilot. It's a great place to be when that kicks in. There are more detailed theories about this phenomenon, often referred to as 'flow'. I see it as a state where rhythm and contentment combine, where no thought, focus or concentration need be expended to keep the engine running. In some ways it's like driving a car without paying any attention to the actions being performed to keep the vehicle moving forward. It's a feeling of great control, where unconscious competence is at play, making whatever task is being carried out seem effortless.

Because of the rocky terrain between the dunes, I wouldn't say I was experiencing full unconscious competence, but it wasn't far away. Flow was also helping me ignore – at least to an extent – what was going on in my stomach, in turn allowing me to keep up momentum.

As I continued pounding the alternate sandy and rocky terrain beneath me, a small village came into sight. This might sound like an exaggeration, but it was the most bizarre thing I've ever encountered. This was the Sahara, a vast and desolate desert, not in any way suitable for human habitat. It was as if this little Bedouin village, made up exclusively of huts, had been lifted from somewhere in civilisation by a massive crane and dropped in the middle of the Sahara. There were kids running about playing, chasing each other and laughing. All I could wonder was – how do these people survive? They can't grow any food out here and their huts wouldn't have any plumbing, electricity or any other amenities we all take for granted. I could only assume that they had some form of access to water, an exceptionally deep well maybe, or something similar.

A couple of kids came up to me and asked for food. It was a horrible situation, because while I really wanted to give them something to eat, I had only packed the bare minimum for my own survival and to keep my backpack as light as possible. Like a cartoonish oversized hammer to my face, it brought home how fortunate I was to live in a developed country with all the essentials at my disposal, alongside many other conveniences and umpteen luxuries. These kids asking for food was ripping my heart out, but there was nothing I could do other than use non-verbal communication to reject them and keep on jogging.

As I jogged on, I wondered what the people of the village did with their time, other than merely try to survive. They had absolutely nothing. Our kids get stimulated all day at school, with further stimulation when they come home and at weekends, via clubs, organisations, sports, TV, games consoles, shopping, cinema, dancing . . . the list goes on. None of these things were available in the middle of the desert. These kids would have to rely on home schooling, irregular food supplies and making their own entertainment. As the distance between the village and me grew larger, I wondered how far the fee I'd paid to enter the Marathon des Sables would go in providing them with a bit more infrastructure and comfort. Thoughts of those kids stuck with me for the duration of day one. They spurred me on, and made me grateful for what I had and the opportunities living where I lived had presented me.

Eleven kilometres* into day one, I reached the first checkpoint. I was given a 1.5 litre bottle of water with my race number on it. A tab on the back of my backpack was also stamped by means of receipt for the water. This was to help protect the environment, ensuring that runners didn't litter the desert with empty water bottles. If anyone did, the support crew could trace it back to the culprit, a time penalty being the punishment. Whilst this system might sound a bit nanny state, I was all in favour of it. The organisers had a responsibility to leave the desert as they found it and to recycle all plastics after use. It would be great if the same approach was taken in the UK as, despite being a developed and powerful country, litter and fly tipping is a national problem. During my football career, I visited many towns in the UK and, in contrast to abroad, the amount of litter on the streets is staggering. It's an odd situation because there are plenty of bins. There will be some sort of explanation or psychological reasoning for it, but if it's something Moroccans can do effortlessly, it begs the question, why can't we?

Because of the scorching heat, the support crew and medical staff at the checkpoint gave runners the option of resting up in the shade for a while. It was certainly tempting, but – mainly because it was the first checkpoint of many – I decided to keep going. I'm not sure if that was the right decision or not, because once I got to the second checkpoint, at 21km†, I felt like couldn't run another step. Unfortunately, my flow had gradually eroded between the checkpoints, not because of ability or mindset, purely because of the temperature.

---

* 6.8 miles
† 13 miles

After checkpoint two, it became increasingly apparent that the human body – or certainly this human body – was not equipped to run in such heat. For fear of heat exhaustion, cramp and/or collapsing, walking was my only option. There was no requirement to run, nor were there any limits to how many breaks could be taken. However, support crew led two camels through the various stages of the race and the rule was, if the camels pass you, you're disqualified. This worked well on two counts. It ensured people didn't end up stranded in the desert after taking too long a break or collapsing, and it was an incentive to keep going. Although the camels merely plodded through the desert, there was always that feeling that something was giving chase and that it was important to keep as much desert between them as possible. After checkpoint two, I was aware that there was already considerable distance between me and the camels, so as long my walking pace was equal to that of the average desert camel, there was nothing to be concerned about.

As I padded forward, my Gaiters shuffling in the sand, I did my best to be positive, but other than the heat, there was something else doing its best to compromise that: the stomach bug. I had done well to ignore it as much as possible between the start line and the first two checkpoints, but things had deteriorated in that department and I could feel myself becoming light-headed and disorientated. I checked the temperature. It was 56 degrees Celsius*. I trudged on, one foot in front of the other. It was all I could do.

I point blank refused to let doubt penetrate my mind. There was a little negative voice in there reminding me that this was only the start of the journey and that

---

* 133 Fahrenheit

there'd be the best part of a week of this suffering to follow. The voice was weak though, pathetic sounding, and I wanted nothing to do with it, so I locked it up in a box in my mind and threw away the key. As messages continued to be sent from my brain to my muscles to propel me forward, I thought back to my 100-mile run between the football clubs I'd played for, and brought the lamppost analogy to the forefront of my mind. Imaginary lampposts were created and I shuffled my way from one to the next, completion of day one being the eventual reward.

Jogging the first two thirds allowed me to complete day one in four hours and 34 minutes, which, given the circumstances, was actually pretty good. The relief was immense, because I was feeling incredibly ropey. A few guys I had spoken to prior to the beginning of the race had mentioned that they'd done heat acclimatisation in preparation for the desert. Stupidly, I hadn't, although I was in Croatia about a month beforehand, where the highest temperature was 37 degrees Celsius[*] and I'd been perfectly fine. I'd assumed the Sahara in October would be roughly the same, but of course I was completely wrong. I never expected it to be almost 20 degrees[†] higher, but then again no-one had. I was only at the end of the first day and already it was the hottest Marathon des Sables on record.

I made my way to the campsite and looked for Tent 54, which didn't take long. Sean had clearly finished before me and had already adorned our temporary home with the red dragon of Wales, which flew high and proud. When I arrived, we congratulated each other on achieving decent times for the first day, proud that our

[*] 99 Fahrenheit
[†] 68 Fahrenheit

guile and determination had kept our engines running and got us through. Sean, however, didn't seem to be affected by the stomach bug, or if he was, it was minor and/or he didn't say anything about it. There are positive thinking theories that talk about ignoring or suppressing the things that could contribute to impaired focus or performance. This might have been what Sean was doing. Even if he didn't have the bug, talking about it in the company of those who did was not going to make things any better, unless of course it was motivational chat about how to minimise its hold and impact.

As I sorted out my cramped corner in the tent, our other tentmates appeared one by one. I quickly noticed that none of them had mentioned the bug or feeling below par. I must have fallen quiet for a while, not wanting to bring any negative energy to the camp by talking about the nick of my insides.

'Hey, Mavis,' said John, 'you alright, mate?'

When I explained – briefly – how I was feeling, my words were garbled and slurred, like I'd expended so much energy that I didn't have enough left to talk clearly.

'You been on the Peroni or something,' Matt laughed, but when he saw my reaction (a forced grimace-cum-laugh), he realised it maybe wasn't something to be joking about. The nausea was kicking in big time and I was finding it equally as difficult to suppress it as I was chatting to the lads. Drained and concerned, I lay flat on my back and looked at the low canvas ceiling in front of me. *I'm going to need another game plan to get through this*, I thought to myself.

In training for the Marathon des Sables, I'd become obsessed with running quickly, which led to picking up injuries, in turn compromising my ability to put in as many miles as I wanted. My right knee began to give me trouble, so I made an appointment with former Celtic physio, Brian Scott to get some treatment and advice. As someone who very much knows his stuff, Brian sorted me out with the level of expertise and professionalism I'd hoped for. Alongside this, I continued to read motivational texts, watch positive mindset videos online and kept in mind the Tam Burns ritual of looking in the mirror and saying, 'You're going to do the best you can today', but with the add-on of, 'without hurting yourself'.

Around this stage in my training, I came across a parable of sorts that resonated with me. Unfortunately, I can't remember the publication or webpage I came across it, or the exact wording, but the sentiment was – Running isn't about the time you do, it's about the time you have. Combining this with Brian's treatment and advice, I started taking things a bit easier, running intentionally slower, but enjoying it more. I could breathe better, was able to appreciate my surroundings more and could think more clearly. I was no longer pushing myself to the limit and, as a result, my knee responded by repairing and strengthening. The human body is a fascinating thing, especially when you listen to it.

As I lay quietly in the tent, banter flying back and forth between the other tentmates, I decided I had to apply the approach I'd adopted during training. If I didn't, I was going to do myself in. Circumstances had meant it was necessary to put pride to one side and focus on the long haul. Achieving a personal best or intended time wouldn't change anything. It wasn't like the donations people had kindly made to Reverse Rett would be rescinded because I didn't complete the race in a certain time. Such things, in this instance, were for the individual and their ego, rather than the greater good.

Setting targets to achieve personal bests can be great for motivation and goal setting purposes, but in my situation – at that very time – it was necessary for such things to play no part in my performance and endeavours over the remainder of the week.

Although I knew this was the right decision, I couldn't help but feel a bit disappointed. I hadn't told a soul beforehand, not even Monica, but prior to flying out to Morocco, the competitive monster that drives me had told me that I was capable of finishing in the top 200. If it wasn't for the stomach bug and the unprecedented heat, this target was – at this point anyway – realistic, as I'd finished day one 81st overall and 18th in my age group. It was a fantastic start, especially for someone who'd never done the Marathon des Sables before, but in order to get through this, I had to rein in my ambition and get real. Maintaining the same pace wasn't an option, especially given how I was feeling. If I was slurring my words after day one, surviving days two, three and four would be nothing short of a miracle if I forced myself to continue as I'd begun. I had to hammer it into my head that being on my feet at the end of the week would be a victory.

That night, I had another dreadful night's sleep. I reckon I got two hours at best, meaning my body and mind didn't get sufficient repair time. The lack of sleep was largely due to the need for visits to the toilet. I was up four or five times that night, although I wasn't vomiting, but the nausea was still there in force, meaning I always felt like I could spew at any moment. A fabulous condition to be in prior to running the second day of a six-day marathon in an oven, I'm sure you'll agree. Day two consisted of 32.5km[*] and a plethora of towering

---

[*] 20.2 miles

sand dunes. Like most challenges of this scope, the demands become more taxing as things progress, so there was a long way to go and it wasn't going to be easy – but it's not like we didn't know that already.

JURASSIC CAMP

As we began to get ourselves ready for day two, it was impossible to ignore the horror film soundtrack emitting from every part of the campsite, which had begun during the night. Retching, coughing, spitting and vomiting echoed throughout the desert. I know there are no echoes in the desert, but the word seems appropriate as the spewing and spluttering was like call and answer. There was rarely a moment of reprieve. The only difference between one spew and the next was the volume, based on the distance between spewers. This made it all the more harrowing, reinforcing that the bug was not contained in a few choice areas within the camp. It was rife. If you excuse the cliché, it had spread like wildfire throughout the night, taking Mark and Chris in its wake. I thought back to the start line on day one when 'Highway to Hell' was being blasted out of the PA. It felt like day one was the highway and we were here. We'd arrived. In Hell.

I tried to push any negativity about what lay ahead to the back of my mind and focussed on my preparation. I had granola and Imodium for breakfast, then slapped on the sunscreen and got ready to walk out into the sun. In terms of distance, day two was similar to day one, but was much, much hillier, with strength-sapping sand dunes up to 350 metres tall to be tackled 13km* in,

* 8.1 miles

directly after the first checkpoint. No, that's not a typo: 350 metres high!

Adding to the feeling of trepidation, I was desperately trying to contain was the fact that the mercury was hitting 53 degrees Celsius[*] before a single competitive step had been taken, and it was only going to get hotter. I was also aware that there were no markings on the course, which was a bit of a concern. On day one, there were rocks marking every half kilometre[†], so there was no chance of ending up off piste. However, it wasn't possible to include these markers in the sand dunes, so day two was almost entirely unmarked, meaning veering off track was always a possibility.

For those who are highly competitive (even more so than me!), knowledge of the lack of markers on day two plays a part in the tactical battle for those out not only to complete the Marathon des Sables, but to win it. The El Morabity brothers, Rachid and Mohamed, came first and second in 2018 and 2019, with Rachid also achieving pole position in 2011, 2014, 2015, 2016 and 2017. Mohamed would likely have finished second in those years as well, but he only started competing in 2018. A key contributing factor to them achieving this so consistently comes from the tactics they employ on day two. The way it works is that the elite runners chase Rachid, who is often in the lead, but Rachid takes them the long way round the sand dunes, thereby tiring out his main competition. While he's doing this, Mohamed takes the shortest possible route over the dunes at speed, outrunning all other competitors.

This formula leads to them always finishing day two in first and second place, which they somehow manage to

---

[*] 127 Fahrenheit

[†] Just under a third of a mile

maintain over the remaining two days. It's superhuman stuff, but I was curious as to how they'd fare with the increased temperatures and stomach bug in the mix. That said, if such things are possible to outrun, it's pretty much guaranteed the El Morabity brothers will be capable. Their approach has so far never failed to drain the legs and minds of the elite competitors who dare to challenge their supremacy and wrestle for the title. In a perfect storm of tactics, endurance and otherworldly fitness, the prodigious El Morabity brothers' plan always succeeds.

With becoming lost and disorientated in the dunes a distinct possibility, and having never really used a compass before – my tuition had come from watching videos online – I was hoping I wouldn't have to use mine. Sean, bless him, gave me a crash course in compass reading just before we got on our way.

As per day one, 'Highway to Hell' pounded out of the speakers, a reality this time, as opposed to anything frivolous or jokey. As the song ended and the klaxon sounded, off we shuffled into the searing heat, ready as much as we'd ever be to climb mountain upon mountain of sand.

I was sticking to my guns and not overdoing it, which I found difficult at first, but I knew it was for the best. When people passed me, I told myself not to be fazed and that it was a common occurrence regardless of the speed I was going. One thing that was impossible not to notice though was the number of people stopping to either throw up or collapse onto the sand, unable to cope with the heat. It was like a battlefield, where members of the Marathon des Sables squadron were being taken out by invisible spears. I half expected to hear a director shout CUT, but what I was living – what *we* were living – was no Hollywood blockbuster.

Despite these unsettling adversaries, I had somehow managed to keep my granola Imodium combo down and was approaching the first checkpoint, situated at the foot of the first sand dune, whose intimidating 350 metre height made me wish, at least for a few seconds, that the checkpoint was actually day two's finish line. The first leg had been relatively flat but it was rough and rocky, so my feet were smarting a little. Looking ahead, the terrain was about to change considerably, but not necessarily for the better.

As I approached the checkpoint, I took a sip of water and let it trickle out of my mouth onto my lips. Despite wearing factor 50 sunscreen and total sunblock for my lips, they were still cracking and cutting up. Who knew a pale Scotsman's lips shouldn't be exposed to 55-degree[*] heat, eh? My intention was to keep them moist to prevent any further cracking and discomfort, but as soon as the water left my mouth, it evaporated. That, as you might imagine, was something I'd never experienced before. If it wasn't so alarming, I'd have laughed at it. There was no moisture to be had, compounded by the fact that my mouth – despite putting water in it – felt as dry as a bone.

The race director, Patrick Bauer was at the checkpoint when I arrived. He doesn't speak much English, but it was clear he was ordering the support crew to give the competitors extra water to take with them en route to the next checkpoint. To be honest, I was in two minds about whether to take it; I didn't want to be weighed down by carrying too much. It was a dilemma, but the conditions made up my mind for me. It was being

---

[*] 131 Fahrenheit

offered not to slow me down, but to help combat dehydration. Even though I'd been going at a steadier pace, my competitive nature still kicked in when I was offered more water. I'm pleased I came to my senses and made the right decision.

It's easy to harp on about the heat, and I appreciate that reading a book is never going to allow you to experience anything close to what my fellow competitors and I experienced, but the following will hopefully give you an idea of how intense it was.

I had two hard plastic water bottles attached to the straps of my backpack, making it easy to take a sip as I was running/jogging/walking. You'll probably be familiar with the kind I mean – most protein shake companies use them, cyclists have them attached to their bike frames and anyone against single use plastic carries their water around in them. What I'd been doing up to this point was pouring water from the 1.5l bottles given to me by the support crew into the two hard plastic bottles attached to my straps. These two bottles, made from hard, durable plastic designed for multiple reuse, were beginning to melt. When I took a sip of water, not only was the water hot, it tasted of plastic. On top of everything else, the last thing I wanted to be doing was ingesting plastic, and any I had ingested up to that point wouldn't have helped my stomach bug. So, I accepted two 1.5 litre bottles of water from the support crew with the intention of drinking directly from the bottle the water came in. However, these bottles were made of thinner, single-use plastic, so they would melt quicker, the difference being that they were for between the first and second checkpoints only. At least that's how I was treating it.

As I set off again, I used the contaminated water from my hard plastic bottles to soak myself, just to bring my core temperature down a little. I think it helped, at least for a while. To be honest, it might have been psychosomatic as the water was so warm and stank of plastic, but I managed to convince myself that it did the job.

The only word I can use to describe the process of ascending and descending dune after dune is 'relentless'. Once I got to the top of my first peak, breathless, under-rested and trying not to throw up, I then had to scramble down the other side, only to be faced with the next one. Not only was this physically torturous, the dunes went on for as far as the eye could see, so the illusion of them being endless was mentally challenging. It almost felt like the one I'd just walked up and scrambled down was pointless, because all that faced me was hideous repetition, like I was stuck in a loop. It was like a scene from something like *Black Mirror*; a glitch in the system that meant my endeavour to conquer these dunes and advance to the next leg was entirely futile; a twisted joke where progress is never rewarded.

I knew, of course, that I wasn't in an episode of *Black Mirror* and that *eventually*, the landscape would change. It was a thing of nightmares though, the only missing feature being a pit of snakes or some sort of mythical beast to duel with. I was half expecting skeletons with swords to emerge from the dunes and try to chop my head off.

As the stubborn landscape refused to change, it felt like my flesh was cooking. Before long, I'd be nothing more than a sizzling human-shaped steak, skin scorched and eyes roasted, a delicacy for some twisted horror film predator. My feet felt like someone was holding a flame under each sole. I soldiered on, using positive thinking as my weapon of choice, but the level of discomfort was becoming as distracting as it was unbearable. In time, a few other competitors appeared on the scene, which gave me something different to focus on. It might sound macabre, but it was a comfort to see they were suffering and struggling as much as I was. I kept my eyes on the person in front of me, tasking myself to either keep pace with them or get up alongside them. I made sure I kept my competitive beast firmly locked up though; it was important to run *with* them, not against them. I thought about the lamppost system again. As there were no markers in this leg, I treated the person in front of me like they were a moving lamppost. It sounds bonkers, but it was refreshing to see something in front of me other than sand dunes.

When I was on my own, I began to notice the sound of the sand parting as I tried to get traction. It became an irritant, an audio confirmation that my human body wasn't designed to run on this type of terrain. When I looked down, the image accompanying the sound always looked like it was in slow motion, all those individual grains of sand dancing around my foot at every step, annoyed that I'd disturbed them. At times it felt like quicksand. If I stood still, I'd end up being buried alive, the sand exacting its revenge by suffocating me to death. I doubt this would be a reality, but I didn't want to find out. Having some people around me helped take away those negative connotations. It's a cliché, but we were all in the same boat, a boat we'd all paid to be crew members of, so there was nothing more to do than keep on moving, praying that our effort and determination would be rewarded by a change in landscape.

I've read in many texts that one of the attributes of a positive thinker is the ability to turn something negative into something positive. It might sound extreme, but survival did cross my mind at one point during that leg of day two. These were uncommon conditions and I wondered at one point if I was going to have to call it a day for fear of death. Thing was, I had a bigger fear of failure. People *expected* me to do this, people with a good grasp of the type of person I am. Shock and surprise would be all over their faces if they learned I'd thrown in the towel. Worse though, I'd be letting Dionne down, even though she probably had no idea what I was doing or why I was doing it. She would never know if I was unable to complete the race, nor would she understand why it meant so much to me. I'd always know though, which is something I didn't want to live with. I'd come this far, battling against every adversary that was thrown at me. If it wasn't for the positive mindset I'd developed and nurtured over the years, it's almost a guarantee that those sand dunes would have broken me. Somehow, drawing on my reserves, I found the energy to keep going. I told myself it was important to give myself credit for what I was continuing to achieve and to lock up those negative thoughts about quitting in that same box my competitive monster was being held captive.

I can't quite decide if it's indirectly positive – or perhaps positive in some guise in the long term – but I have a tendency to be my own hardest critic. This was certainly the case during my football career, none more so than the biggest match of my career at Kilmarnock, the 1997 Scottish Cup Final against Falkirk at Ibrox. When the final whistle sounded, confirming we were 1-0 winners, the first thing that came into my head was, *You weren't good enough today, Mavis, especially in that second half.*

Every Killie fan was jumping for joy, but the overwhelming emotion for me – if you can call it an emotion – was relief. Years later, it was a boost to read that Frank Lampard experienced the same emotional response when Chelsea won the Champions' League in 2012. For me, the relief morphed into a brief moment of guilt – why am I not grateful? – followed by the onset of joy. Ten minutes must have lapsed between the final whistle and me beginning to celebrate. Nobody cared that it wasn't our best performance and that we were hanging on by a thread at the end; all that mattered was we'd won. When I had the trophy in my hands, there weren't any Killie fans screaming, 'You don't deserve that, Mavis, you were rubbish in the second half!' They were ecstatic. We'd won the Scottish Cup! In their eyes, I was a hero.

I don't think that aspect of my personality will ever change though. For good or for bad, I've always been tough on myself, regardless of how hard the circumstances are. The Marathon des Sables had dished out the hardest conditions I'd ever encountered, and despite appreciating that failure is part of life – a part that great learning can be gleaned from – it wasn't something I was willing to consider on this occasion. Regardless of how tempting it was at this juncture, it wasn't in the script, so on I continued, my thoughts on my little girl back home and that glorious day we paraded through the streets of Kilmarnock in an open top bus, showing off our silverware.

Some of the competitors around me had hiking poles. The way they were using them to ascend the dunes made me think I'd missed a trick. I'd decided to travel as lightly as possible, as advised by Rory Coleman, so I'd written off anything that wasn't deemed essential. In hindsight though, not taking hiking poles was a mistake. *Oh well, next time*, I thought to myself, laughing at the notion.

Soaking with sweat, feet feeling like they were being slow-cooked on a barbecue, I was becoming more and more aware of how much the people around me were struggling. A lot of them were looking for any form of shelter. Between the dunes, the occasional bush could be found, along with as many people as it was possible to get round it, some of them having used their hands to dig into the sand like dogs so they could crouch down into the shade. It was like a scene from a film where victims are tortured, put into situations where it's impossible to escape a sinister force tasked to destroy them.

As tempted as I was to take a break behind a bush, if there was any room, my concern was that if I stopped, I wouldn't start again. Stopping wouldn't get me out of the heat, it'd only be a temporary reprieve. Paying the price of extending my time on the dunes wasn't one I was prepared to pay. Due to the stomach bug, I hadn't eaten much, so I had to strike a balance between continuing at a pace I could manage and going quickly enough to get to the end of this leg as soon as possible.

As I forced myself to keep moving, I thought back to my many years of pre-season training. These were the days before sports science, so things were quite different to how they are now. More than one manager had me and my fellow squad members run until we threw up. In those days, no-one questioned it; it was the norm, the spewing an indicator that 100 percent had been given. We'd go home that night, do whatever we did in the evening, then get up the next morning and do it all again. It was common, at one point in my career, to throw up four or five times a week, not through bad food choices or excessive alcohol consumption, but purely through exertion to prove myself to my current gaffer. Those days were tough, but nothing compared to what I was enduring in the Sahara, albeit the spewing was because of the bug rather than exertion.

After a heavy week of football training, which sometimes included a closed doors pre-season friendly, I'd wake up with sore legs and hobble my first few steps of the day. Compared to what I was experiencing in the Sahara though, I'd take those sore legs at the drop of a hat, times ten. It wasn't diagnosed, but I guessed I had some sort of heatstroke. I could've consulted the medics at the last checkpoint, but I was concerned they might have diagnosed me with a list of things that would mean I'd have to pull out of the race. I suppose it was dangerous, and Monica wouldn't have been pleased at that decision if she'd known about it, but despite everything, my determination to keep going was the only part of me that was at peak strength.

As I continued to play Mavis versus Sand Mountains, the competitors that were around me had thinned out, either falling behind, stopping to take a break, or picking up the pace until they became dots in my never-changing horizon. This meant I was back to being on my own, fighting the campaign solo, just me and my own thoughts. I tried to block out the pain by thinking about Dionne, not so much in an emotive way, more in a motivational way, telling myself, *I only have to deal with THIS*. At other times, my mind would be completely blank. I know this sounds odd, but I think it must've been an autopilot thing, like my brain had decided that all my energy had to be spent on moving forward and surviving, and that thinking about stuff was only going to use energy that was badly needed elsewhere.

Occasionally, someone would catch up to me or I'd catch up to them. Few words were exchanged, but when they were, they were always words of encouragement and support. The wordless moments weren't at all awkward, mutual respect clear as we breathed the same boiling hot air, the only sounds our laboured breath, the occasional cough and the swooshing of our feet in the sand. These shared moments, in silence or otherwise, offered a strange sort of comfort. We each had the same goal of the next checkpoint, and while distance would inevitably extend between us again soon, it was nice to have some company while it lasted.

I had no concept of the amount of time I'd been on the sand dunes, but eventually I saw something I at one point didn't believe I'd ever see: a change in the landscape. The checkpoint wasn't far away; I hadn't veered off track due to the lack of markers, the camels hadn't caught up with me and I hadn't collapsed from heat exhaustion, dehydration or lack of nutrition. When I got there, the relief was enormous, even more so than when that final whistle sounded at the end of the 1997 Scottish Cup Final.

There was a final leg to complete before I could put day two behind me, but thankfully it was the shortest of the three and was void of sand dunes. Much like the first leg, it was rocky, gritty and unwelcoming, but I managed to get through out without too much trouble. This didn't mean I felt great, because that would be a lie. My legs were still working though and apart from all the things I'd been suffering up to that point, none of which had gone away, there was nothing fresh that presented any great cause for concern. Taking my foot off the accelerator had been the right call. My right knee, which I'd twinged in training felt in the same condition as the

234

other – weak and tired, but working as a knee should. Looking back on day two, I think I can say with a fair degree of certainty that if I'd gone full pelt like I had done at the beginning of day one, withdrawing or being advised to withdraw would have been the reality. I had given myself a talking to, listened, and actioned my own advice in a way that got me to the stage where I could say that, against all odds, I was about a third of the way through the Marathon des Sables. There was no medal for that though, only the lamentable return of the sound of knackered competitors throwing up.

My tentmate, John, had crossed the finish line with me. I'd heard his voice just as I was approaching and held back so we could cross together. As we were congratulating each other, we spotted Chris and Mark. Wow! I thought, they must've navigated those dunes at an impressive pace, but I was quickly told that the constant vomiting had become all too much and both of them had pulled out. They were only at the finish line before me and John because they'd been picked up in a Land Rover and taken there so they could recover and consult the medics.

As you know, I checked my placings after day one, but this time I didn't bother as I'd decided it wasn't important. I was solely focussed on being able to continue into the next day of the race, rendering any placings meaningless.

John, Mark, Chris and I headed back to the tent, where Sean's red dragon looked as vibrant as ever. Barely a word was shared between us as we shuffled towards the low entrance. We'd all been put through the wringer, video game characters with energy bars so low, it wasn't even possible to see which colour represented energy. I was proud of myself though. I'd managed to shoulder everything that was thrown at me. I'd come out the victor. The only worrying thing was I still had a long, long way to go and I'd heard – as I'd expected – that as the day numbers go up, so does the level of challenge. As we neared the tent, Terry appeared behind us, looking equally as drained. Using as few words as possible, we shared our day two experiences and he was filled in about Chris and Mark getting picked up in the Land Rover because they'd collectively decided they could go no further.

Inside the tent, Sean was sitting sipping water and we were taken aback to see Matt lying on the ground on top of his sleeping bag. That wasn't like him at all.

'You alright, mate?' I asked him.

'Not really,' he replied.

Sean looked like he already know why. I assumed that, like Mark and Chris, he'd also been hit badly by the bug and I wondered if he was about to say that he too had pulled out because it had been too difficult to manage on top of the heat and the dunes.

'What's up?' Mark managed to say, coughing and holding his stomach. 'You had it bad too? I'm done by the way, and so's Chris. It's like hell out there.'

Matt came across as calm and collected when he replied. 'Nightmare, guys,' he said. 'I'm out too, but not just because of the sickness bug.' We all looked at him. 'My heart packed in out there today, a full blown cardiac arrest.'

For a second, I thought he might be joking. Buying a donkey on a night out and taking it home on the tube was one thing, but joking about his heart stopping beating was another, yet I still wouldn't have put it past him. There wasn't a flicker of a smile on his face though. This was for real.

236

Everyone was dumbstruck by the news, rendered speechless. Wide-eyed, shaking heads and sipping bottles of sun-cooked water, we knelt on the ground around him to get more details.

'It was at the start of the sand dunes,' he said. 'I felt breathless, but put that down to the heat. Then my legs just buckled from beneath me and I landed face first in the sand.'

'Oh my God,' said John.

'Next thing I knew,' Matt continued, 'I was surrounded by doctors and medical staff, with no recollection of anything that happened in-between. They told me I was dead for one minute and 57 seconds.'

We all exhaled heavily, followed by a few of us coughing and retching. 'That's unbelievable, mate,' I said. 'How are you feeling now?'

'Alright, considering,' he said, 'but I was lucky. There were people around me when I collapsed, who were quick to get help, so I owe my life to them really. One of the medics said that if I'd entered the dunes, I wouldn't have come out the other side alive. Sorry to let the side down, lads.'

'Don't be ridiculous,' Terry said, 'you're a winner, mate. You're going back to your wife and kids alive. Based on what you've just told us, that's a good result.'

'Yeah,' John chuckled, lightening the mood slightly, 'I mean, if a cardiac arrest isn't enough for you to call it a day, I don't know what is.'

'Just make sure you don't take a camel back to her,' Chris laughed, holding his stomach.

There we were, after a brutal day of running, three men down, but still finding it possible to have a laugh. That was commendable, but it drew even more attention to our vulnerability. I had to remind myself that this was

237

essentially a leisure pursuit, not a war zone I was obliged to be part of, and I certainly didn't want to be going home in a body bag. What had happened was a wake-up call, but I was still determined to keep going – for Reverse Rett, for Dionne, for myself, and to honour this great group of guys. They had done all they possibly could before deciding or being told it wasn't safe to continue. As Terry had said, that was a win – and it's not like Matt was the type to call it a day flippantly. This was someone who had represented Great Britain 19 times in Ironman competitions, had completed an Ironman in less than nine hours and at one point had held the British record for the fastest bike leg. He was a seriously fit guy with a great record so, on paper, the Marathon des Sables should have been doable for him, but the conditions had taken such a toll on his body, its reaction was to warn him not to enter those monstrous sand dunes by having a cardiac arrest.

'By the way,' he said, carefully sitting up, 'anyone who needs wet wipes or toilet rolls or that, help yourself.' He pointed to a pile of stuff next to his bag. 'There's bits and pieces of kit in there, so if it's any good to anyone, fire in.'

This was a great mark of the man. He had nearly died and, although not showing it outwardly, would be deeply disappointed at having to pull out of the race, yet his focus was on helping those of us who were still crazy enough to run at least another day in hell.

It was going to be tough going on without three members of our troop. We had spoken about the celebration we would have after all of us crossed the day four finish line. It was a moment we were all looking forward to that had now been snatched away. Marathon running is very much an individual sport, but we had become a team, bonded by our shared interests, indomitable spirit and sense of humour. It was a grim realisation that – at that stage – a maximum of five of us would be able to share that moment. It would be hard seeing members of our army leave, but soldiering on was the only option for me. That's not to say I was feeling great. I had the bug too and was knackered, sunburnt and weak, but I knew in my heart of hearts that I still had some fuel in the reserves. Hopefully a night of rest and recuperation would fill my energy bar, at least a little bit, meaning I could take on day three with fresh drive. Such thoughts were perhaps a bit ambitious, but the one thing I made sure I had on my side was positivity. Despite day two throwing every possible weapon at me, my survival was made possible through mental strength and refusing point blank to let my physical exhaustion impact my mindset.

I wouldn't quite call it a consolation, but it's not like it was just our tent that had people dropping out. It was obvious from walking around the campsite that each tent had fewer occupants as the race progressed. The tent directly across from us definitely had fewer occupants than it did at the beginning of day one. It was weird to think that that was just the previous morning, a time where everyone was still in the race, geed up with excitement, raring to go. A lot had happened in that short intervening period, the buzz around the camp distinctly different, depletion and dread hanging heavy in the blistering air. Retching and vomiting continued to echo around the camp, like sound files from a *Jurassic Park* film, an unrelenting audio reminder of the horror. In and around the medical tent, there were competitors lying around attached to IV lines, like soldiers taken down in the line of duty. The smell in the toilets was so rancid, it's difficult to find words to describe it. If you've ever been to a music festival, imagine the toilets on the last day and times that by about 100. That's not to say the smell in the tent was all roses and lavender. Eight guys with no access to showers, who have been running in 50+ degree heat does not create a pleasant scent. At this stage in the race, it felt like there was nothing positive to drink in. Even breathing was difficult due to the heat. I felt, on a number of occasions, that my nostrils were burning when I breathed in through my nose.

Conscious that Aiden was yet to return, the rest of us did our best to recuperate, doing what we could to block out the horrific sights, sounds and smells surrounding us and focussing on keeping any food we'd consumed in our stomachs. It was at this time that we received a notification that there'd be a briefing from Patrick Bauer at 7pm. We all attended, even Matt, Chris and Mark, despite the fact they were no longer in the race. When we arrived, the number of attendees was noticeably lower due to people dropping out because of the bug, the heat, or because they were still receiving treatment at the medical tent. Patrick, as always, was standing on top of his Land Rover, microphone in hand. We thought the briefing would be something to do with the bug and/or the extreme heat, maybe something like one of the day three or four legs being shortened due to the unprecedented circumstances.

Patrick began speaking in his native French, which meant we didn't know what he was saying, but it was clear from his tone and body language that something wasn't right. As he continued to speak, he grew more and more emotional until his voice cracked and tears ran down his cheeks. People who spoke and/or understood

French put their hands over their mouths, inhaling audibly.

Patrick's translator, also choked with emotion, revealed that a French competitor, Pierre, had collapsed and died towards the end of the second checkpoint.

It was difficult to process, even though I had said to Sean before the announcement was made, 'Somebody's died here.' Looking back, I suppose I predicted it because of how barbaric the combination of the dunes, the heat and the bug had been. A few runners, one of whom was a British doctor, had tried their best to resuscitate Pierre, but despite working on him for 45 minutes, their attempts were futile. It was a deeply sad moment and a stark reminder that enthusiasm and drive did not mean invincibility. Apart from the fact Pierre was married and had kids, very little else was revealed about him, including his surname. This would be to offer a degree of anonymity, which of course we fully respected. The remaining competitors stood silently, heads dipped, paying their respects to Pierre.

Despite this horrendous news and his clear distress, Patrick Bauer was adamant that the race should continue.

Naturally, once we got back to the tent, the atmosphere was sombre. Whether still in the race or otherwise, we spoke about day four, deemed to be not only the longest, but the hardest and most demanding day of them all. This was the first year that details about day four, titled the 'Mystery Stage', were held back until completion of day three. So, while we knew it would be extensive and arduous, we knew nothing about the route, the terrain or the number of kilometres we were expected to tread. Given what day two had entailed, it was difficult at that stage to comprehend anything more challenging.

I needed to be honest with myself. I had to detach myself from what I wanted to do and assess my situation impartially, taking into consideration my age and what my body was and wasn't capable of. I was in my 50s, a pale-skinned Scotsman running this race for my daughter and a charity doing exceptional and inspiring work. Sure, I couldn't do what I could when I was 26, but I always had my positive mindset to fall back on. Cheesy as it may sound, it was my rock and – as many a philosopher and theorist has surmised over the years – the mind is the most powerful muscle in the human body. Despite the difficult day I'd had, three of my tentmates pulling out and the devastating news about Pierre, I still felt like I had this. That I was capable of completing this race.

I hadn't been eating much because of the bug, but if I could keep some food down and get some sleep, there's no reason I couldn't continue. If you change the way you look at things, the things you look at change. I kept looking at the Marathon des Sables as something Mavis Reilly could do. I was a physical wreck, but my mind kept saying 'Keep going, Mavis. Do it for Dionne and everyone who's sponsored you. Just think of the buzz when you cross the finish line. It'll be brilliant.'

The organisers made a satellite phone available to competitors, which meant I could phone Monica. I knew she'd be following my journey because there was a live tracking feature on the Marathon des Sables website that allowed people back home to track an individual runner's progress.

Although I wasn't 100 percent, I had assumed the death of Pierre would have been posted on the Marathon des Sables website, so I wanted to assure Monica that I was okay. Pierre wasn't the first Marathon des Sables fatality. In previous years, two other competitors had died and, in 1994, an Italian competitor, Mauro Prosperi, had veered off track to the extent that he'd crossed the Moroccan border into Algeria, spending nine days lost in the desert, surviving by drinking his urine. When he was found, it was calculated that he'd ended up an astonishing 289km* off course. What a terrifying prospect. Every scream unheard; no shelter from the blazing sun; no water for miles and miles; only sand as far as the eye could see. It's reported that the experience was so harrowing that he attempted suicide by slitting his wrists with a knife. His attempt was futile though, on the grounds that he was too dehydrated. I can't bear to think what he was going through – both physically and mentally – before he was finally found and taken back to camp to recover. I believe there's a video about this poor guy's tribulation, but I've avoided watching it in the interests of protecting and maintaining my positive mindset.

When I spoke to Monica, I played down how much I was struggling with the bug. I didn't want to worry her, nor did I want to enter into a conversation about considering pulling out. This might come across as a bit selfish or stubborn, but I was adamant I wanted to continue, so it was important to let her know I was well aware of what was going on around me, but that I was fit enough to keep going.

I phoned my mum too, because I knew she'd be worried. Although not great with technology, she had managed to find out what had happened to Pierre and that there was a stomach bug wreaking havoc throughout the camp. As someone who worries a lot, it took a bit more to reassure her that I was okay and that I knew what I was doing. Despite the nature of the

---

* 180 miles

conversations, it was great to hear the voices of my wife and my mum, two of the most supportive people I had in my life. I focussed on the people the voices were coming from rather than specifically what was being said, which was my way of turning concern into comfort.

Late at night and much later than we expected, Aiden turned up, looking drained, frail and colourless. No-one had specifically said they were concerned about him, but it's guaranteed we all were, especially given the impact day two had already had on Tent 54 and the announcement about Pierre. Gingerly, Aiden lay down on his sleeping bag. Sean asked him how he was doing and how he got on out there, but he was barely able to talk. He had taken a lot longer than me, John, Terry and Sean to reach the finish line of day two, but not to the extent that the camels had caught up with him. We thought it best to save him the energy of talking and let him rest. However, it wasn't long before he was up, out of the tent and off to see the medics.

Shortly after, Jack Fleckney (the 30-year-old former Marine mentioned in the prologue and the first Coisty chapter) came over to say hello. He and his tentmates were all military or ex-military, doing the Marathon des Sables to raise money for Walking With The Wounded. Despite the events of the day, his naturally pleasant demeanour helped me keep as positive a head on as possible. Sean joined in and we chatted for a while, sharing stories and common interests. There was an instant connection there and the three of us chatted away as if we'd known each other for years.

After Jack had returned to his tent, I lay in a position where I could stare up at the stars, hopeful that that I could keep down what little food I'd consumed. Any time I lie on my back and look up at the sky, regardless of whether it's daytime or night-time, I'm struck by how vast it is and how small I am in comparison. *Every human on Earth is under this sky*, I thought to myself, zooming in on a cluster of stars. I split my attention between the stars and my breathing, cancelling out the sounds of retching and vomiting, replacing those distressing sounds with an imaginary soothing synth, the type commonly found on meditation videos. The stars were innocent and beautiful, brighter than any stars I'd looked at in Scotland, yet entirely unaware of the chaos that was going on beneath them. I continued to focus on my breathing and repeated a few positive affirmations in my head, grateful that I had made it through day two, that I had spoken to Monica and my mum, and that I was alive. Using the most powerful muscle in my body, I'd managed to create a moment where despair had been pushed aside to make way for peacefulness.

Unfortunately, positivity wasn't capable of cancelling out the forces of microbiology, and the peacefulness I'd found looking at the stars was soon put paid to by the bug beginning to take a proper hold on me. I was up a number of times during the night and the camp was rife with groans, gipping, retching, coughing and spewing. The sound of bile and vomit splattering onto the ground, coupled by the stench of illness en masse, generated an infinite loop of chain reaction puking, meaning there was no single silent moment throughout the night. As a result, sleep didn't come easily to any of us.

The next day, I was in zombie land. Sleep deprivation and the stomach bug made the camp look like a set on a zombie film. Aiden had returned, having been on a drip in the medical tent for most of the night. The bug had got him bad and he was advised to pull out, a recommendation he agreed with instantly. Day two had reduced our army of eight, in one fell swoop, by 50 percent.

Battling both stomach and mind, I had my usual granola and Imodium combo for breakfast, washed down with a recovery shake I hoped and prayed would stay in my system. Competitors still in the race were getting themselves ready, while those who had pulled out prepared for home. A comfy bed and a temperature that wasn't trying to bake me like a sponge sounded like utopia. But I was staying. For one more day at least.

Putting my days as a Water Rat to the test at the Barcelona Ironman, with my cousin, Mark Bailkoski (L) and his mate, Jim McLuckie (R)

Support from the family at the Barcelona Ironman: (L-R) Monica, my daughter, Nicole, and my mum, Kathleen

Getting prepared for the Marathon des Sables, with my training buddies, Milo and Manny

Six Englishmen, a Welshman and a Scotsman: (L-R) Mark, John, Chris, Sean, Terry, me, Matt, Aiden

Navigating the sands in blistering heat

156 miles can only be achieved one step at a time

Traversing a sandy decline with Jack

Flying solo on rocky terrain

Tent 54: Easily recognisable with Sean's red dragon of Wales

Always time for a smile: (L-R) Sean, me, Terry, Jack

Competitor 710 feeling the pressure

Struggling with the stomach bug, but determined to keep going

Happy days in the sun: Part of the Killie squad who beat Falkirk 1-0 at Ibrox in May 1997 to lift the Scottish Cup

Party time in John Finnie Street, Kilmarnock

Letting it all sink in: me with the Scottish Cup

WHAT YOU FOCUS ON EXPANDS

As was expected, the mood around the camp was low as people tried to process what had happened to Pierre. I imagine they were thinking about the mismatch between his fitness levels, his excitement and enthusiasm at competing in the Marathon des Sables, and his untimely fate. Not that I ever saw or met him, but he would've looked no different to any of the rest of us – a fit, healthy guy with a love of outdoor exercise, taking on a challenge that would push him outside his comfort zone. This made us all realise that this desert could claim anyone. None of us could be considered 100 percent safe. I admitted to myself that continuing was dangerous, but that I'd take great care, make good decisions and think – if necessary – about the bigger picture, beyond finishing the race for Dionne and Reverse Rett.

As Sean, Terry, John and I got ourselves ready, Jack appeared. His pleasant demeanour was once again instantly uplifting, quite the gift considering the hellish place we were all in. It's amazing how something as simple as a smile and a positive tone can raise the spirits. He asked if he could tag along with me for day three. I explained that I'd walked and jogged the first two days, but that it'd be great to have some company if he was happy to go at my pace. John, Terry and Sean had a different pace to each other (and me), so while we'd all start together, we'd inevitably drift apart as the race progressed. Having Jack around would be ideal for taking my mind off what had happened to Pierre and Matt, but not only that – if anything happened, I wouldn't be alone.

The five of us made our way to the start line where, in contrast to the adrenaline-fuelled start to the previous two days (day one in particular), the only sound that could be heard was the shuffling of Gaiters on sand. These shuffles were all the more audible due to the lack of talking and, more specifically, the lack of AC/DC's 'Highway to Hell' blaring through the PA. Its absence emphasised the permanent absence of one of our fellow competitors.

From atop his Land Rover and with a neutral tone, Patrick Bauer explained that, as a mark of respect, Pierre's tentmates would lead the race for the first 100 metres. He made it clear than no-one, including the elite athletes, were permitted to overtake them during this period. As expected, there was absolutely no resistance to this, even from those who had run before and had a personal best in their sights. There was no klaxon, but the movement from those in front of me indicated that day three was underway. Due to the heat and the bug, but more so Pierre's tentmates, no-one was running. Fast walking is about as pacey as it got, which was totally understandable under the circumstances.

After the 100 metres had been reached by Pierre's tentmates, some people picked up the pace, but my increase was minimal. Without saying anything, Jack respected this and stayed by my side. We were by no means the slowest of the competitors that remained, but the only thing that was important to me was completion. If I sped up a little, that was fine, and if I had to slow to a saunter at times, that too was fine. As long as I was safely ahead of the camels, that was good enough for me.

A welcome distraction to becoming increasingly weakened by the bug was learning more about Jack. He had been a Marine between the ages of 17 and 23 and had gone on to open a number of gyms in the Northampton area, evidence of his commitment to, and promotion of, a healthy, athletic lifestyle. At 6ft 4in, I gave my neck a mini-workout any time I wanted to make eye contact with him. He loved pushing himself and at one point held two 24-hour world records, one for the assault bike and the other for the ski machine. I can't imagine being on the same piece of gym equipment for more than a couple of hours, never mind 24! He had also been on track to achieve 5500 pull-ups in 24 hours, but suffered a tear in his shoulder at the 21-hour mark, meaning he had to pull out. Despite this, he managed to smash the previous record of 4000, held by former Navy Seal David Goggins, and raised £50,000 for charity. *Anyone who can do more than 4000 pull-ups must be in with a good chance of completing the Marathon des Sables*, I thought to myself, but then again, pull-ups are done in a controlled environment where the temperature can be adjusted and as much fresh, cold water as needed can be drunk.

The one thing Jack was struggling with was the heat. He wasn't alone, but I wondered if there being more of him meant that he was feeling the heat even more than I was. What an unbearable thought. He said that, as a Marine, he had done tours in Afghanistan, but the heat in the Sahara was more intense and suffocating than he had ever experienced.

As we continued to distract ourselves by chatting about our achievements and ambitions, Jack mentioned that paddleboarding the length of the Amazon was on his bucket list, along with mushing in the North and South Poles. He came across as the kind of person who can achieve anything he puts his mind to, so I was in no doubt that, in time, he'd have everything ticked off his bucket list. When we were talking about this stuff, he never came across as conceited or full of himself, as some ambitious athletes can. I never at any point thought he was blowing his own trumpet, more just sharing experiences and ambitions with someone who had similar interests. What came through loud and clear, though, was the positive impact of belief, specifically self-belief. So many people talk themselves out of things because they think they're not good enough, or because they think they'll fail and look stupid in front of their peers. I'm reluctant to call it a pandemic, but it's probably accurate.

Limiting beliefs stand in the way of umpteen people's dreams, ambitions and aspirations. Thing is, if you believe in yourself, your life will be fruitful. I *believed* I could win a national keepy-uppy competition. I *believed* I could be a professional footballer. I *believed* I could get the ball off Paul Gascoigne. I *believed* I could run 100 miles. I *believed* I could complete an Iron Man. I *believed* I could continue to live a successful life after my football career finished. When I first became aware of the Marathon des Sables, I *believed* I could not just compete in in, but complete it successfully. Without self-belief, none of those things would have happened and I would never have made it to the Sahara, nor would I be writing this book.

With Jack, his self-belief was boundless. His energy and enthusiasm for life was like a form of medicine as we trundled our way, bit by bit, towards the first checkpoint. Positivity breeds and what you focus on expands. If you focus on negative things, more negative things will present themselves, but if you turn that on its head, you'll find positivity and opportunity everywhere you look. It's just my opinion, but I think people's lack of self-belief often comes from failure or a fear of failure.

In the modern day, where nearly everyone has access to video features via their mobile, failure is recorded and shared far more than it ever has been before. These failures remain online for eternity, a constant reminder that whoever was centre stage did not achieve what they wanted or failed in their pursuit. To me, this says more about the people who record and share the failures than those who experience them. Failure is a fundamental part of becoming successful in pretty much everything you do. Without failure, there's no opportunity to learn. No-one has their first driving lesson on the motorway. No child's first attempt to walk leads to them strolling down the road in a perfect line displaying perfect balance. It's not possible to win every football match you play in. There will be failures and there will be disappointments, but the mistake so many people make is that they lose belief. Failure isn't being unsuccessful with something, it's being unsuccessful once and then instantly chucking it.

Personally, I couldn't imagine doing 1000 pull-ups, never mind over 4000, but if I put my mind to it, trained well and learned through failure, I'd develop the belief that I could set an ambitious target and achieve it. Whatever you think your limit is, it's almost always higher – and all that's required to appreciate that limits are essentially limitless is self-belief. Sometimes it's necessary, for safety reasons, to shift the goalposts from time to time, but that's just reading the room and nothing to do with capability. My goalposts had shifted because of the stomach bug and the excruciating heat, but that didn't mean my belief that I could finish this race had wavered. It wasn't going to be easy, but I *believed* I was capable, as was Jack, so onward our feet continued to go.

Before long, I encountered a new problem: blisters. I had never been bothered by them in my football career, during any of the Ironman events, or my 100-miler, so I hadn't taken any measures to prevent them as other competitors had, including my tentmates. I was now suffering from that decision, because they were all over my feet: heels, soles and between my toes. I'd feel new ones forming, knowing that in time they would burst, followed by the rawness of the fresh wound rubbing against my trainers. What I'm about to say might sound nuts, but I actually grew to welcome them. The terrain in the first leg of day three was stony, a world apart from the soft sands of the previous day's gargantuan dunes, which led to blisters forming frequently. Since the previous night, I had constantly been feeling nauseous, so the blisters gave me something else to think about. The pain in my feet was impossible to ignore, so it took centre stage, thereby taking the attention away from what was happening in my guts. It sounds masochistic to welcome such pain, but I convinced myself that those blisters served a purpose, perhaps even a dual purpose, the second being to take the necessary precautions next time I was running a long, physically demanding race.

Once we got to just under the 8km* mark, not too far from day three's first checkpoint, we were faced with another area dominated by dunes. Not that I wasn't expecting to see them, but my heart still sank as all thoughts of the previous day's struggle flooded to the

* 5 miles

forefront of my mind. There was a bright side though (there always is if you look for one) in that they weren't as colossal as day two's, nor did they stretch on for an agonising 13km*. This time, it was only 3km†. They would still be tough, that was for sure, but I told myself that, in contrast to the dunes I'd navigated 24 hours ago, conquering them shouldn't be a problem.

Chatting away, encouraging each other and retaining a collective positive frame of mind, Jack and I made it across the dunes successfully and welcomed the first checkpoint with open arms. The bug and the blisters were doing their best to derail me, but I wasn't having any of it. The heat, however, was so overpowering, Jack and I had decided to make a few tactical changes, as a football commentator might say when a manager makes a few unexpected substitutions.

On the first two days, I hadn't spent any length of time at the checkpoints, using them to rest briefly, hydrate, pick up fresh water and then re-join the race. On day one, I did this because I was keen on maintaining pace and achieving a decent time, and on day two it was because I was concerned that if I stopped for any length of time, I might seize up or feel so ill that I'd be tempted to call it a day, especially at the checkpoint after the sand dunes. Whilst these things were still on my mind, I was conscious of how vicious the sun was. Together, Jack and I agreed that checkpoint breaks should be a minimum of 15 minutes and a maximum of half an hour. We agreed this based on the need to get our core temperatures down. I was no expert in this area, but it felt dangerously hot, an environment unsuitable for humans to be exposed to for any length of time. Safety

---

* 8.1 miles
† 1.9 miles

was important, especially given what had happened over the first two days. Each checkpoint had a few tents where competitors could shield themselves from the ferocity of the sun's unyielding rays. I know us humans need sunshine to get vitamin D, but it felt cruel that this essential vitamin was being provided by a flame-thrower.

We poured fresh water over our heads and down our throats, feeling its replenishing effects instantaneously, but when we made our way to the tents, they were chock-a-block and getting a space was difficult. However, a space in one of the tents did finally become available. I lay down and took a couple of tiny wipes out of my pocket. They were only about 1cm in diameter, but they expanded when they were soaked in water, creating a cold compress. I placed them on my head, which was bliss. Short-lived bliss, but bliss nonetheless. I felt utterly drained. I could happily have fallen asleep there and then, but I knew that wasn't on the cards.

I had considered going to the medical tent to get my blisters seen to, but decided against it. I figured that my feet would be so raw that taking my trainers off and putting them on again would be more painful than the blisters themselves. I also didn't want to hold Jack up any longer than necessary, as I had no idea how long it'd take to get them checked out. I didn't want to exceed the 30 minutes max we had just recently agreed on, so whilst a longer break and a new pair of feet would've been nice, we ventured back out into the furnace and took on the route to the next checkpoint, an agonising 12km* away.

On this leg, I told Jack about my football career and more about Dionne and Reverse Rett, and he told me stories about his time as a Marine and some of the characters he'd had coming into his gyms. The

---

* 7.5 miles

conversation and occasional laugh was instrumental in distracting me from the pain in my feet and the turmoil in my stomach. I had been retching and puking from time to time and could feel myself growing weaker and slower by the step. I've used the horror film analogy a few times already, but at one point when I threw up, it was like the sun cooked my vomit as soon as it hit the sand. Although it was a small amount, due to there being hardly anything in my stomach, it sizzled like it had landed on a frying pan greased up with half a block of molten lard. The smell was enough to make me want to throw up again, but the image reminded me a stomach-churning scene in *The Fly* where Jeff Golblum's character, Seth Brundle, is at the stage of transition when he has to puke up acidic bile to break down his food before he can eat it.

Jack, like the bulk of those still left in the race, hadn't managed to avoid the bug and had stomach issues of his own, but he was stronger than me at that stage, or that certainly appeared to be the case. I was conscious that I was over 20 years older than him, which might have been a contributing factor to energy levels, but whatever the reason, I began to feel like I was holding him back.

As we approached the second checkpoint, I heard the voice of my Terry, my tentmate, who had reached the checkpoint not long before us. Some of Jack's tentmates were there too, so they mustn't have been too far ahead of us either.

'Jack,' I said, guzzling water like it was the first time I'd consumed any for weeks, 'why don't you march on from here with your mates? My wee legs are taking three or four steps to your one.'

He chuckled at my turn of phrase. 'You sure?' he asked. 'I don't mind.'

'It's fine, mate,' I said. 'I'll do the last bit with Terry. He's not as tall as you.'

Jack took it in the spirit it was intended. I was admitting I was slowing him down, only without using those words, and he read me correctly. He knew I wasn't ditching him because I was fed up of his chat. On the contrary, his chat might well have kept me in the race. I had a positive mindset, but I was up against it. Two positive mindsets, however, meant that what the desert had thrown at us, whilst powerful, wasn't enough to knock us down.

Sticking to the rule I'd set with Jack, Terry and I stayed at the checkpoint for about 20 minutes, recuperating, drinking water, sheltering from the sun and mentally preparing ourselves for the remainder of day three, which consisted of one stretch of 9km* and then one of around five and a half, with a checkpoint in-between. In comparison to other parts of the race, it felt doable, even in my current condition.

Once Terry and I got going, he told me more about his time in the North and South Poles. He'd mentioned it before, but this time offered more detail, probably in the hope that talking about such low temperatures would do something to us psychologically, taking at least a sliver of the sting out of the burning desert sun. He told me about the time he was pulling his sledge in temperatures as low as minus 40 degrees Celsius†, over 90 degrees* lower than the temperature we were exposed to as we plodded across the 9km stretch that would take us to the next checkpoint. Such a low temperature was difficult to imagine, yet even though minus 40 is equally

---

* 5.6 miles
† minus 40 Fahrenheit
* 194 Fahrenheit

as inhumane as over 50, I would have taken ten minutes of it in a heartbeat.

'You've never seen anything like it in your life,' Terry said. 'When we stopped for a break, we boiled a kettle, filled a cup and then threw the water in the air.'

'I think I know what you're going to say,' I said. 'The water froze, right?'

'Before it even hit the ground,' Terry added. 'It was like something out of a science fiction film, or the kind of thing an illusionist would pull.'

While the sun did its best to melt my sunglasses and grill my eyeballs, I wondered how Terry's eyes didn't freeze over in such low temperatures. I was going to ask, but I assumed it'd be high-quality eye gear, so it'd be a silly question. No-one would take on such a challenge if their eyes were going to freeze over.

As well as having taken on both Poles, Terry had been a boxer and had developed a high standard of physical fitness as well as great mental resilience, so it was no surprise he wanted to do the Marathon des Sables. At this stage in the race, he was talking a lot more than me and I thought he was looking strong. Everyone was lagging because of the intensity of the sun, but considering everything that had happened up to that point, Terry looked like someone who was doing well. As someone who had been successful in pretty much everything he'd done in his life, his resilience and enthusiastic approach, along with chatting away to me, were getting him through.

The remainder of that leg up to the next checkpoint was largely uneventful, but I do remember getting an unusual and intense craving for an ice-cold pint. I take a pint from time to time, but I certainly wouldn't call myself a big drinker. That day though, for several kilometres, all I could think of was downing a cold, crisp lager. I wouldn't call it a mirage because I was only seeing it in my mind rather than before my very eyes, but I imagined running towards a parked Jeep and thinking nothing of it. Then, when the Jeep pulls away, a tiny bar is revealed. It has a solitary Peroni tap on it, the condensation glistening in the sun. Behind the bar is a Moroccan wearing a white shirt and black bow tie, awaiting my arrival so he can pour me the tastiest, most satisfying pint of my life. Even if he charged me 200 Euros for a half pint, I'd have taken it.

At one point, Terry was talking about something, but I found myself responding with nothing more than throat noises bordering on the dismissive, because all I could think about was how utterly fulfilling that pint of Peroni would be. If such a thing became a reality, I'd be hammered after a few glugs and would probably spew up within ten minutes, but as a fantasy, there was nothing more I wanted at that moment in time.

During the final leg of day three, we came across another Bedouin village, which, just like the last one, seemed to emerge from nowhere. This one was derelict though, proof of how difficult it is to live and survive in such conditions. The huts that were once the humble abodes of Arabian citizens who, despite being far more acclimatised than a baldy white guy from Bellshill, still had to give up the ghost.

My blisters were starting to give me serious grief during this last five and a bit kilometres*. They had been a problem for a while, but had advanced from being a welcome distraction to causing me pain on every step. I only had myself to blame for this though, because I'd made the decision to wear trainers one size too big for

---

* Around 3.2 miles

me, a decision I'd come to bitterly regret. I'm a size eight, but because my feet swell up a little bit when I do long-distance challenges, I tend to go up half a size. This time, however, I'd gone up a full size, thinking the heat would mean more swelling. There was extra swelling for sure, in the shape of multiple blisters, created by the constant movement of my feet inside my trainers, chafing away. In hindsight, it was a careless mistake, but it was too late to do anything about it. All I could do was suffer the pain and try to get some treatment at the medical tent later on.

I can't speak for Terry, but when I reached the finish line, all I felt was relief. There was no elation, no celebration or high fives, no victorious punching of the air and gritting the teeth, joyous at overcoming the third day. I was exhausted. Totally and utterly exhausted. The referee had blown the half-time whistle on my Marathon des Sables experience; three days down and three to go, but there was no rousing half-time talk or orange. All I wanted was water, sleep and my guts to stop doing somersaults. I also knew that the second half was going to be tougher than what had come before – and at that stage, it didn't feel like tougher was possible. Day three had taken me seven hours and 47 minutes and had come directly after the misery of the sand dunes on day two. Naturally, day four was next, but this was the 'Mystery Stage', so I had no idea what was in store for me. One thing I did know though was that day four was the longest day, so long that it lasted longer than a day.

Confirming that Sean has once again finished before those of us who remained, Terry and I walked towards the red dragon, every step painful. My blisters were so intense that I was limping. For a few seconds, I felt sorry for myself, but I quickly shrugged it off by thinking about Dionne. All I had were blisters. Blisters don't need thousands of pounds of funding and decades of intense academic research to remedy or cure. All they need is time. After a while, it'll look like they were never even there and I'll be able to walk effortlessly again. If only things could be as straightforward as this for Dionne.

John arrived back not too long after us, looking equally as knackered and plagued with blisters. Later on, I asked John if he fancied chumming me up to the medical tent so we could get our blisters seen to. He said yes, so we hobbled our way there, sharing our experiences of day three on the way. The chaotic choruses of vomit had thinned out slightly, but only because of the number of people who had withdrawn. It was still a deeply harrowing sound though, one of desperation, misery and lack of control. Athletes and competitors work and train hard for years in order to be fully in control of what they're doing. This bug had compromised that control for so many of these poor competitors, myself included.

When John and I arrived at the medical tent, it was packed out, so much so that there was a queue because of the number of people requiring medical assistance. We stood in the queue, but I soon felt like I was going to pass out, nausea and dizziness taking a hold on me. I lay down on the ground and managed to elevate my legs. It was bedlam. There were others lying on the ground too, while doctors buzzed from one person to the next, somehow managing not to trip up on the lying wounded in the process. I managed to get up after about five minutes and got some water in me, but I had to lie down again because the heat in the tent was unbearable.

'Doctor?' I said as one passed. 'Can I get a scalpel and some iodine so I can treat my blisters?'

I was surprised the doctor heard me among the hubbub and pandemonium, and equally surprised that my request was honoured. They were so snowed under, any quick fix was welcomed.

My right foot was a hideous bloody mess. When I first took my trainers and socks off, it looked like I'd accidentally stepped in a blender. The left wasn't great either, but not quite as bad as the right, not that it felt much different. The iodine stung like hell, but it was a necessary part of getting some relief for the biggest challenge of them all: day four. I'd already put myself through the wringer, the hellish heat and noxious stomach bug teaming up to try and take me out. Knowing that the challenge was only going to get tougher was almost unthinkable. I had to think about it though. I had to mentally prepare myself. I couldn't let anything stand in my way of keeping going. Winning the Scottish Cup with Kilmarnock in 1997 was my professional cup final. The Marathon des Sables was my personal one.

TOXINS V THE MIND

Although they still looked like they'd been gnawed on by a beaver or a zombie, or a zombie beaver, my feet felt a little better, at least to the extent that walking wasn't as excruciating as it had been a few hours earlier.

When John and I returned to our tent, we were met with the good news that emails had been sent by friends and family. The messages were printed out by the event organisers and delivered to the respective tents. This was made possible via the Marathon des Sables website. As long as they knew my race number, anyone could log on to the website, key in my number and then click on a link that allowed them to send a personal message.

Reading these messages of support from home, especially those from close family, gave me a much-needed lift. It reinforced that while I was running solo in a desert, sometimes for prolonged periods, I was never truly alone. They might be thousands of miles away, with blister-free feet and far more tolerable temperatures, but they were very much with me in spirit, which gave me great comfort. It was a nice feature of the Marathon des Sables set-up and I'm pretty sure these messages of support made a difference to everyone in the camp as a prelude to the longest, toughest day.

That spiritual comfort was – unfortunately – not extended into physical comfort during the night. For one, strong winds did their best to blow the camp away, the canvas flapping and fluttering aggressively, hardly a lullaby to help me nod off. At one point, a gust was so strong that it blew some of my kit away, meaning I had to get up and chase after it. Thankfully, I managed to recover everything, which I then secured in my sleeping bag, forcing upon me an unwelcome and uncomfortable sleeping partner. To add insult to injury, 15 minutes never went by without the sound of people throwing up. It was a sound I had heard so often over the past few days, but I hadn't become immune to it. Despite the wind, it sounded as loud and as agonising as ever. Dollops of puke splatter could be seen on the sides of tents, the competitors' stomach contents blown there by the erratic wind, as if some kid had attacked the camp with a toy gunge gun.

As well as me, John and Terry were among the spewers that night and, despite looking strong during day three, neither looked anything like as strong when we were side by side chucking our guts up. I also had some issues with the other end, which meant a couple of trips to the horrendous toilets, the smell of which was enough to make you sick even if you didn't have the stomach bug, but you don't need any more details than that. All of this led to me getting a maximum of about two hours' sleep, hardly ideal given the three days I'd just had and what was to come next. Somehow, Sean managed to get a bit more sleep than the rest of us and didn't seem to be affected by the stomach bug. I wondered what his secret was and if he was prepared to share it. Maybe the red dragon of Wales was protecting him in some way. If I'd brought my Lion Rampant, maybe I'd have been in better nick.

When the sun came up, John announced that he was pulling out. Having been so sick during the night, he

271

didn't think running 82.5km* in the desert was the best way to take care of himself. It was a real shame because he was a great guy and had done really well. It also meant that our army of eight was now down to just three: me, Terry and Sean. Terry wasn't looking great, but Sean displayed no signs of weakness. If he was struggling in any way, he was hiding it exceptionally well. As the Berbers dismantled the tents, the three of us shuffled our way in the direction of the start line, Jack falling into step alongside us. Like Sean, Jack was looking alright. He had youth on his side, not that that made him immune to the heat and the stomach bug, but he certainly looked more spritely than me and Terry.

We'd been given the details about day four, the 'Mystery Stage' the previous night, so we knew we had 82.5km ahead of us over a period of a maximum of 32 hours. If you're thinking *That's nuts!*, you'd be right. It meant not only running a full day, but also a full night and a few more hours on top for good measure! It'd be a daunting prospect for anyone fit, healthy, hydrated, well rested and with a belly full of fuel-providing, nutritious nosh. That wasn't us though. Although there were a few exceptions, most of the competitors who remained were dehydrated, burnt, exhausted, ill, riddled with blisters, sleep-deprived and anxious about the distance they were about to attempt to run, with any fuel they tried to put into their bodies being brought up soon after.

As someone with a lot of interest in health and fitness, I had read a few things over the years about the importance of sleep. Without sufficient sleep, concentration and decision making are severely compromised, as is the ability to learn and create new memories. Sleep, especially deep, rejuvenating sleep,

* 51.3 miles

plays an important cleansing role, one where toxins that build up in the brain during awake time are flushed out. I had had three consecutive nights of heavily broken sleep, meaning the completion of a full sleep cycle (made up of light, slow wave and REM) had either barely happened or hadn't happened at all.

There are different theories out there, but there's general consensus that, for a period of sleep lasting seven hours, the average person completes the cycle three times, which fosters the detoxification process. If I was at home, I'd have had nine full cycles over the previous three nights. In the Sahara though, I'm lucky if I'd had nine hours' sleep over three nights, meaning my brain had had insufficient rest and therefore more toxins than it should have. Toxins in the brain, toxins in the stomach and toxic blisters on my feet – what a combination! If I was going to get through this day, I was going to need as much positivity and belief in myself as I could muster. I'd had more granola, Imodium and water, but I knew my main source of fuel was my mindset. I was relying on it to get me through.

As we approached the start line, I had noticed that Terry had barely said a word since we set off. As someone who is usually quite chatty, his silent suffering only added to the sense of foreboding in the air. The sun hadn't decided to give us a break. It might have been the level of exhaustion and lack of sleep at play, but it felt fiercer than ever. I had worked out that the distance we were about to run was the same as running from Glasgow to Edinburgh plus around another three and a half miles*. A key difference, of course, was the terrain and temperature in the Sahara being distinctly different to that of Scotland. I classed it as negative thinking

---

* 6km

though, so shook it off and tried to divert my attention towards something more positive.

That wasn't easy though. People were standing in quiet contemplation, knowing they were about to put their bodies and minds on the line. There was no atmosphere, no excitement, just a soundless, soulless sense of dread. On day one, the atmosphere was electric. People were laughing even when nothing was funny, some even singing and dancing, unable to contain their excitement, like kids at a carnival. Videos were taken and good wishes were shared as the party in the desert built like a crescendo to the sound of the first klaxon. In contrast, the day four start line was like a wake. I clocked a few competitors taking deep breaths, the expressions on their faces asking, *Why am I doing this?* It was a good question. After all, it's not like we were being held captive, forced to endure days of torture. All of this was voluntary. I knew my answer though: Dionne.

A number of competitors may have had Pierre on their minds. He certainly popped into my thoughts from time to time, his death a timely reminder of how savage a footrace the Marathon des Sables was. I reminded myself of the vow I'd made to push all competitive notions to one side and focus solely on completion. As long as the camels didn't pass me, even if I finished last, that would be a victory.

When 'Highway to Hell' pounded through the speakers, it never felt so apt. In a strange way, it was as appropriate as it was inappropriate. We hadn't heard it the previous day because of what had happened to Pierre, so its return was another reminder of that tragedy. It was also a reminder that we had put ourselves through hell over the previous three days and continued to do so, voluntarily, for fun and/or to raise funds for charity. I decided to put a positive spin on it. This wasn't the highway to hell, it was the highway itself that was hell; where we were going was the finish line of day four, which was heaven, because that'd mean the longest, hardest day would be behind us. There you go, positive thinking at its best! This was the highway to heaven, even though the highway itself was certain to be hellish.

When the klaxon sounded, the vast majority of competitors began with a walk. There was next to no running, the need to conserve as much energy as possible on everyone's minds. Everyone's batteries had already been heavily drained, so pace was essential if we were going to get through what lay before us.

THE DOOR OF DOUBT

Terry, Jack and I managed to get into our stride and found a pace that collectively suited us. It was steady and ensured we kept moving in the right direction, but not to the extent that we were using too much energy early on. Despite saying that he'd march alongside us, Sean had broken into a run and was already out of sight. What a guy! His batteries must have been those max strength power seal ultimate lithium advanced plus ones. How he'd managed to avoid the stomach bug was anyone's guess, but I was pleased for him, if not a little envious.

There was very little conversation between me, Terry and Jack, which was unusual as we all liked a chat, but we were in our own wee worlds, putting one foot in front of the other. I put it down to the weakness brought on by the sickness and diarrhoea during the night. Terry, however, was particularly subdued. Fairly early on, he dropped off to sit under a little tree, desperate to get some shade from the sun. Given that we were all supporting each other as much as possible, I did wonder if I should've joined him, but while we were a team, we were also on our own personal journeys and I decided it was too early on to stop, so Jack and I kept going, leaving Terry to recuperate. If he felt he couldn't continue, there were plenty support crew Land Rovers shuttling around that could pick him up and take him to the nearest medical tent to be checked out. Like every other competitor, he also had an SOS button, so if he decided to carry on but ran into trouble in a more isolated area, he could press his button to alert the emergency crew to come to his aid. There were plenty of options in place for Terry, so whilst I was concerned for him, I felt okay about leaving him behind.

Jack and I plodded on, chatting occasionally, but also sharing lengthy periods of silence. I wasn't exactly feeling great, but I managed to get into a decent rhythm as we navigated the stony terrain and a stretch of small sand dunes that took us to the first checkpoint at just under 13km. With day four being so extensive, I had decided to avoid thinking of it as one huge task, opting instead to place my focus exclusively on the next checkpoint. The brutal distance of 82.5km was likely intended to intimidate and test competitors' resolve, but splitting it up into bite-size chunks made it feel more manageable. The way I saw it was that the first chunk had been bitten, chewed and swallowed. The next chunk, up to checkpoint two, I would treat like a new race altogether. Yes, it came almost directly after the first one, but treating it as six shorter challenges felt better mentally.

It was perhaps a symptom of everything else that was going on, but my sense of time seemed to have vanished. If someone had told me I'd taken four hours to get to the first checkpoint, I'd have believed them, but I'd also have believed them if they'd told me I'd taken only two and a half hours. It was early doors and even though I'd managed to find a rhythm, I was feeling quite disorientated.

Despite the number of dropouts over the previous three days, the checkpoint was jam-packed with people, like Christmas Eve in a popular high street shop. This did nothing for my disorientation, so I flopped down onto the ground and covered my face and head with more of those little expanding wipes, which were a godsend because my core temperature was through the roof.

We stayed at the checkpoint for around half an hour, or maybe 40 minutes; it was hard to tell due to my disorientation, but it felt longer than I had spent at a checkpoint before. I was actually keen on the idea of staying there longer, but I was already in breach of the time agreement I had made with Jack the other day, plus he was keen to get moving again. This was probably a good thing as the longer the time spent at a checkpoint, the bigger the temptation was not to bother continuing. That wasn't a real consideration to be honest, but hanging around wasn't going to help, so I got myself to my feet, washed down a few salt tablets with some fresh water and made moves to take on the next bite-size chunk.

However, when I put weight on my feet, my blisters fired up like someone was stabbing my feet with knitting needles. I was in two minds about whether to get them quickly checked out by the doctors, but not only would that delay Jack further, it'd also mean taking my trainers and socks off and, worse, putting them back on again. I decided I was in enough pain as it was without adding another layer into the mix, so I gave myself a shake, recited a few positive affirmations in my head and, hobbling at first, we set off.

I was still struggling to keep food down, but I was drinking plenty of water and the salt tablets I'd been taking were helping my energy levels. It was nice to know that I was hydrated and my body salts had been replenished without being rejected. Anything that gave me any boost, regardless of how small, I hung on to.

Once I'd gotten into my stride, ignoring the pain from my blisters as much as possible, we navigated some more small sand dunes and a gorge over the next 5km*. After the gorge, we clocked a small, solitary tree, which looked like it had sprouted out of nowhere at random, which had about a dozen people gathered round it, trying to get some shelter. I've called it a tree, but it was sparse and small, more a bush with a few spindly branches than anything else, offering about a foot and a half of shade.

'Do you want to rest under that tree for a bit?' Jack asked.

He wasn't asking for himself, so I assumed he had noticed how I was looking and thought it would be a good idea. There were no mirrors in the desert, so I couldn't check, but I got the message and appreciated his concern. I'd never stopped between checkpoints before, but a bit of shade did sound like a good idea and it's not like the camels were anywhere close.

As we arrived, a few people who had been there for a while got up and headed off, freeing up a little space for us. By this point, the temperature had exceeded 50 degrees Celsius† and it was clear people were struggling with such unforgiving heat. The bush offered hardly any shade, but it was better than nothing, so we sat down for ten minutes or so, trying to get ourselves together. I say ourselves, but it was mainly me. That's not to say Jack looked fresh, more that he looked and felt at least slightly better than I did.

Chris Gaskin, a guy from Jack's tent soon joined us at the bush. I was taken aback by how unwell he looked and assumed Jack had seen something similar in me prior

---

* 3.1 miles
† 122 Fahrenheit

to us stopping. Sweat was pouring down his ashen face, his expression one of weariness.

'I think I'm done,' he said to Jack. 'I can take on water okay, but I can't keep any food down.'

It sounded horribly familiar.

'Rest up here for a bit and see how you feel,' Jack said, his tone indicating he was supportive of whatever decision Chris chose to make.

Once we reached the second checkpoint, I collapsed under the canvas. I lay there, utterly drained, nothing left in the tank. Then, going against my former frame of mind, I thought about how only 25.5km* had been covered so far, meaning there was an incomprehensible 59.6km† still to go. I'd let the big picture creep into my thoughts and it was overwhelming. At the flick of a switch, I was drowning in dread, submerged in self-doubt. The only way I could continue was if I ate something and kept it down. My body needed fuel now more than ever before. The bug meant I didn't feel hungry, but I felt the weakness associated with not eating, that's for sure. Even if eating something made me feel nauseous, as long as I didn't spew it up, it'd give me the energy to walk, march and hobble my way to the next checkpoint.

After lying in a heap on the ground for about 20 minutes, Chris appeared, much to my surprise. Given the state of him back at the bush, I was pretty certain he was going to pull out.

'You made it,' I said.

'Only just,' he replied, collapsing down next to me.

---

* 15.8 miles
† 37 miles

I covered his face with a cold compress. 'We use these all the time in Glasgow,' I said, 'because it's always so hot there. That's you an honorary Scotsman now.'

'Thanks, mate,' he mumbled, a slight smile on his lips. I'm not sure if he was too knackered to realise I was only having a carry-on.

Ex-special forces, Chris was an ultra-runner who, in May 2021, had broken the world record for the Wainwright Challenge, a challenge consisting of running and climbing all 214 peaks and fells in the Lake District over a distance of 318 miles*. I'm only telling you this to illustrate how tough a guy he was.

'That's me out. I'm finished,' he said, matter-of-factly.

'Really?' said Jack. 'Look, why don't you tag along with us and see how you go. I can carry your gear for you if you like.'

This was a nice moment, proof of the camaraderie and togetherness an event like the Marathon des Sables develops. Jack already had a torn shoulder due to his pull-ups record attempt, yet he was willing to carry two sets of kit to help out his tentmate.

'I appreciate the offer,' said Chris, 'but when darkness comes, I'll be a liability and I don't want to compromise your chances of finishing.'

We accepted and appreciated his reasoning and knew that it wasn't a decision he would be taking lightly. As someone who had been in the SAS and held a world record, he would've come to Morocco fully intending to complete not just day four of the Marathon des Sables, but the full thing. It proved just how debilitating the stomach bug had been and how incomprehensibly oppressive the 50+ degree heat was.

---

* 511.8km

As we said our goodbyes to Chris, I pulled out a packet of macadamia nuts from my backpack and forced down a couple of handfuls. I could feel my power bar increasing almost instantly, but that would only continue if I managed to keep them down. *Come on, Mavis, think positively*, I said internally to myself. *You've been keeping food down for over 50 years, so what's a few handfuls of nuts, eh?*

Just before reaching the first checkpoint, Jack and I had got chatting to a South African guy called Ian. He'd run with us between checkpoints one and two, even though there wasn't a lot of chat at times due to how Jack and I were feeling. He was a nice guy though, and it was always good to hear a different voice and set of experiences. He waited for Jack and me at the second checkpoint because we all got on and had a similar pace, so it made sense to run together, especially since we were later going to be running in darkness, so it felt safer to have a gang, albeit only a gang of three, but that was still better than a gang of one.

However, after we set off to take on the third leg, I felt distinctly ropey. I tried to stay positive and ignore what was going on in my guts, but it was futile. Only a few kilometres in, I had to stop to be violently sick. This was the worst bout of sickness yet; it was projectile stuff, like I'd been possessed like the girl in *The Exorcist*. Clumps of half-digested macadamia nuts flew through the air and splattered onto the sand. It was so powerful and all-consuming that I fell to my knees. As I continued to chuck up the nuts I so desperately needed energy from, I directed my mouth towards the sand to try and keep everything in the same place, but the heat cooked my vomit like I'd puked up onto a grill, sending the putrid reek directly back up towards my nose, causing me to spew again.

The only comparison I can make is when I had food poisoning a number of years ago. I had a basin next to my bed because I knew I'd be vomiting again soon. What I was experiencing was similar to that, but instead of being in a comfy bed in a temperature-controlled environment, I was in an oven with no possible means of escape, depleted and sleep-deprived, trying my best not to become tearful or angry. Tears and anger weren't things that had featured much in my life, but I was close to experiencing both in that moment.

Anger usually occurs when someone feels out of control and is a mask for fear. When someone is angry, it's usually because they're scared or fearful of the reality of something. It was this that I was close to experiencing. The control had gone. The stomach bug had taken over, like a dark force out for some sort of unjustified retribution. Knees burning on the sand and chucking up jets of nuts and bile, I can safely say that it was one of the worst moments of my life.

I'm no doctor or nutritionist, but I reckoned I might have had heatstroke of some description, possibly a bit of hyperthermia with the heatstroke too. Macadamia nuts are quite high in fat, but they're also high in energy, which is why I ate them. The high fat content might have played a part, I don't know. What was for sure was that they were no longer in my stomach, and the combination of all these ailments conspired to make my Marathon des Sables experience a living nightmare. I had done well to keep the door of doubt closed, but it was during this period of suffering that I let it open; I couldn't help but think how far I still had to go. That alone was intimidating, but adding the imminent threat of darkness and the fact I'd never felt so weak in my entire life, I wondered if I was still capable. I didn't want to quit, but nor did I want to be the next Marathon des Sables fatality. If Monica was with me, she'd tell me stop; if Nicole or Dean could see me in this condition, they'd tell me to stop. Probably even Coisty would tell me to stop. He'd take the piss out of me afterwards of course, but he'd still see it as the sensible decision.

Jack and Ian watched on, unable to do anything except console me and ask daft questions like 'Are you okay, mate?', not that I held that against them. It's all I would do in the same situation, despite it being obvious that things weren't okay. The only thing in control at that point was the bug. With all the will in the world, there was nothing any of us could do.

'Just go on without me, guys,' I spluttered. 'I don't want to hold you back.'

'Are you sure?' said Jack, 'we don't mind waiting, honestly.'

'No, please, just keep going,' I replied with a dismissive hand. 'I'll try and sort myself out and catch up with you both later.'

'Okay, if you're totally sure,' said Ian. I momentarily looked up at them, concern in their eyes, before turning back to the sand to shoot some more pungent, nutty slime onto the sand.

Jack and Ian gave me their best wishes and then jogged off into the distance. My stomach felt like it had nothing left in it, but I continued to cough, splutter and spit, my core contracting and abdominal muscles aching, desperate to get rid of every last bit of the stuff my mind was telling me to retain for energy. It wasn't possible for this to go on forever, but there were no signs of these violent convulsions abating, regardless of whether there was anything left to spew up. I had to face facts. I had to think about safety. For a couple of seconds, my mind was made up – I was pulling out. I couldn't go on like this. Then, out of nowhere, Tam Burns popped into my head.

When Tam was our manager at Kilmarnock, I remember him saying that he learned more about his players in times of adversity than he did when they were playing well and everything was hunky-dory. He also told us that tough times presented opportunities for learning, that they were sent to test our mettle and resilience, and that our responses to tough times would ultimately determine whether we had what it took to play regular top-level professional football. These weren't his exact words, but I remember at training one day, he said something along the lines of, 'Are you someone who can keep pushing yourself when your body and mind are telling you enough is enough?'

These memories of Tam Burns did just enough to push the door of doubt shut. It was a feeble push that took all the strength I had left, but it was enough. This was a good outcome, but it didn't mean the darkest place I'd ever been in had become any brighter. The vomiting, at last, had subsided, but I was suddenly desperately lonely. Looking ahead, there was no-one in front of me, just desert. Even during periods when I'd been lagging, like during those horrific sand dunes on day two, I could always see someone in front of me. To see no-one, it was like they had all fallen down holes or evaporated in the heat. My heart had been pounding during my bouts of projectile vomiting, but it was pounding even harder now. I looked behind me and, to my horror, there wasn't a soul to be seen either. Now, I'm not someone who's prone to being scared, but at that precise moment, I was utterly terrified that I was entirely alone in the world's largest hot desert, left there to fry to a crisp, my remains a meal for scorpions and snakes.

I did the only thing I could think to do – think about Dionne and those words of wisdom the late great Tam Burns had uttered all those years ago. I had to keep that door of doubt firmly closed. *There are people behind you and in front of you, Mavis, there has to be. Just because you can't see them, it doesn't mean they're not there.*

I fumbled to my feet and looked straight ahead. I took a few sips of water to get the taste of spew out of my mouth. Roasting hot water that tasted of plastic wasn't much better, but it's the only thing my stomach would retain. Squinting my eyes, I looked into the distance. *Is that a lake?* It was! A beautiful oasis on the horizon! I quickly checked I had everything and shuffled off towards it, eager to throw myself into its glorious cooling waters. Jack and Ian would probably be there, swimming and splashing about, recharging for the remaining 50-odd kilometres* we still had to run. Panting and sweating, still struggling from what I'd just been through, I managed a little smile. A dip in the lake was going to turn things round for me. It was perfect timing and exactly what I need.

However, I began to notice that although I was moving in the direction of the lake, it wasn't coming any closer. I managed to draw on some energy from deep within the reserves of my reserves and upped my pace, blisters smarting as the chafing resumed. The smile fell from my face when the realisation hit me that I was seeing a mirage. Of course there was no lake. I had read the road map. There are no lakes in the Sahara. In fact, I knew that before I signed up for the Marathon des

---

* 31-odd miles

Sables. Everyone knows there are no lakes in the desert. If there were, it wouldn't be a desert.

The disappointment was crushing. I let out a groan and was close to tears, but like a switch was flicked in my head, it quickly dawned on me that the lake that never was had got me moving again. Tam Burns, an imaginary lake and hanging on to my positive mindset by a thread had pulled me out of my stink and pushed me closer to the next checkpoint. I'm reluctant to call this a nice moment, because I still felt like hell, but I was out the other side of the bubble, one foot in front of the other happening automatically, to the extent I barely felt present. Only minutes ago, withdrawal was a serious consideration, but now it was off. *Surely that was the worst of it?* I thought, consoling myself. *Projectile vomiting and a mirage. It can't get any worse than that. Surely?*

LIMITS DON'T EXIST

I n Scotland, especially in the summer months, it can take hours for darkness to fall. In the desert, however, it takes a maximum of ten minutes. On my first night at camp, I was taken aback at how quickly the sky turned black, but didn't think anything of it because I didn't have several hours of running ahead of me, nor was I so hideously unwell. When I conceded there was no lake, it was still light. Now, ten minutes later, it had turned so dark that I could barely see anything in front of me. The adversaries were stacking up, individually and collectively doing their best to knock me down. I was alone in the desert, desperately ill, and in darkness. The sense of loneliness and isolation became unavoidable as I somehow managed to trundle on, telling myself that the only way to get out of this situation was to keep on moving.

Although I had heard a few guys at the campsite talking about them, I hadn't encountered any scorpions or snakes, but I had no reason to believe they didn't exist just because I hadn't seen them with my own eyes. For all I knew though, I could've been surrounded by them, oblivious to the threat. Proof of the mind's power, I began to hear scuttling and hissing, which should have been terrifying, but I told myself that since my eyes were able to play tricks on me, so too were my ears. I shook it off, determined not to let my fragile mind convince me

288

that being accosted by venomous foot-sized insects and slithering carnivorous reptiles was a possibility.

Stifling my fear and relying on a combination of inner compass and intuition to keep me running in the right direction, I fought hard to stop my mind from going where it would only make things worse. By this I mean thoughts of Mauro Prosperi, the Italian who drifted off course by 289km*, leading him to suffer so much that he attempted suicide. The fundamental facts were there in my mind, but thinking about the possibility that I could suffer the same fate would only send me down a darker rabbit hole than I was already in.

Then it occurred to me: I had a head torch in my backpack! I had been running in near pitch blackness for – well, if I'm honest, I had no concept of time; it was probably only a few minutes, but it felt a lot longer because I was fighting to keep panic at bay. My mind clearly wasn't right though. I had been running in the dark, my body hanging in tatters and my ears playing tricks on me, when all along I had a head torch at my disposal. I stopped, took off my backpack, fished it out and put it on my head. I fumbled my backpack back onto my shoulders and stood up. The head torch only served to illuminate my desolation, but at least I could see where I was going, despite my view being so changeless, it might as well have been a photograph.

Before I started moving again, I stood still and noticed the silence. I had never felt so alone. The nothingness was so deeply intimidating, but at the same time there was an awesomeness to it. I don't mean this in the sense that it was in any way good, more that it was so immense, so colossal. If I'd used all my strength to shout at the top of my voice, no-one would've heard me. Think

---

* 180 miles

about where you are right now while you read these words. If you want to hear different things, you can no doubt achieve that with ease. If you want to change your environment and give your eyes something different to look at, you can achieve that with ease too. My environment was identical regardless of which direction I looked in, and any penetration of the silence was only made possible by the movements I made. I was so used to the sound of my Gaiters on the sand and even when I stopped, I could still hear the sounds being made by the people around me. At this moment, though, apart from the sound of my breath and my heart beating in my chest, the quietness was so brutally apparent, it felt like another adversary to contend with.

As I got moving, blisters smarting as ever, the sound of my feet on the sand was, for the first time since day one, comforting to hear. Actually, comforting is probably pushing it, but it was better than silence. As I trudged on, I had the reassurance of the SOS button if I got to the stage where I needed it, but I didn't want to go down that route, nor could I be certain I was findable. Somehow, though, I got the sense that I was heading in the right direct and that my inner compass had my back. After a while – although exactly how long is anyone's guess – my head torch caught sight of a tree. It was an actual tree this time, nothing like the little bush I had taken cover under earlier in the day. This one had a proper trunk and branches. *Brilliant*, I thought, *I can rest here for ten minutes and get some shade*. As there were very opportunities to get some cover from the sun, this one was very much welcomed.

Then I realised my error of judgement, my brain not quite firing on all cylinders. Unlike the lake, the tree wasn't a mirage, but I was 100 percent in the shade already because it was dark. The tree would've been a godsend earlier in the day when the temperature was mid-50s, but now it served no purpose whatsoever. It was another blow, but in the big scheme of things, it was as minor as they get. I considered lying down for a while, mainly because I was still feeling dreadful. The vomiting had subsided, but the nausea was obstinate, point blank refusing to give me a break. However, as I made a half-move to take off my backpack, it occurred to me that lying next to a tree in the dark in the Sahara might make me a target for scorpions and snakes. That didn't sound in any way relaxing or rejuvenating and although I had never seen any and had only heard them when my mind was playing tricks on me, I decided that's how I wanted it to stay. *Your brain isn't completely fried after all, Mavis*, I said to myself and traipsed on, tank empty, unsure how it was possible I was still moving.

After a while – again, no idea how long, but it didn't feel extensive – my head torch caught the sight of a couple of silhouettes. The relief was all-consuming. The silhouettes looked exactly like I wanted them to; like Marathon des Sables participants. A sound escaped from my mouth that was meant to represent some form of joy. I was going in the right direction and as long as I continued to do so, I would reach the safety and security of the next checkpoint. Running until I collapsed, to either be consumed by snakes or cooked by the sun was now off the cards, as was running in the dark and coming across the same tree again, in some horrific *Blair Witch Project* loop, the darkness toying with me until I expired. Instead, it would be medical attention, rehydration and living, breathing human beings to speak to. I was still in a bad way, exhausted and unable to eat, but I was another step towards reaching my goal and the door of doubt was still closed.

When I finally reached checkpoint three, I was given a fluorescent light by one of the support crew, who told me it was to be attached to my backpack to help prevent people becoming lost in the dark. I couldn't help thinking that these should've been given out at the previous checkpoint, but I had no energy to bring it up. In fact, I had no energy at all. I got some fresh water in me and tottered to the doctor's tent, pleased to see there was only one competitor there, who was being attended to at that time, meaning I was next.

Knowing I was mere feet from safe hands, I collapsed onto the floor, backpack still on. I had sand all over me, including up my nose, in my ears, between my teeth and embedded in my stubble. Once it was my turn to be seen, I took my backpack off and told the doctor that I'd been sick, had had diarrhoea and asked for an anti-sickness tablet. I put a cold compress on my face. It was less necessary with the sun was away, but that didn't take away from its soothing and refreshing properties, and I needed as much of that as possible, that was for certain.

The female doctor returned with an anti-sickness tablet and an Imodium chaser. I washed them down with several mouthfuls of fresh, cool water that this time didn't taste of a plastic soup.

'They'll take about 20 minutes to take effect,' she said. 'Rest up and I'll be back to check on you later, but you will have to eat something if you want to continue.'

'Thanks,' I managed to slur, and lay back with my eyes closed.

There were no beds in the medical tent, just rugs the size of a single mattress on the floor. There wasn't even a ground sheet, so underneath the rug, it was sand. Inescapable, omnipresent sand.

It sounds ridiculous, but I was concerned about the doctor returning and not being satisfied with my health and energy levels. To be fair, if the tables were turned and I was the doctor, I'd be reluctant to let me continue. That was the thing though – the doctors had the power to withdraw competitors on medical grounds, especially if continuing was considered life threatening. There had already been a fatality and no-one wanted another one, so the doctors would understandably be practicing great caution, especially since the stomach bug was rife and well. As I lay there, this became a great concern because I didn't want the decision taken out of my hands. If I was going to pull out, it had to be *my* decision and no-one else's. *You will have to eat something if you want to continue.*

I'd be lying if I didn't say the temptation to stop was massive. There were so many cracks in my armour that I was on the cusp of admitting defeat. I thought about Chris. He was a tough guy, ex-SAS and a record holder, someone far tougher than me, yet there was no shame in him pulling out, so there'd be no shame in me pulling out either; none whatsoever. The door of doubt was shaking, its latch flimsy. Maybe it was time. Between my ears, mind games were actively at play – voices of reason, of doubt, of safety, of consolation, they were all in there, loud and irritating. Lying on that pathetic rug, I'd never felt so weak and so low in all my life. *It might be time, Mavis. It might be time.*

Then, in my mind's eye, smack bang in front of me in 1080p high definition, was an image of Dionne, her loving smile as captivating as it's always been. Instantaneously, tears flowed, stinging my sandy sunburnt cheeks. I was so utterly dehydrated, I don't know how such an onslaught of tears was even possible, but they kept coming as I thought about my little girl and others like her, who need 24-hour care and can't do anything for themselves. I gave myself a shake. I was still capable of putting one foot in front of the other, so why was I even considering quitting? My stomach bug wouldn't last forever and neither would my blisters. In two weeks or less, they'd be gone or there'd be little left to show. That wasn't the case with Rett Syndrome. It's not like Dionne simply had to tolerate it for a couple of weeks until it went away. I wasn't feeling great, which is an understatement, but in the big scheme of things I had no business complaining about anything.

As my tears abated slightly, I made the decision there and then that, come hell or high water, I was going to complete the Marathon des Sables. There was no high water in the desert of course, so it was only the hell in front of me that I had to contend with to prove my resilience and fulfil my ambition. It wasn't going to beat me. The decision was made and there was no turning back. Thanks, Dionne. You saved the day, Princess.

I wiped the tears on my face with the back of my hand, the sand on both my hand and my face providing an unwelcome abrasive sensation as I sorted myself out. I needed to look as fit as possible for the doctor returning and I didn't think tear tracks would do much for proving my levels of strength and mental stability. There's nothing wrong with being tearful, and even though it wasn't something I was prone to, impressions were important. Having made my decision, the last thing I wanted was the doctor to force withdrawal because it was clear that not only I was in poor condition, but it was evident that the challenge was all too much for me.

'Limits don't exist,' I said out loud, even though the only person who could hear it was me. I had read something like this in one of the many books on motivation and self-improvement I had picked up over the years. Those weren't the exact words[*], but that was the message, loud and clear, one I began to say over and over again in my head. *Limits don't exist. Limits don't exist.*

I kept it rolling, knowing that the repetition of any positive affirmation could only be a good thing. I had used these techniques before, pretty much ever since Tam Burns told me to speak to myself in the mirror back in the 90s. I reinforced it further by closing my eyes and using visualisation. I imagined Monica saying it. 'Limits don't exist'. I then gave Dionne a voice, based on the tones and inflections she uses when she's petting Manny. 'Limits don't exist, Dad.' A fresh tear threatened to escape, but I wiped it away, somehow managing to avoid putting more sand in my eye.

Limits don't exist. Limits don't exist.

The slightest of smiles graced my face as I continued to repeat the mantra, drinking in its message. Despite lying in a heap in a tent in the Sahara waiting for medication to kick in, I had just locked the door of doubt, thrown the key into the sand and added an industrial strength bolt for good measure.

I had covered 37.5km[†], meaning I still had a mountain to climb. Looking on the bright side, I was nearly half way through and at least the sun had gone to bed. The remaining 43km[*] were going to be tough, that was a certainty. My visualisation and positive affirmation

---

[*]The exact words were: 'Life has no limitations, except the ones you make.' – Les Brown.

[†] 23.3 miles

[*] 26.7 miles

295

techniques had helped, but I couldn't deny that I was in a dark, dark place. It was going to be a long, agonising day, but I had committed to it, so there was no turning back.

When the doctor came back to check on me, I used visualisation again, to present as healthy a version of myself as possible. I doubt it made me look any better or stronger, but there was no harm in trying it.

'What have you been eating?' she asked.

'Macadamia nuts,' I replied, 'and fruit pastilles.' I showed her my roll of pastilles, which had only two missing.'

'That's not food,' she replied, a scowl on her brow.

I had eaten a couple of pastilles when I'd stopped briefly at the tree, and because I'd managed to keep them down, I felt it worthy of celebration. It was clear that the doctor thought otherwise. It perhaps wasn't my best move, but a bell can't be unrung, so there was nothing I could do about it. Regardless, not continuing was no longer on the cards. I owed it to myself, to Dionne and to everyone who had sponsored me to keep going. It was going to be horrific, but I think pulling out (or being forced to pull out against my will) would put me in an even darker place.

As the doctor continued with her examination, I thought about the word used to describe a Marathon des Sables participant: a competitor. Sure, it was a race, so that meant we were all in competition with each other, but for me, the competition had become a battle of myself versus myself, or as fitness spokeswoman Ali Vincent puts it, 'The only battle to win is the battle within.' In 2008, Ali lost a whopping 112lbs in weight, a colossal achievement and a fantastic example of mind over matter.

My mind then drifted to boxing. What I was about to do was like walking into the ring for the biggest fight of my life, but without a cornerman. I was going to take a battering, but I was prepared to respond to it as best as I could. The only way I'd be leaving the desert was if I had to be carried out. I had made peace with myself that I was going to finish this race and, despite the dark place I was in, that gave me a great mental boost.

It didn't hit me at the time, but looking back, my decision making could have been classed as selfish and reckless. I was dangerously weak and, although my mind had played a few tricks on me, I was perfectly aware that someone had died, my tentmate had suffered a cardiac arrest and the general attrition rate was high. If Monica and my kids were there in that tent with me, there's no way they'd let me continue. The Marathon des Sables is a race that is capable of killing, yet I was still prepared to keep going with off-the-scale nausea and ripped-up feet. I'd be no good to Dionne and Monica dead, yet I couldn't seem to get over the fact that I was doing this for Dionne and Reverse Rett and if I pulled out, they would be disappointed in me. It was totally irrational, but it was what I had decided, so there was no turning back. Rightly or wrongly, I saw it as no different to telling Tam Burns that day that I wanted to be a footballer. To me, these things – even though they're between myself and myself – are contractual. That's part of the battle I suppose. This approach had let me fulfil so many of my life ambitions that I had come to trust it as bulletproof. This was the first time the possibility of death was in the mix though, but even that wasn't strong enough to sway me.

The doctor had momentarily transferred her attention to someone else. Conscious that she had the power to force me to withdraw, I saw her absence as an opportunity to hold on to my autonomy, so I got to my feet, quickly checked I had everything and legged it back onto the course.

KING OF THE MOUNTAIN

From this point on, fluorescent markers were used to keep competitors on the right track, but they were few and far between so it'd still be possible to veer off and end up lost. Maybe the organisers thought that the combination of head torches, the fluorescent lights on the back of our backpacks and the occasional markers in the sand would be sufficient. To me though, especially because I was feeling disorientated, it felt like I was playing some sort of twisted game where my vision was compromised and I was relying on other people to guide me in the right direction – only those people didn't exist. It was then that I said a couple of prayers, asking the big man upstairs to help me stay on course, protect me from any further threat and allow me to regain some strength.

Having completed the vast majority of the previous leg up to checkpoint three by myself, I decided it was essential that I find some company. That leg had been so horrific, I had to ensure that I never experienced anything like it again. It was also necessary to keep hydrated and take my salt tablets at regular intervals. They were no substitute for real food, but they at least replenished me, in turn providing me with small amounts of energy. I still had my packet of fruit pastilles too, so there was always the option of trying to eat a few of them. The sugar alone would give me a boost, as long as it stayed in my stomach long enough to be digested.

Confident I was well ahead of the camels and had plenty time on my hands, I made the decision to do something that went against pretty much everything I had done in any other competitive event I'd entered: slow down. I knew I wasn't sitting in last place, so it was guaranteed there'd be people behind me. Slowing down meant the end of this most brutal of days would be further away, but the consolation was that I'd have company.

Before long, I heard the familiar sound of Gaiters against sand and was joined by two guys, Simon and James, with a younger guy, Andrew, catching up to us about ten minutes later. It was nice to hear some new voices, or any voices for that matter, and we chatted away as we alternated walking with slow-paced jogging. After a while, James and Andrew pulled off slightly, leaving me and Simon behind, although we could still see James and Andrew with our head torches, the beams regularly catching the fluorescent lights on their backpacks. Simon and I distracted each other by chatting away about our jobs and how we'd fared over the previous three and a bit days. I told him how ill I'd been and that I'd scarpered away from the doctor at the last checkpoint in case she deemed me unfit to continue.

'I've got something that might help you,' he said, slowing to a saunter. It was at this point he gave me the Shot Bloks, the little gel capsules designed to give athletes an energy boost. Having managed to keep down a couple of pastilles, I figured there'd be no harm in trying them. They were only 33 calories each, but I needed all the energy I could get. I placed one under my tongue to let my saliva slowly break it down, meaning it'd be introduced to my stomach gradually rather than suddenly. This gradual approach worked, meaning my body was receiving and processing some degree of nutrition. Although nowhere near as extreme as other things that had happened that day, it was another turning point. It might have been psychosomatic, but I could feel myself growing that little bit stronger as the Shot Bloks were not only retained, but digested and distributed as well.

Realising they were helping, Simon gifted me a full packet, containing six gels. I didn't know how many he had in total, but this act of kindness from a stranger had a profoundly positive effect on me, not just physically, but mentally too. It seems odd to give a packet of little gels such credit, but they were providing fuel and there was only so long I'd have been able to carry on with nothing in the tank.

Whilst I was keeping the Shot Bloks down as well as regularly hydrating and taking my salt tablets, it would be inaccurate to say I was feeling great. I was still weak and ill, but I felt like I had turned the corner. This was proven by the remainder of that leg being largely uneventful. The terrain was reasonably flat and more sandy than rocky, so nothing I hadn't encountered before. Don't get me wrong, it was still weird being in the desert in the dark and surviving off water, salt, Shot Bloks and the occasional fruit pastille, but my automatic pilot was in full activation mode, as was Simon's, allowing us to walk and occasionally half-jog our way to checkpoint four, 50.8km* in with only 31.7† to go.

As well as seeking out company and making sure I took in sufficient levels of water and salt, the other thing on my checklist was to get some sleep. Time wise, I was doing fine. There was no threat of the camels catching

* 31.6 miles
† 19.7 miles

up to me any time soon, so this allowed me to have an hour's kip at the checkpoint. There are theories out there that suggest an hour of sleep can be damaging as it means waking up during the slow wave part of the cycle, which is where deep sleep occurs. This is prior to the first REM stage where all the filing cabinets of the brain get sorted out, and preventing this from happening is not advised. The sleep world is an enigma though, and it's an area that is regularly researched, so there are many different trains of thought out there. It would be great if we could just turn ourselves off like an electrical appliance, then boot ourselves up again whenever we liked, ready to go.

Regardless of the theories though, my body was screaming out for rest and I couldn't afford much more than an hour. There was also a concern that if I slept any longer, I'd wake up with the camels passing me and I'd be disqualified from the race. After everything I'd been through, that was the last thing I wanted.

I lay down on a rug in the sand and fell asleep almost instantly. When I woke up an hour later, Simon and James had already left, but Andrew was still there. He had decided to have an hour's kip as well and was still knocking out the zeds. Feeling refreshed but a little groggy, I decided to sort out my gear and replenish my water supplies before giving Andrew a nudge. During this, I got chatting to Lynne, a girl from Linlithgow. I hadn't heard any other Scottish voices since I arrived in the desert, so it was nice to hear one. Like the majority of competitors left in the race, Lynne was feeling terrible, but was doing well nonetheless. With a few exceptions, like the El Morabity brothers and our Sean, I think that applied to the majority of us – we were doing well to stay in the race, but felt terrible due to the illness and heat. At least the heat wasn't a factor at that moment, but we all knew it would return. I wished Lynne all the best with the next leg and said I'd look out for her later on.

When Andrew got up and got himself sorted, we made a pact to stick together until we reached the finish line. Andrew, a Cheshire lad in his late 20s, got a real boost back at checkpoint one. He was struggling badly in the early stages and the medical staff at the first checkpoint had deemed him unfit to continue and used their authority to withdraw him from the race. At the last minute though, as if through some sort of divine intervention, he made enough of a recovery for them to change their decision and allow him to continue. There were parallels to what happened to me at checkpoint three. It wasn't a carbon copy, but if I hadn't done a runner, I think I might have been faced with a similar situation.

The 11.2km* to checkpoint five covered fairly standard, consistent and flat terrain, which Andrew and I completed with barely a word spoken between us. As two competitors who were nearly pulled out of the race for medical reasons, we were both shattered, so expending energy on talking seemed unnecessary. There was no awkwardness though, the pair of us knowing that we were there to support each other and, should the need arise, to be there if one of us takes a turn for the worse. Head torches illuminating our path, we maintained a steady pace which, for the duration, was nothing more than a brisk walk, but that suited us fine; it was all about getting to the next checkpoint in one piece. Having studied the roadmap, we knew that checkpoint five was at the foot of a jebel, so climbing that was going to require all the effort and energy we could muster. We

---

* 7 miles

worked out, though, that based on the progress we were making, we could factor in a couple of hours' sleep at the checkpoint, meaning we'd be as prepared as we could be to take on the jebel, which was about 2000 metres high and had a 25 percent slope to the summit. It wasn't what we needed, but if the Marathon des Sables was easy, everyone would be doing it.

Factoring in a couple of hours' sleep at the checkpoint also meant that we'd be taking on the jebel as the sun rose. This would naturally increase visibility, which would ultimately be safer, but it'd also mean that the temperature would increase gradually rather than being the interminable furnace we had endured on day two when navigating hilly terrain. I was delighted that my stomach was accepting and processing the water, salt tablets, Shot Bloks and fruit pastilles I had put in it. I still felt nauseous, but the absence of spewing meant my system was beginning to recover. At least that's what I was telling myself.

As we plodded on, the lights illuminating the foot of the jebel became visible.

'We're nearly there,' said Andrew, a sense of triumph in his tone.

'We've done well, mate,' I said, meaning it wholeheartedly. The pair of us had been dealt difficult cards, but we'd managed to stay in the game, the sight of those lights a marker of our endurance, success and unyielding spirit. Those lights didn't seem to be coming any closer though, making me wonder if I was hallucinating again, stuck in some cruel loop, a treadmill under my feet, its presence invisible, masked by billions of grains of sand.

Andrew was clearly thinking the same. 'It doesn't feel like we're getting any closer,' he said.

'I know,' I replied, 'but we have to be, unless we're part of some crazy, sadistic joke.'

Andrew laughed, but given my mind had played tricks on me all too recently, I did wonder if my sense of perception was out. It didn't matter how fast we were moving, the checkpoint and jebel looked like they were the same distance away. It made me think of one time when I noticed a little bit of black fluff on the kitchen floor. At first I thought it was an insect, probably a spider, but because it wasn't moving, I changed my mind and decided it was a bit of fluff. While the kettle was boiling, I looked at it intently, still in two minds as to what it was. Then it moved a little bit, so I went back to deciding it was an insect. To get closure, I bent down to inspect it properly, a plastic tumbler in my hand so I could take whatever it was out to the garden, only to discover it was a bit of fluff after all! My mind had made it move, convincing me it was an insect. By this rationale, the lights Andrew and I could see before us *were* coming closer. It might not appear that way, but the ground we were covering was definitely taking us to where we wanted to be, regardless of what my mind was telling me.

When we finally arrived at checkpoint five, we got some fresh water down our throats and then lay down for a couple of hours of sleep. I drifted off almost instantly and got a solid two hours. In contrast to my attempts to sleep over the previous four nights, this was a blessing. My prayers were being answered and I woke up feeling as refreshed as I possibly could in the circumstances. According to the literature out there, two hours is at the tail end of slow wave sleep, just before REM kicks in. I think it's best to go for a full cycle, but that would have meant sleeping for around two and three quarter hours, which was a bit lengthy. I was aware

305

that sleep theory is an ongoing and ever-changing beast and that, regardless of what was the most appropriate, I felt better having had a couple of solid hours in the land of nod.

Unlike at the previous four checkpoints, this one had Moroccan tea at it, which came highly recommended by the support crew as an energy boost for taking on the jebel. Moroccan tea is extremely sweet, so the energy boost came almost exclusively from the sugar content. I was wary because of how dicky my stomach had been, but I took a cup anyway. It was so sweet, I got an instant sugar rush, which gave me a few moments of euphoria. I don't think I had tasted anything quite so sweet before. It was up there with Scottish tablet, which isn't something I can take much of. Only time would tell if I'd be able to keep it down.

As the sun rose, Andrew and I tackled the jebel, our first obstacle en route to the final checkpoint. It was crazy to think we'd been running through an entire night, but the couple of hours' sleep I got was comparable to what I'd managed the previous four nights anyway. This, along with feeling a little better, meant I was as ready as I'd ever be to tackle the jebel.

The incline was extreme, steeper than the sand dunes on day two, but there was the security of rock being underfoot rather than just sand. I think our automatic pilots had kicked in again and we just got on with it. It was tough, but the temperature was bearable and the Moroccan tea had remained in both of our systems, so once again it was just a case of keeping moving, knowing that we'd inevitably reach the summit. There was a really sandy section up the middle where we clocked the footprints of the elite athletes who had taken the direct route. The alternative, taken by the majority of competitors, was to take a rocky path marked out by ropes, which could be used to haul ourselves up the steep incline.

When Andrew and I got to the summit, the view was spellbinding. Miles and miles of desert bathed in the pinks and oranges of sunrise. The air smelt fresh and clean, like a washing powder advert would portray. I had had one of the worst days of my life, but this was a moment to be cherished. Only a matter of hours ago, Andrew and I were seconds away from packing our bags for home, yet here we were, standing atop a mountain like kings, conquerors of everything that had been thrown at us, masters of mind over matter. I'd gone from thinking I might die to standing victorious and proud, looking out over the desert that had pushed and tested me to the hilt. I drank it all in, taking photographs with my mind, savouring it for the beautiful thing it was.

I couldn't help thinking it would've been a cracking place for the finish line, either for day four or for the entire race. That wasn't the case, though, and there was still work to be done, so I gulped down some water (while it was still relatively cool), placed a Shot Blok under my tongue and got ready for descent. Despite the lift reaching the summit had given me, as well as successfully keeping down the Moroccan tea, I was still pretty weak, limbs heavy at times, but the nausea that had been ever-present, with varying degrees of bite, was finally beginning to pass. It was a great feeling knowing that the worst of it was over. This didn't quite cancel out my weakness, but it made it more tolerable as we journeyed on towards the final checkpoint. The only thing that stood in our way was a passage of sand dunes, not huge ones thankfully.

It was at checkpoint six that I received the makeshift shower I mentioned in the prologue. After that rejuvenating experience, Andrew and I decided not to hang about for too long. The end of day four was in sight and the pair of us were keen to get to that finish line as quickly as we could so we could draw a line under a day of such brutal challenge neither of us would ever forget.

The six kilometres* of flat, sandy terrain that made up the final leg was as pedestrian a leg as I'd experienced so far. It still seemed to take forever to complete, but the challenge – in comparison to pretty much every other leg so far – was minimal. It was just a case of covering the ground and knowing that finish line would eventually appear. And when it did, the overpowering feeling was one of relief. Dionne was the catalyst in completing a momentous, gruelling day that actually ended up being longer than a day, 26 hours and 45 minutes to be exact. I was doing it for her and it was her who kept me going and got me through it.

Due to being so exhausted and relieved, I didn't anticipate a change in my emotions, but as I sat there in the sand, it dawned on me that not only was I past the worst of my illness, I had also completed the most taxing parts of the race. Euphoria set in and a smile graced my face. I knew there and then that I was going to complete the 35th edition of the Marathon des Sables. The final two days would still be challenging, but they'd be nothing compared to the savagery of day four. I was going to do this! Nothing could stop me now.

'I'm finishing this,' I said to no-one in particular, fists clenched, smile growing wider. As electric pulses of joy and ecstasy rippled through me, energising me like a

---

* 3.7 miles

battery charger, I thought about Dionne and everyone who'd sponsored me. *You're not letting them down now, Mavis. Not a chance in hell.*

SEAN'S MARVELLOUS MEDICINE

F eet throbbing and with Dionne on my mind, I faltered my way towards the red dragon of Wales to see my last remaining tentmate, Sean, a machine of a man who was beasting his way through the Marathon des Sables, laughing in the face of the unprecedented circumstances.

'Alright, mate,' I said, walking into the tent.

The shock on his face was priceless. 'You made it!' he cried, sheer delight in his voice. He high-fived me, grinning from ear to ear, and rattled off sentence after sentence at 100mph in his strong Welsh accent. My exhaustion would've been a contributing factor, but I had great difficulty following what he was saying. In those moments, I felt like Manny and Milo, unable to understand what was being said but fully understanding the message from the tone, inflection and body language. Essentially, he was telling me how happy he was that I'd made it.

I had a lot of time for Sean. He was a tough guy, but when he was smiling and laughing, he was like a big teddy bear. His career had been pretty diverse, incorporating building houses from scratch, owning and running a pub, working in the ambulance service and serving in the military, not to mention competing in more than 70 ultra-events. He was well-built, sturdy and strong, the kind of guy you could imagine excelling at rugby or American Football. He also seemed to have a fortress of a constitution, somehow immune to the stomach bug that had ripped through the camp, taking out competitors left, right and centre. Certainly, if he had been suffering from it in any way, shape or form, he never showed it. Maybe there was a secret ingredient in his hot chocolate. Yes, you read that correctly, *hot* chocolate, in a desert where the temperature regularly exceeded 50 degrees Celsius*. He was one of the few who had brought a little stove with him, so he could have a hot chocolate every night before bed. The whole desert was a stove, but there was Sean, firing it up each and every night to make his hot chocolate, the soundtrack of retching and vomiting in both foreground and background inescapable. A kind soul, he always offered to share, but most of the time whoever was still left in the tent was too knackered or ill to take him up on it.

'Is that a Scottish voice I hear?'

I turned round to see Jack standing at the entrance of our tent. 'It sure is,' I said with a smile.

Jack looked equally as shocked as Sean did to see that I'd made it, probably more so. After all, Jack had seen the condition I was in when I couldn't stop being sick and had told him and Ian to carry on without me.

'It's so good to see you,' Jack said. 'I honestly didn't expect you to make it. I'm over the moon for you.'

Whilst it was heart-warming to see how happy Sean and Jack were to see me, I think the overwhelming emotion was relief. If I hadn't made it, Sean would've faced three nights in the tent on his own, which I don't think he would've liked. He was happy enough being solo out on the sands, focussed on the task at hand, but

* 122 Fahrenheit

he liked people around him afterwards, not just for safety but for company as well.

As for Jack, I think his relief came from seeing a) that I hadn't withdrawn, and b) that I was still alive! I didn't think about it at the time, but if I'd died back there, he would have felt terrible, maybe even culpable. My insistence on him and Ian continuing without me was down to me not wanting to hold them back. It was their race as much as mine, so it wouldn't have been fair to ask them to stay with me until I felt able to soldier on. I hadn't fully considered the risk at that point, but the combination of relief and joy in Jack's expression told me everything I needed to know. We congratulated each other without ever speaking about those details, focussing instead on the fact that the three of us had come out victorious from the most monstrous challenge this hazardous, torturous, completely bananas race had thrown at us.

What happened next was one of the oddest moments of my Marathon des Sables experience, which is saying something! Adding to Jack and Sean's elation and relief, a Dubai-based Londoner by the name of Joseph appeared at the tent to offer his congratulations.

'I can't believe you got through that,' he said.

'Thanks, mate,' I responded. 'Neither can I!'

I did my best to recall meeting Joseph out on the battlefield, but there was nothing there. He was a complete stranger to me, which made me feel bad, because we'd obviously had some sort of interaction, to the extent that he'd acknowledged how depleted I looked and was concerned for my safety. I put my lack of recollection down to how fragile my mind had been during certain points over the course of the 82.5km slog, the lake mirage being a significant low. I must've chatted to Joseph at some point, but for how long and about what is anyone's guess. Only Joseph will know. Regardless, I appreciated his hosannas, proof that I must have looked horrific and highly likely to withdraw or be withdrawn. That, of course, was accurate, which only added to how fantastic it felt to be out of the other side.

Overall, the atmosphere in the camp had improved markedly. The camaraderie was back and the atmosphere in the air was more positive than it had been for days. Everyone who was still in the race knew that the worst was over. That didn't mean that the remainder would be a walk in the park – no-one was complacent – but knowing the biggest challenge of the week was behind us shifted the scales, the dread and desperation being countered by hope and excitement. The stomach bug was still hanging around like an uninvited troublemaker at a party, but it wasn't as prevalent, its reign under threat, the retching more sporadic than constant.

It was just after midday when Joseph and Jack headed back to their respective tents. It was day five, our rest day, and a rest was definitely something I needed. I lay down on my sleeping bag, Sean on his, and we set our sights on the land of nod. There was plenty of time to rest and recover in preparation for day six, a four-leg stretch totalling 42.2km*.

'Is it just me, mate,' I said to Sean, lying on my back looking at the canvas, ' or is it even hotter out there than it has been at any other point this week?'

'You might be right,' Sean replied. 'Just be grateful you're not out there running in it.'

'Too right,' I said and we shared a laugh. With the buzz of what I'd just achieved still simmering, I closed my eyes and managed to drift off to sleep.

* 26.2 miles

Unfortunately though, I woke up after only an hour, my body seemingly unwilling to allow me the sleep I craved. Maybe I was still in survival mode, body and mind in conflict, my mind denying me what my body needed. Sean was in the same boat, so we decided to head to the medical tent to have our blisters looked at. There was always the option of patching them up ourselves, or working on each other's, but because they were in such poor condition, we thought it best to consult the experts.

When we got there, we took off our socks and shoes and lay on our backs on the ground next to each other. We chatted away, feeling quite good despite the blazing heat and our unsuccessful attempts at prolonged rest. Two female doctors, both French but with impeccable English, each positioned a chair at our respective feet, sat down and raised a right leg each onto their laps, making the process look like well-rehearsed, synchronised choreography. Sean's feet were a state, but mine looked like I'd been running barefoot on nails for four and a half days. Blisters covered each foot to the extent it looked like there were more blisters than regular foot. I assumed my doctor would lacerate them, douse them in iodine and bandage them up. Instead though, she reached down, opened one of the drawers in the plastic box of medical kit that sat on the floor next to her chair, and pulled out a great big syringe, about 10cm in length. I figured she was going to use the syringe to pop the blisters rather than a scalpel, but instead she plunged the needle right into my heel.

'Ouch!' I yelped, jerking in response to what she'd just done.

'Stop that!' she blurted, her tone authoritative like a schoolteacher. From her reaction, she must have thought

I was a wimp and expected better from someone who had made it through day four. Sean was in fits of laughter, unable to contain himself, until his doctor reached down and pulled out an identical syringe. The smile fell from his face, instantly transferring to mine. His feet might have been in slightly better condition, but the same fate awaited him. He grimaced as it went in, but he made sure not to jolt and twitch, to avoid being told off like I had. We had faith the doctors knew what they were doing and if getting our heels syringed meant improving the state of our feet, we were all for it.

After returning from the medical tent, Sean and I just lay about for the rest of the day, keeping the weight off our feet to allow them to recover as much as possible. The organisers had promised an ice cold can of cola to every valid competitor on the evening of rest day. I had wondered if it was a wind up, but was overjoyed when I discovered it was genuine. When I received my can, it was covered in condensation, like it belonged on a TV advert rather than in the hands of a sand-skelped Scotsman with feet that looked like they might need amputated in the not-too-distant future. All I'd drunk for days was tepid, lukewarm, or roasting hot water, so to have something chilled, sweet and bubbly was like a lottery win. I'm not even a fan of fizzy drinks, but drinking down that nectar was sheer bliss.

Before attempting to get more shut-eye, I used the satellite phone to call Monica. I knew she'd have been worried about me, so it was important to assure her that I was okay. Being cut off from the outside world was part of the Marathon des Sables, but Pierre's death, the insane temperatures, the stomach bug and the brutality of day four had changed the circumstances.

It occurred to me that Monica would be tracking me on the website or via the app on her phone and might have become concerned when she saw the little dot that represented me stop moving. These periods of inactivity would be my sleeping, resting or vomiting time rather than me collapsing, fainting or dying, but a dot on a screen thousands of miles away doesn't differentiate between these things.

When I spoke to her, she confirmed that her mind had gone into overdrive when my little dot had remained static for any length of time. Overall, the tech is impressive, but it was also responsible for generating unnecessary panic. I didn't tell Monica all the details of what I encountered on day four as I didn't want to add to her worry. I instead focussed on the fact that the biggest hurdles had been overcome and that I was not only still living and breathing, but that I was on track to complete my mission, honour my sponsors and make her and Dionne proud.

We spoke for a while and I relayed some of the highlights and lowlights of the race so far, pleased that I'd put her mind at rest. At least I think I had. If I'd told her everything that had been going on, that wouldn't have helped, so whilst I didn't brush over how brutal the race had been, I assured her that the worst was behind me and that I had everything under control.

I doddered back to the tent via the revolting toilets, pleased that the bug had waned, but not to the extent that I was feeling great, or anything close. I still had a bit of diarrhoea, hence the pit stop, but I had stopped vomiting, which was fantastic. Keeping things in my stomach long enough for them to work their way into my system – like that luscious can of ice-cold cola – was a total boon. This pleasure was topped up when I returned to the tent to be welcomed by the smell of hot chocolate.

Since the puking had ceased, I thought there'd be no harm in trying Sean's go-to bedtime treat. Maybe it would protect me from now until the end of the race like it had protected him since the start line on day one. I'm not someone who believes in hocus-pocus like this, but there was no reason not to try it, if for no other reason than it smelt terrific. I had almost become used to the pungent reek of sweat, spew and squirty bums, so it was nice to have something appealing to cloak those unpleasant smells. The difference this time, though, was that I wanted to drink it. I had smelt it on previous nights, but the thought of consuming any was out of the question as I'd just chuck it up again. It had been a tease, but now I was in a condition to be able to drink it down, retain it and enjoy it fully. So that's exactly what I did, and it was delicious.

'One last push,' said Sean, draining the dregs of his cup.

'Yes, mate, the finishing line is in sight,' I smiled.

'You've got it in the bag,' Sean replied, pointing at me, his tone suggesting the remaining kilometres were nothing more than a formality.

'So have you, thanks to your miracle hot chocolate,' I chuckled, straightening and flattening my sleeping bag.

'Don't tell anyone, Mavis,' he laughed. 'It's our little secret, okay?'

We wished each other good night and settled down with the hope of a decent night's sleep. That only applied to me, right enough, as Sean had managed to sleep better than me or any of our other tentmates. One of those lucky ones who can go out like a light no matter where

317

he is, what he's been doing, or what he has ahead of him when he wakes.

I lay there looking up at the canvas, completely knackered but unable to drift off. I couldn't help thinking about the dark place I had found myself in at checkpoint three. I'd never felt like that before and never wanted to again. I'd had to dig deeper than I'd ever dug before during those moments, helped of course by Dionne. It was like a massive God-like Dionne had found the ability to grip and reached down to me there on that rug, pulling me out of the darkness.

Without her, I was done. With her, I was finishing this thing.

COISTY AND THE CONVERTIBLE

I got up early on the morning of day six, not through choice, but because it was a 7am kick-off, meaning we had to be at the start line for 6.55am at the latest. Despite being over the worst it, both in race and stomach bug terms, my sleep had still been erratic and inadequate. This meant the filing cabinets in my brain would be all over the place, some of them containing the wrong files, others left open with files spilling out onto the floor. Expecting myself to perform to a decent standard during the 42.2km that lay before me was the equivalent of expecting a computer to perform as normal during an essential system update *and* a defrag. Although getting more than two and a bit consecutive hours of sleep would have been nice, I had come to expect the broken pattern that had impeded me since the night before day one. Regardless, although I was bushed and still a bit ill, I was buoyed at the end being in sight. This didn't mean I expected day six to be a piece of cake – 42.2km is the length of a full standard marathon after all – but because I had conquered day four, it felt like I was on the home straight.

The earliest I had set off was 8.15am – the dreaded day four – but setting off at 7am was actually a good thing as the sun wouldn't be at full strength at that time. It would, of course, grow hotter kilometre after kilometre, but it meant we could cover a decent whack of ground in more tolerable conditions before the scorching heat came along to slow us down. Also, considering I wasn't sleeping well anyway, I might as well be up and getting on with what stood between me and the finish line.

Jack and I agreed to tackle day six together, which was great. We were happy to go at each other's pace and got on well, so it made sense, plus I had no plans to abandon him this time due to becoming possessed by the vomit monster. The hot chocolate I'd had with Sean the previous night had stayed down, as had my morning recovery shake and regular granola and Imodium breakfast, so it looked fairly certain that there'd be no repeat of that ghastly, asphyxiating experience.

When we arrived at the start line, the mood was markedly different to how it was at the beginning of day four. It wasn't quite the level of excitement and euphoria as day one, but that was because the numbers had dropped significantly and many of those who were left were still feeling pretty ropey. That aside though, the party atmosphere had definitely returned, the vibe positive as the feel-good factor bounced from competitor to competitor. Positivity breeds positivity, so the good vibes were infectious, the chatting and laughing growing louder and more prominent the closer we got to the klaxon that would kick-start the second last day of the 35th edition of the Marathon des Sables.

Bizarrely, the medals are handed out at the end of day six, rather than on the final day. The final day is only 8.5km* and is run for Solidarity, an urgent aid charity supported by the Marathon des Sables. Interestingly, it's still necessary to run the final 8.5km even though the medals are handed out the previous day and the awards ceremony takes place the same night. A few competitors

* 5.3 miles

had asked if they could forsake the final day and were told they could, but that they'd be disqualified. It'd be crazy to soldier through the mammoth sand dunes of day two and the utter mayhem of day four to then be disqualified for not running eight and a half kilometres on flat land on the final day. I'm not sure if medals would be taken back if anyone opted out of the final day or withdrew during the race. I doubt anyone will ever find out to be honest, because it's not something that'll ever happen.

After the customary pre-race chat from Patrick Bauer and 'Highway to Hell' being blared across the shimmering sands, the klaxon sounded and we were off. My blisters were raging but, as I had done previously, I tried to use the pain positively. The agony gave me a sense of being alive and helped detract my attention from my guts and the anticipation of the temperature rising to furnace levels.

There's not too much to say about day six, or certainly nothing that hasn't been covered already. The terrain was relatively flat, a short pass of small, manageable sand dunes being the only exception. Jack and I took it easy, chatting away to each other to pass the time, every step pushing us closer to fulfilling our goal. It was the most chatty I'd been in days, another sign that I was over the worst of the bug and starting to feel like myself again. I decided to tell Jack a couple of football stories, the first being a Coisty classic that makes me laugh every time I think of it:

Jim Lauchlan, a really likeable big guy from the east end of Glasgow, had broken into the Kilmarnock first team as a centre half and was delivering the goods. He worked hard, gelled with the rest of the team and communicated well with his keeper and fellow defenders.

He was, however, pretty gallus and sometime over-confident, bordering on the cocky, something Coisty picked up on instantly. As a gallus character himself, I knew it wouldn't be too long before some sort of carry-on or prank was dished out. Bobby Williamson was the gaffer at that time and he, naturally, was wise to Jim's characteristics and traits and had to regularly rein him in to keep his feet on the ground.

Despite his gallusness, Jim – or Lauchie as we called him – performed well enough on the pitch for Bobby to offer him a three-year extension on his contract. Delighted, Lauchie snapped up the offer, signed all the necessary paperwork and, to celebrate, went out and bought himself a brand new burgundy Peugeot convertible with a private number plate. Next day, he turned up to training in it and, as you would expect, everyone noticed. This was exactly what Lauchie wanted of course, but with McCoist in the team and Bobby Williamson as the manager, it was a careless move. By all means, buy yourself a nice car if that's your thing, but don't show off your private number plate and soft, retractable roof in front of these guys.

Bobby took him into his office and, according to what Lauchie told us later on, he was completely slaughtered. He'd sat there taking pelter after pelter, the pride he'd had in showing off his convertible instantly downgraded to regret and embarrassment as the slaggings came thick and fast. As part of his annihilation, Bobby had called him a big-time-Charlie, but I'm guessing that was one of the milder insults thrown at him.

Twenty minutes later, Coisty appeared, bursting into the dressing room, full of life as usual, instantly making his presence known. Most of us were surprised to see him because being 20 minutes late was early by his standards.

'Right, Mavis,' he said with a grin, 'what's the big news this morning then?'

I nodded over to a sheepish looking Lauchie, worn down by Bobby having hauled him over the coals. 'Big Lauchie's gone out and bought himself a convertible to celebrate his new contract,' I replied. 'Private reg plate and everything.'

Coisty's face lit up, the cogs already turning. Something was definitely brewing and I knew it wouldn't be long before I found out what.

At that point, Kilmarnock didn't have their own training ground, so we were always scouting out different locations, sometimes even using public parks if they were in good enough condition. Many a Killie fan probably walked past their heroes while out walking their dogs, assuming it was a junior or reserve team being put through their paces.

That day, Bobby announced that he'd found a suitable open grass area in Irvine and asked us to follow the coaching staff in a convoy of cars.

'Right, Lauchie,' said Coisty, instantly, 'me, Mavis and Bunion will come with you so you can show us your new motor. I hear it's a belter.'

'Nae bother, Coisty,' Lauchie said, visibly pleased to have his approval.

As we got ourselves ready to go, Coisty revealed where his thinking had been going.

'Right, lads, before we go to training, let's have a wee sweepstake, a tenner each,' he said, a glint in his eye. 'Instead of following the convoy, we'll go into Irvine town centre and stop some punters to ask for directions to the training ground.'

'Okay,' I said, inquisitively, raising an eyebrow.

'The punters have got to mention my name though, 'Are you Ally McCoist?' or something like that. We'll each pick how many punters we think'll recognise me and whoever's closest wins the dosh. Yous up for it?'

'I don't know, Coisty,' Lauchie said, pursing his lips and shaking his head slightly. 'We might end up late for training.'

'It'll be fine,' Coisty said, dismissively, a cheeky smile on his face. 'You're with me.'

So off we went in Lauchie's shiny new burgundy convertible, Coisty and Lauchie in the front with me and Bunion in the back, detouring into Irvine town centre. Everyone we stopped to ask for directions recognised Coisty, most of them instantly, all of them asking for his autograph.

'Bet you wish you were as famous as me, eh?' he laughed, looking back at me and Bunion. We just laughed back, knowing fine well it wasn't a question that warranted an answer. At this point, I still didn't know what his game plan was because the focus was on him rather than Lauchie. However, after we'd stopped a few more punters and had a chat and a laugh, it clicked that the sweepstake was nothing more than a distraction to make us late for training. I looked at the clock on the dashboard and we were already 20 minutes late.

'We should really get going, Coisty,' Lauchie said, a touch of panic in his voice. 'The gaffer won't be happy at us being late for training.'

'I didn't realise that was the time,' Coisty lied. 'Get the foot down, Lauchie. Let's see what your new motor's made of.'

Soon enough, we were out of Irvine town centre and heading towards the training ground. We turned into a wide open grass area – which we shouldn't have been driving on – and could make out our teammates in the distance, just short of a quarter of a mile* away, already going through their drills. This served only to panic Lauchie more. The gaffer had already been through him once that day, so he didn't want to give him an opportunity to go through him again.

Totally deadpan, Coisty turned to Lauchie and said, 'D'ye think you could get 120 out of this?'

'No way,' Lauchie replied. 'This is turf we're on, not tarmac, and anyway, the garage told me to keep it below 70 for the first few weeks.'

'Ach, that's a load of crap,' Coisty nipped, 'that's just something they guys always say. I reckon you could get at least 115 out of this. What do you think, lads?' Coisty looked over his shoulder.

'Maybe,' Bunion said, in as neutral a tone as possible.

'Listen, Lauchie, I've got a brilliant idea,' Coisty chirped, clapping his hands together. 'The boys and the gaffer will love it and it'll get you back in the good books with him.'

This was it. This was what he had planned all along.

'We'll get the roof down,' Coisty continued, pressing various buttons, 'get the tunes on full blast, hit the gas and blast this bad boy right onto the training ground.'

'Coisty, wait a minute, don't you think–'

'The boys will see us coming,' Coisty continued as the roof retracted, 'and they'll scatter at the last minute. Then I'll yank the handbrake and we'll do a handbrake turn and arrive in style, like something out of *The Dukes of Hazzard*. Then, casual as anything, we'll get out the car and join in with the training as if nothing's happened.

---

* 0.4km

The gaffer'll love it. The boys'll love it. What do you reckon, lads?'

Bunion and I looked at each other, wordlessly agreeing that it's not the kind of thing Bobby Williamson would even like, let alone love.

'Coisty, I do *not* think that is a good idea,' Lauchie said, doing his best to be assertive.

'Aw, come on!' Coisty countered, irrepressible as ever. 'It'll be a great laugh! The boys'll love it, trust me!'

There were a few moments of silence between us until Lauchie uttered, 'Aye, alright then.'

'Yaaas!' Coisty rejoiced, cranking the volume on the car stereo, Lauchie's CD of pounding dance tunes penetrating the Irvine air, turning a few heads in the process.

With no-one in front of us, Lauchie put his foot to the floor.

'Faster, faster!' Coisty shouted, like a kid on a fairground ride. I leaned over to look at the speedometer, which was approaching 110mph. 'Faster, faster,' Coisty continued, laughing like a lunatic.

Despite our speed, everything felt like it was in slow motion as we rocketed closer and closer to our teammates, their bodies increasing in size by the second. A few stopped what they were doing and looked up, conscious that a car was careering towards them at over 110mph. I can only imagine what it must've been like to be one of them, the roar of the engine and the pounding dance tunes growing louder and louder as the distance between convertible and squad became less and less.

From where I was sitting, it looked like they all froze, transfixed at what they were witnessing, unable to accept that a convertible coming at them at great speed was something that would even be possible at a Kilmarnock training session. At what looked like the last second, the reality hit home and they scattered in all directions, some shouting and probably swearing, not that I could hear anything over the thump of the four-on-the-floor. Coisty reached down and, with great force, pulled on the handbrake. We spun like a waltzer, up on two wheels at one point, tottering on the brink of upending, narrowly avoiding death or at least a trip to A&E followed by months of physio. It felt like we were hanging up there on two wheels for ages, but it'd be a couple of seconds at the most. Mercifully, gravity took over and put us back onto the turf on four wheels.

Danger over, Coisty got out of the car, followed by Lauchie and then me and Bunion. A livid Bobby Williamson ran towards the car. 'Lauchlan, you arsehole!' he bellowed. 'It's always you, isn't it?'

If he hadn't been held back by some of our teammates, I reckon Bobby would have swung for him.

Then, as if it was scripted, Coisty puffed out his cheeks and shook his head. 'Gaffer, I tried to tell him,' he reasoned, 'but he wouldn't listen.' He put out a hand. 'Look, I'm shaking like a leaf!'

Lauchie was fined two weeks' wages for his antics, even though he was heavily egged on by the club's ultimate practical joker. He could've refused to put his foot to the floor certainly, but it's always difficult to say no to Coisty. The bit I can't get over, though, is him believing that the boys and the gaffer would love it! But that was Coisty all over, an expert at convincing people to believe the opposite of the truth.

Stories like this kept Jack and I going as we maintained our steady pace. The sun was growing hotter – not that this was a surprise to us – but we ploughed on, keeping each other entertained as we went. The party atmosphere hadn't died down any, competitors cheering each other on as they passed or were passed by others. It was invigorating and kept the positivity alive and well, something that had been very much an uphill struggle earlier in the week but was now made much easier because it was en masse. If everyone maintained the upbeat and encouraging atmosphere, not only would it not die, but it'd become the default, in turn increasing everyone's chance of success.

Jack shared a few stories from his time in the Marines, including being taught how to calculate distance without any technology. I followed his explanation as best as I could but I found it tricky to carry out. It wasn't known to be easy though, so I persevered, quizzing Jack when necessary. These activities ate up the time and, given that we were in a race, that time meant distance, meaning we were always edging closer to where we wanted to be.

I decided to tell Jack another funny story, this time about something that happened during my probation period with the police:

It was a Saturday afternoon and Kilmarnock were playing Motherwell at Fir Park. My partner and I were working across Motherwell and Wishaw that afternoon and were contacted by officers at Fir Park because a Kilmarnock fan had been arrested for a minor offence and they needed him to be taken to Motherwell Police Station.

We didn't know, nor were we told, what he had done to be arrested, but when we turned up, it was clear he'd had a skinful as his words were slurred, his balance impaired and he reeked of alcohol. Thankfully, he wasn't aggressive and was largely compliant with what we asked him to do, which was a bonus as it didn't always play out like that. The officers at Fir Park had cuffed him, so we switched their cuffs for ours, got him into the van without a struggle and made our way to Motherwell Police Station.

When we arrived, my partner and I took off our hats – as is customary when entering a police station – and tucked them under our arms. Civilian staff searched the perpetrator and, once satisfied, gave me and my partner the green light to take his cuffs off. During this process, the duty officer was asking questions from behind the charge bar[*] and entering the garbled, slurred responses into a computer. The search now over, my partner and I stood either side of the perpetrator, holding an arm each, in case he attempted to escape or kick off – not that he was in any condition to be able to do either to be honest, but sometimes alcohol fuels those beliefs, despite it being the root of the impairment in the first place.

As the duty officer continued to ask questions, the perpetrator, now no longer distracted by being searched, threw me a sideways glance. With my hat having been removed, the expression on his face said, *I know him from somewhere.* He chanced a second look and his face lit up as if it was a surprise birthday party we'd taken him to rather than a police station.

'Mavis Reilly?' he shouted, pointing at me, his tone a mixture of jubilation and disbelief.

I ignored him like nothing had happened, continuing to look at the duty officer, who had just been rudely interrupted, not that these processes were renowned for being interruption-free certainly. I knew the duty officer wasn't interested in football, nor had he any idea that I'd played for Kilmarnock for 11 seasons, so he was totally baffled by the perpetrator pointing at me and shouting the name of a character from *Coronation Street*. I'd been

---

[*] The reception-style counter at a police station

given the nickname Mavis by former Killie centre half, Paul Flexney, who claimed that everyone needed a nickname and that Mavis suited me because, like the *Corrie* character, I was a wee moaner. It stuck, so much so that the only person who still calls me Mark is my mum. Even Monica has me in her phone as Mavis!

'I've just been arrested by Mavis Reilly!' the perpetrator rejoiced. 'Wait till I tell the lads who gave me the jail.' He burst out laughing as if he'd just heard the funniest joke in the world. 'This is the second best day of my life after the cup final in 97!'

It was a surreal moment for me. I maintained the professional demeanour expected of a police officer, refusing to entertain or encourage the perpetrator's celebrations, but inside I was humbled by how much that victory meant to him all those years ago. He was clearly a Killie die-hard and had great affection for the club and its alumni. It was also hard not to laugh at the two best days of his life being Kilmarnock winning the Scottish Cup and being arrested by me. If he was married, I felt sorry for his wife as their wedding day could only peak at number three in the countdown of best moments of his life.

Regardless, I – somehow – managed not to laugh, the switch in my head set to 'professional' and 'on duty'. It became more and more difficult to maintain this, though, especially when the perpetrator burst into song.

'One Mavis Reilly! There's only one Mavis Reilly! One Mavis Reiiiiiily! There's only one Mavis Reiiiiiily!'

My partner, who knew about my footballing past, couldn't hold it together and burst into fits of laughter. I'd be lying if I said the faintest of smiles didn't appear on my face, but I managed to remain composed and serious, which no doubt made it all the funnier for both my partner and the perpetrator. Everyone in the station was looking over, wondering what the hell was going on. It was one of the most bizarre moments of my life and that's coming from someone who used to get sent bucketloads of Jaffa Cakes from McVitie's and who once believed there was a lake in the middle of the Sahara.

The duty officer, still clearly in the dark about what was going on before him, was getting really cheesed off.

'Do you want to charge him?' he barked over the singing, my partner still buckled with laughter.

'Yes, Sarge,' I replied, a tinge of guilt jabbing at me. This guy was treating me like a rock star, but I had to do what was right. I told him that, under the circumstances, I had to issue a caution and charge him. He was too focussed on singing my praises to absorb what I was saying, but I made sure the duty officer witnessed me following the correct procedure. Part of the script is to inform the perpetrator that they have an opportunity to reply to the charge, which is written in the arresting officer's notebook and can be used in evidence if the case goes to court.

'Now that I've explained everything to you,' I said to him, 'do you have any reply to the charge.'

'Aye,' he said, instantly, finger in the air. 'One Mavis Reilly! There's only one Mavis Reilly! One Mavis Reiiiiiily! There's only one Mavis Reiiiiiily!'

So that's what I had to write in my notebook: *There's only one Mavis Reilly.*

The perpetrator continued to sing and my partner continued to laugh as we took him down to the cells. As we made our way back up, we could still hear him, in full voice, his adulation unwavering, despite the fact I'd just locked him up. Even back at the charge desk, he could still be heard, albeit faintly. I offered a quick explanation to the duty officer before my partner and I returned to the streets of North Lanarkshire, where I could finally let out a hearty laugh. Thankfully, the case didn't go to court, but I do wonder what judge and jury would've made of *There's only one Mavis Reilly* as a piece of evidence!

Jack had let out a series of hearty laughs during that story as we continued to make our way through the desert, properly enjoying ourselves for the first time since day one.

As far as day six was concerned, there were no mirages, sky-high sand dunes as far as the eye could see, or vomit-fests teetering on the deadly. In comparison to other parts of the race, it was fairly straightforward, but the one thing that didn't relent was the heat. The remorseless sun never gave up, its strength as inescapable as it was intimidating. A quick search on the internet suggests temperatures in the Sahara can reach as hot as the high 40s (Celsius), but we had been exposed to 50+ the entire week, a temperature unsafe for human habitation, never mind mobility. It might have been my mind playing tricks on me again, but day six felt like that ominous, omnipresent sun was trying to beat its personal best. I've run out of adjectives to describe how hot it was, but to be honest, no words exist to describe the level of heat we experienced. At the checkpoints, even the fresh water was warm and between them, we had to endure the taste of plastic again.

Cooking like rashers of bacon, Jack and I – eventually – had the finish line in our sights, not just metaphorically, but for real this time. It should've been a moment of true elation, but I was split as to how to feel. It was the finish line, but there was still another mandatory 8.5km to complete the following day. It was going to feel weird receiving a medal for a race that wasn't quite finished. Regardless, 8.5km was literally a walk in the park (a sandy, grassless park) in comparison to the brutal distances we had already covered. Rightly or wrongly, I decided that, despite crossing the finish line on day six meaning I'd be awarded a medal, my personal cup final wasn't over yet.

Jack and I crossed the finish line together, the pair of us utterly drained, exhaustion blocking the euphoria we knew would come in good time. A super-animated Patrick Bauer greeted us with a grin as wide as his face, a celebratory fist pumping the air. He awarded us our medals, placing them over our heads, followed by more cheering and jubilation. After Jack and I congratulated each other, caught our breath and drank down some lukewarm water, I had a few moments of quiet contemplation and personal reflection. My thoughts were with my tentmates who didn't make it, six of them in total. Like me, each of them had trained for 19 months under Rory Coleman, as had Sean. They'd put their hearts and souls into conquering the Marathon des Sables, but it just wasn't to be. Not this year anyway. Silently, I toasted them with my lukewarm water, hoping they were well and would one day return to the Sahara to achieve what they'd set out to do.

Smiling, I looked at my medal and, naturally, thought about Dionne. The emotions swelled as elation set in, but I put a lid on them for now because there was still another day to go. Yes, I had the medal to prove I'd completed the 35th edition of the Marathon des Sables, but it wasn't over. Failure to complete the final 8.5km rendered the medal void, so it was like being given a brand new Ferrari for doing an exceptional job, but without the keys. The keys would only be passed over upon completion of one final, straightforward task. I didn't anticipate anything going wrong the following day, but I couldn't be complacent. I had just done 42.2km* in the Sahara and it had taken me eight hours and 16 minutes; the exact same distance in Nice took me a staggering five hours less! There was no place for complacency in the desert, so while I still joined in with what was going on, I decided to park my personal celebrations until I was 100 percent over the line.

That night, there was an awards ceremony, where the El Morabity brothers were awarded first and second place, as we all anticipated they would. There were other awards as well, age and gender categories and such like, but I didn't pay a great deal of attention to it all. It was obviously a great moment for those who achieved hard-earned recognition but, as far as I was concerned, everyone was a winner. That might sound trite, or a bit corny, but 47 percent of those excited, fired up competitors at the start line on day one had dropped out – not because of insufficient preparation, poor fitness or lack of mental strength, but because of the unique conditions the 35th edition had dealt out. A certain level of dropout is expected in any extreme event, but over the previous 34 editions of the Marathon des Sables, the dropout ranged between five and ten percent. Even considering the top end of that window, the 35th edition saw a 38 percent difference. It wasn't my intention and I'm not the owner of a crystal ball, but I had managed to pick the year when the toughest footrace on Earth was much tougher than usual. In my book, getting over the finish line this year was as much of an accolade as finishing first in any of the previous years. Every one of us had won and I'd never see it any other way.

* 26.2 miles

INJURY TIME GLORY

Having had the best sleep of the week and my general condition improving by the hour, I woke up on the final day feeling better than I had for a long time. But then I stood up. As soon as I placed any weight on my feet, they throbbed, pulsating like the toes of a cartoon character who'd just had a ten ton weight dropped on them. I knew this would be the case though, so I did my best to ignore it and get on with what the day had in store for me.

The previous night, after the awards ceremony, each competitor had been given a yellow Marathon des Sables charity T-shirt, to be worn on the final leg of our journey. I found mine and dragged it over my head, looking out over the camp, pleased to hear only the very occasional retch. It seemed cruel that the bug was at its most potent during the most challenging parts of the race, but at least it was on the way out, that was the main thing. The spirit in the camp after the awards ceremony had kept the positive vibe going and I had a smile to myself at the possibility of positivity being the bug's Achilles' heel.

Sean, as ever, was in good spirits, he too doing his best to ignore the condition his feet were in. He was going to have to go at my pace for this final stretch, whether he liked it or not, as it's traditional that tentmates run it together. While he got himself ready, I looked at his Welsh flag, gawking at the red dragon, wondering if there was anything in my theory that it had provided Sean with some form of protection. Generally, I find mythological stuff like that to be nothing more than conjecture, but at the same time I have no issue with anyone who treats it seriously, especially if they find it helpful. I was just conscious that, apart from blisters almost as grotesque as mine, Sean had body-swerved the stomach bug, had achieved some impressive times and didn't seem to be as affected by the heat as most. It was more likely to be personal strength, a never-say-die mindset and a level of resilience that would make superhero villains envious, but if that dragon had anything to do with it, it had done its job well. I decided there and then that the next time I decided to take on a mammoth personal challenge, there'd be no harm in packing a Lion Rampant.

When we got to the start line, all wearing the yellow charity T-shirts like we were members of a massive band, Patrick Bauer, from the roof of his Land Rover as always, burst into an enthusiastic speech. The atmosphere was vibrant and high-spirited, everyone knowing the finish line – the *actual* finish line – was only eight and a half kilometres away, a mere 5.3 miles. Having enjoyed the football stories the previous day, Jack decided to join me and Sean for the duration, but would split off and join his tentmates during the last couple of kilometres.

I appreciated Patrick's unyielding enthusiasm, but his speech (including translation) had hit the 20-minute mark and we all just wanted to get going. The jovial atmosphere was at risk of being impacted if he didn't draw things to a close soon. Strangely, just as I was thinking those thoughts, he said his final words and 'Highway to Hell' thundered out of the PA for the last time. In a pedantic way, the song had never really worked for me. It was the highways themselves that were hellish, especially on days two and four, and on this day – the charity day – it felt especially weird because, as soon as that klaxon went, we were on the highway to victory. The final 8.5km was known to be fairly flat and, in contrast to earlier parts of the race, relatively undemanding. This wasn't hell, a highway to or otherwise, it was our lap of honour, where, upon completion, we'd get to celebrate conquering the most challenging footrace on Earth in its most challenging year to date.

I shrugged off the lyrics of the song and instead focussed on its high energy and pounding beat, using that to help propel my obliterated feet across the sands for the final hurrah.

The klaxon blared for the last time and we were off, feet agony but spirits high, confident that nothing would stand in our way of getting where we wanted to be. The sun was as bright and raging as ever, but it was exhilarating to know that we'd be done and dusted by the time it reached peak strength. Knowing that Jack had enjoyed the football stories the previous day, I decided to tell him another one to pass the time:

Referees are often known to be a law unto themselves, but there were two I got on with really well during my playing days, Willie Young and Bobby Tait. If Willie made a poor decision or looked like he was favouring the opposing team, I'd get right up in his face and, living up to my nickname, have a right good moan at him. On one occasion, he looked right at me and said, 'Look, Mavis, you know you're having a shocker, mate, yet you're the one slagging *me* off?' It's funny looking back at these moments, because we were good friends off the pitch, yet you'd never know that based on the way we spoke to each other on match days.

Off the pitch, I got on equally well with Bobby Tait, but our relationship on the pitch was much like it was with Willie Young. I got the better of Bobby during the penultimate game of the 1997/98 season, though, a tie against Rangers at Ibrox where the outcome bore great significance for both clubs. A point behind Celtic at the time, a Rangers victory would mean the final game of the season (Dundee United v Rangers and Celtic v St Johnstone) would be a league decider. This was no regular league campaign for Rangers though, their ultimate goal being to break the record for consecutive number of league victories, the record at the time being nine, held by their city rivals. This meant a win over Kilmarnock was key in keeping their league and record-breaking hopes on track. Killing off Killie wasn't going to be a formality though, because victory for us would massively increase our chances of qualifying for Europe and competing in what was then the UEFA Cup the following season.

For two reasons, Bobby had been in the papers on the morning of the game. Firstly, he had announced he was retiring at the end of the season, meaning Rangers v Kilmarnock would be his penultimate professional gig as a referee and his last opportunity to officiate at Ibrox as Rangers' final game was away to Dundee United. The other reason was that it was no secret Bobby Tait was a massive Rangers fan, having supported them religiously since he was a kid. Allegedly, the SFA had gifted him the fixture as a retirement gift, which, naturally, had put the noses of anyone of a Kilmarnock or Celtic persuasion out of joint. We would be playing to win though. This wasn't about standing in the way of Rangers' success, it was about increasing our chances of qualifying for Europe – and if that meant wrecking the Rangers party, so be it. It wouldn't have mattered which team we were playing, we'd have had the same drive and determination.

I couldn't escape three facts, though: Rangers were at home; they'd be buzzing at the prospect of getting one up on their biggest rivals by achieving ten league victories in a row; and, of equal relevance, they had Bobby Tait on their side. It was going to be 11 v 12, so we knew before a ball was kicked that we'd be up against it. Not unjustly, some punters, pundits and players were calling it corrupt, but I put all that to one side and focussed solely on the game.

One thing I saw as being in our favour was that we were playing at Ibrox. Rangers had been the dominant team for the majority of the 1990s, but for whatever reason, Kilmarnock had a good record at Ibrox, beating them on their own turf on several occasions. Given they were so powerful in that era, our success in front of 49,000-odd Rangers fans could be considered unusual, especially since we struggled against them at Rugby Park, occasionally salvaging a point but regularly suffering defeat. Ibrox was also where the 1997 Scottish Cup Final took place, Hampden being unavailable because it was being renovated at the time.

Whether it was a contributing factor to our victory that day, I couldn't say, but I'd never enjoyed playing at the national stadium due to the distance between the crowd and the pitch. Ibrox was still a big stadium of course, but it was more compact, which made for a better atmosphere. I was sitting in the dressing room thinking about this when Bobby Tait appeared.

'Did you read the paper this morning, Mavis?' he asked me, winking.

He was looking for a bite, but I didn't entertain it. I just chuckled and said, 'I'm sure you'll be entirely fair today, Boabby. I wouldn't expect anything less from a professional like yourself.'

He walked out of the dressing room with the kind of cheeky grin you'd only see in a comic. *Ibrox might be an advantage*, I thought to myself, *but maybe not when it's him who's got the whistle.*

It was a pretty even game, the Killie defence holding strong, limiting Rangers to only a handful of opportunities, which they failed to capitalise on. A solitary shot on target, courtesy of Brian Laudrup, was saved comfortably by Gordon Marshall. I had a great chance in the first half to put us ahead, but I shot wide, much to the relief of the Rangers faithful.

At the 67-minute mark, Bobby Williamson took off Alex Burke and brought on Ally Mitchell, hoping fresh legs would give us a bit more threat. It's not that any of the play – from either side – was particularly poor, it was more a case of the defences being solid, neither back four willing to accept any responsibility for conceding. Time wore on and it remained 0-0, chances for both sides few and far between. I could hear the Rangers fans murmuring, collectively creating a sound that suggested they were beginning to become concerned. Noticing a lack of penetration, Bobby Williamson substituted Mark Roberts with Kevin McGowne. While this was going on, I looked up at one of the digital scoreboards (there's one at either end), which, as well as displaying the score, also showed how much time had been played. The number 84 had just turned to 85 as Kevin McGowne ran on, determination in his expression, relaying instructions from the gaffer to the players around him.

Five minutes later, the 89 on the big digital clock had turned to 90 and we were in injury time. Kevin McGowne had made a difference since coming on and a ball that had begun in our half had found its way to his feet. He ran up the wing, using his strength and skill to fend off a midfielder who was tracking back. He then worked his way past the Rangers left back and whipped in what could only be described as a David Beckham cross, perfectly weighted with an elegant bend, high enough to clear the heads of the opposition and descend to its target: the middle of the Rangers box. Ally Mitchell could've timed his run better, but he managed to sclaff it home from close range, silencing 99 percent of Ibrox and sending the remainder into raptures.

After the celebrations, it was essential that we didn't lose focus. We had an advantage to protect and Rangers still had all 12 men on the pitch. As they were getting ready for the re-start, their faces despondent, I looked up at the digital scoreboard to discover it had been turned off. Rangers had kicked off, so I couldn't contest it, but it was clearly done intentionally so we couldn't tell how much additional time had been played. The only person who'd know was Bobby Tait.

We battled away at protecting our lead, naturally focussing on making sure our defence was as solid and impenetrable as possible. Not that I could tell exactly, but it felt like four minutes had gone by and there hadn't been many stoppages throughout the game.

'Boabby, blow the whistle, time's up,' I yelled into Bobby's face, but he just ignored me like I wasn't there; didn't even make eye contact.

A minute or so later, I'm in his ear, shouting, 'Haw, Tait! The game's finished!' He looked at me this time, but continued to dish out the silent treatment.

Another minute went by and I'm cracking up now. 'Do you think we're zipped up the back, Boabby? Think we wouldnae notice the clocks going off? The game's done! Get that whistle blown!'

At least this time I got a reaction out of him. 'Mavis, I asked you if you'd read the paper this morning,' he nipped. 'We're playing until Rangers score!'

He ran away with a smirk on his face, continuing to officiate a game that should've been finished more than five minutes ago. No doubt he had added five minutes for our two-minute celebration.

Eventually, he blew the whistle. We must've played about eight minutes of injury time, but it didn't matter. Our fans went nuts, our chances of getting into Europe significantly increased. All we needed was to get a better result than St Johnstone in our final game against Hibs, and St Johnstone were away to Celtic.

With the exception of the Killie fans, who were overjoyed, Ibrox was eerily quiet. The only way they could achieve ten consecutive league victories was if Celtic faltered against Dunfermline or St Johnstone.

When I shook Bobby Tait's hand, I returned the smug expression he'd cast me after telling me we were playing until Rangers scored. I was tempted to say, 'Hard lines, Boabby, looks like your newspaper got it all wrong, eh?', but I decided to be the bigger man and say nothing, which probably wound him up more anyway.

Jack and Sean totally loved that story. 'I think that's even better than the Coisty convertible one,' Jack laughed.

'The Coisty convertible one?' asked Sean, intrigued.

'Tell it again,' said Jack. 'It's not the kind of story that gets old.'

So I did – and I think Jack enjoyed it even more the second time. He knew what was coming, so his eyes were fixed on Sean, anticipating his reactions.

These stories, as well as plenty other general banter, kept us ploughing through the sands and, before long, the finish line was in sight and Jack peeled away to find his tentmates. It was a bittersweet moment. In a matter of minutes, Sean and I would cross the finish line together, having successfully completed one of toughest challenges of our lives, but the absence of Matt, Terry, John, Mark, Chris and Aiden was pronounced, our army heavily depleted, each of them taken down by a desert devoid of pity. Despite knowing each other only a short time, the bond in the group was unmistakable and we'd all been looking forward to that moment when we crossed the finish line together.

I had to put that out of my mind, though, and focus instead on what I was about to achieve. I'd successfully navigated the highway through hell and was about to come out the other side, knackered but victorious. It was proof that as individual warriors, indomitable spirit, resilience, self-belief, motivation and positivity were forces to be reckoned with, but packed a bigger, stronger, more defiant punch when they worked collectively.

Definitely not a mirage this time, the finish line appeared in my line of sight. It was a moment I'd thought about regularly and, at one point, a moment that felt out of reach. But here it was at last, only a matter of seconds away. I'd be crossing the line with Sean but, in my mind, all our tentmates were there as well, each of them grinning with pride. The key people in my life fluttered through my thoughts – Monica, Nicole, Dean, my mum, Tam Burns, Coisty and big Kevin McGowne –

before my focus was consumed entirely by my little princess, Dionne.

I imagined the smile on her face as the same smile she had that day on the Chain Carousel – one of sheer joy, one that tells me she trusts me and loves me and knows I want her to have as good a life as possible.

Eyes damp, I crossed the finish line, my surroundings blurry.

We did it, Princess.

We did it.

EPILOGUE

What follows is a handful of extra pieces that missed out on the final cut, but were too good not to include.

THOSE DUNES

From reading about the sand dunes I had to navigate on day two, you'll know how taxing I found that that 13km stretch. Upon completion of the three legs that made up day two, I checked my time and learned that I'd come in at six hours and 36 minutes. In contrast, I completed the three legs that made up day one in four hours and 34 minutes, a full two hours and two minutes less. This might be understandable if day two was a good bit longer in distance than day one, but it was only longer by 0.3km*. There's no doubt the bulk of that extra two hours was spent in those dunes. They were horrendous!

TAXI FOR REILLY

At the finish line on the final day, about a dozen taxis were parked alongside the coaches that would cart us back to civilisation. However, those coaches did not

---

* Less than 0.2 of a mile

have air conditioning and would be packed with sweaty, exhausted competitors who hadn't had a shower for a full week. The taxi drivers were wise to it being mandatory for each competitor to carry 200 euros on their person, so they knew their comfortable, air-conditioned cabs would be attractive to any competitors willing to part with their cash.

Neither of us keen on stewing in a coach for the best part of six hours, Sean suggested going for it. We had stewed enough over the past week, so it was time to embrace some luxury and knock two hours off our journey time. After a bit of negotiation, Sean managed to secure a fee of 300 euros for our journey, so we hopped in and kissed goodbye to the Sahara.

About an hour and a half into the journey, I asked the driver, whose English was excellent, 'Does it ever rain here?'

'Oh yes, of course it does,' he replied, nodding. 'In fact, it rained just four years ago.'

Laughter erupted from the back seat, the driver laughing along with us, enjoying the moment. Part of the hilarity came from not knowing if he was being serious. About half an hour later, we asked if we could stop at a shop to get a cold drink, to which he duly obliged. As I decided what to buy, I clocked Sean with his head in the fridge. The air-con in the taxi was delightful, but the temperature was still ridiculously high, so he took the opportunity to chill his face while he could.

When we got chatting to the shopkeeper, he was intrigued by our accents. 'Are you Irish?' he asked Sean.

'No, Welsh,' Sean replied, looking at me as if to say, *At least he didn't say English*, something the Scots, Welsh and Irish get regularly when visiting other parts of the world.

'And what about you?' the shopkeeper asked, shifting his attention to me.

'I'm Scottish,' I told him.

'Ahhhh, I know someone from Scotland,' he said. 'A famous guy. Maybe you'll know him?'

I laughed. 'What's his name?'

'William Wallace,' he replied, cheerily. 'I saw him on television. Braveheart! You must know him.'

THE BERBER PALACE

Even though John had pulled out of the race after day three, he decided to stay at The Berber Palace in Ouarzazate to greet any Tent 54 members who made it to the end. Ouarzazate is the Moroccan city closest to the Sahara, aptly nicknamed 'The Door of the Desert'. A night in The Berber Palace was part of the Marathon des Sables package, so John, having learned that Sean and I were the last men standing, organised it so the three of us could share a room and spend a final night together relaxing and talking about our experiences. This was a kind gesture and said a lot about the camaraderie we had built as a group.

This was only made possible because Sean's mobile was capable of sending and receiving text messages. He was very much in the minority as far as that was concerned – my phone might as well not have existed – so that was handy. I decided it had something to do with his general luck or the combination of that red dragon and that luscious hot chocolate. I had noticed significant improvements in my appetite since I'd had that hot chocolate. What was his secret?

Rory Coleman had told me it takes two showers to get all the sand and dirt off. At the hotel, I had a 45-minute shower and loved every second of it. For ages, I just let the water batter me. It was so refreshing and rejuvenating, and reinforced how much I take for granted as part of everyday life in Scotland. When I eventually turned the shower off and began towelling myself down, I discovered what I had been told to be true. Even after 45 minutes, there was still sand behind my ears, buried deep in my leg hair and in the corners of my eyes.

It was great to see John again and the three of us ate like kings that night, gorging ourselves on as much food as our stomachs could hold. It might have been this overindulgence or it might have been my body being unwilling to allow me to unwind, but, much to my dismay, I had another night of broken sleep. Maybe it was too much to expect my body and mind to revert back to pre-Sahara. Maybe my body was still in survival mode, while my mind tried to make sense of what I had put myself through over the past week. Regardless, I was in a lovely, clean and comfortable bed with an actual roof over my head, so for that, I was exceptionally grateful.

BLISTERS

Given I had eaten my body weight in fresh, delicious food at The Berber Palace, the stomach bug that had plagued the camp was, by then – for me at least – a thing of the past. Having done Ironman events, plenty long-distance running and many years as a professional footballer, my body healed in good time. Fatigue and muscle ache disappeared in a matter of days and my sleep pattern sorted itself out after about a week. I just wish I could say the same about my feet. The ill-fitting running shoes had done me in big time, leaving my feet in quite a state. Not only did they take months to fully heal, I also got the impression that I might have done some lasting damage.

I was working at the Rangers v Hibs League Cup Semi-Final on the 21st of November, 42 days after returning from the Sahara, and my deployment was foot patrol from Cathcart Police Station to Polmadie. All I was doing was walking up and down, but after only a few hours, I began to get blisters. It had taken me three days to get them in the Sahara, but only a matter of hours on Polmadie Road in Glasgow, and that was with shoes that fitted me! So, if you're a runner planning on doing any ultra-events in the near future, if there's one piece of advice I can offer you, it's . . . make sure you wear shoes that fit you.

BIGGEST ACHIEVEMENT?

Once I got back to Scotland and settled back into a semblance of normal life, I posted a number of blogs on Facebook about my experience. The response I got was phenomenal, but one person posted a question that took me aback a little. *Does your Marathon des Sables medal mean as much to you as your Scottish Cup winners' medal?* It was a great question, and one I found extremely difficult to answer.

The fact is, those medals were earned through two entirely different experiences. Completing the Marathon des Sables was a massive personal accomplishment, driven by Dionne and my desire to raise funds and awareness for Reverse Rett. However, shortly after leaving checkpoint two during day four, it'd be inaccurate to say my life wasn't under threat. I was alone, in darkness, desperately weak, disorientated, dehydrated and undernourished. It was utterly terrifying, much more terrifying than playing midfield for Kilmarnock in *any* game, Scottish Cup Final or otherwise. Like boxing, the Marathon des Sables is an individual pursuit. Sure, boxers need an opponent, just like any race needs several participants to make it competitive, but it's very much a you versus yourself battle. All the training and positive thinking in the world doesn't take away from the fact that success is determined entirely by the actions and decisions of the individual.

In contrast, football is a team game, one opponent made up of 11 individuals. Success lies in teammates knowing each other's strengths and weaknesses, and playing to strengths. If part of the machine is weak, the whole machine can suffer. This is one of the reasons success tastes so good in team sport: it provides confirmation of excelling not just individually but as a key part of a well-oiled force to be reckoned with.

Completing the Marathon des Sables raised over £21k for Reverse Rett, which is more important to me than a medal, but the medal confirmed completion and ensured I was able to collect all the sponsorship money that would contribute to discovering a cure for the disease that has trapped my lovely wee girl. This might lead me to say that the Marathon des Sables medal is more meaningful, but it isn't as simple as that.

Winning the Scottish Cup Final in 1997 was a tremendous achievement on a personal level, but I didn't win it on my own. I was part of a tight-knit team that succeeded collectively, bringing sheer joy not only to the team but to so many other people as well. John Finnie Street was rammed with Killie fans as far as the eye could see as we made our way through the throng in an open top bus. I was one member of a team of players that generated that massive, monumental celebration, and that is something that will stay with me for life. Apart from the Ayr United fans, it felt like the whole of Ayrshire was there that day, all decked out in Killie blue and white, beaming with pride to be part of a Scottish town whose football team had just won the Scottish Cup.

Although Falkirk would've been disappointed on the day, I was seriously impressed by how many fans the two towns packed into Ibrox. It was the first time in 40 years that a Scottish city hadn't featured in the Scottish Cup Final and the stadium was absolutely buzzing. It was another aspect that made that day – and win – all the more special. Interestingly, the Scottish Cup Final in 1957 was also between Kilmarnock and Falkirk, won 2-1 in extra time by Falkirk in a replay after the original tie ended 1-1. It's been a while since finals weren't decided on the day, one of the many things that has changed in the game over the years.

Another consideration when thinking about that Facebook user's question is that anyone can enter the Marathon des Sables as long as they pass the medical and pay the entry fee. This doesn't apply to playing professional football or winning a cup final. Those experiences can only be earned through commitment and hard graft.

I decided it wasn't possible to answer the question one way or the other. That may come across as sitting on the fence, but because the two experiences were so different, yet equally meaningful, for me, they'll just have to co-exist.

THE LIVES OF REILLY

A few weeks after returning from the Sahara, a card addressed to me, but for Dionne, arrived in the post:

Hi Dionne,

Your dad told me some amazing things about you and it helped get me through the race when I was really struggling. I thought of you and it inspired me, so I just want to thank you.

Sean.

ACKNOWLEDGEMENTS

To my mum, Kathleen, a strong, hardworking woman who showered me with unconditional love and instilled in me the importance of faith, integrity and humility. She worked day and night to make sure I always had a pair of football boots. I never went without.

To my dad, Terry, who introduced me to the beautiful game. Little did I know it would bring me so much joy and become my profession.

To my children, Nicole, Dean and Dionne. Each of you have given me strength to keep going and never give up.

To Tam Burns, who taught me the importance of striving to be the best version of myself I can be every single day.

To Ally McCoist for reminding me that a smile can be found in every situation.

To Kevin McGowne and Andy Millen for having my back every Saturday on a football pitch – and every day since.

To all my friends who have supported me through good times and bad.

To Tent 54 and all the characters I met in that merciless desert. Thanks for the memories.

To Andy and Rachael Stevenson for their drive and determination to give everyone suffering from Rett Syndrome a better life.

To my co-writer David McCarthy for his time, creative writing and selfless kindness in helping me tell my story.

To my co-writer and editor Dickson Telfer for his creativity, hard work, attention to detail, and for making this book happen.

To Emmanuel Lamarle, the MDS Foundation, *The Daily Record* and Kilmarnock F.C. for their assistance in acquiring photographs for inclusion in this book.

To all the celebrities who posted or shared messages about any of my fundraising endeavours.

To everyone who has sponsored me and donated to Reverse Rett. A heartfelt thank you.

To my wife, Monica. I'm blessed to be surrounded by strong women and none more so than you. My rock, I'm so fortunate to have met you.

To my ultimate inspiration, Dionne. You have taught me the importance of appreciating the simple things in life and the real meaning of gratitude.

Mark 'Mavis' Reilly is an ex-professional footballer player and ultra-event enthusiast. He has played for Motherwell, Reading, St Johnstone and St Mirren, but spent the bulk of his career at Kilmarnock. He helped St Mirren secure promotion to the Scottish Premier League in 2006 and was a mainstay in the Kilmarnock starting 11 that won the Scottish Cup in 1997.

Mavis regularly seeks out ways to test his resilience and challenge his mind. He enjoys stepping out of his comfort zone and embraces any opportunity to raise awareness and funds for Reverse Rett, a charity with the goal of reversing Rett Syndrome, the condition his daughter Dionne suffers from.

Currently working as a police officer for Police Scotland, Mavis has plans to continue to push himself in all aspects of his life, driven by his hunger for personal growth – both physical and mental – and his endeavour to raise as much money for Reverse Rett as possible.

He lives in Uddingston with his wife, Monica, and two dogs, Manny and Milo.

In a sportswriting career spanning almost four decades, **David McCarthy** has covered numerous World Cups and European Championships, as well as Wimbledon, The Masters, the Olympics and the US and Australian Opens (golf and tennis).

He is currently Associate Sports Editor for *The Daily Record*, where he has worked for 27 years. Earlier in his career, he wrote for *The Falkirk Herald* and attended the 1997 Scottish Cup Final where, in his own words, 'The Bairns were robbed blind!'

Prior to working on *The Lives of Reilly*, David collaborated with former Rangers defender Lorenzo Amoruso to co-write his autobiography, *L.A. Confidential*.

Father of two boys – one a promising runner, the other a budding footballer – David's admiration for Mavis's ability and dedication in both spheres made working with him one of the highlights of his career.

He lives in Glasgow with his wife, Kay, and two sons, Sam and Jamie.

Dickson Telfer is an editor, author, publisher and ghostwriter with a lifelong fascination of language, both written and spoken. He is the author of two short story collections, *The Red Man Turns to Green* and *Refrigerator Cake* (Fledgling Press) and has edited work for clients all across the globe, including in Bengaluru, Qatar, Fife, Seattle, California, Florida, London and Camelon.

When he isn't writing or editing, he enjoys hosting book launches and performing at spoken word events. Also a keen bassist, he plays (or has played) in a number of bands and recording projects, most of which have had airplay on national radio.

Dickson works part-time in Learning Development in Higher Education, where a lot of his time is spent providing advice to Health & Life Sciences students on academic writing and critical analysis.

He lives in Falkirk with his wife, Lucinda, and his two dogs, Ruby and Dasher.

SAY HELLO

Twitter:
@ReillyMavis1
@ReverseRett
@NamelessTownLit
@DicksonTelfer

Instagram:
mavis_reilly1
reverserett
namelesstownbooks

TikTok:
@mavis_reilly1

Facebook:
Mavis Reilly
Reverse Rett

Web:
reverserett.org.uk
namelesstownbooks.com

nameless
town